Get the eBook FREE!
(PDF, ePub, Kindle, and liveBook all included)

We believe that once you buy a book from us, you should be able to read it in any format we have available. To get electronic versions of this book at no additional cost to you, purchase and then register this book at the Manning website.

Go to https://www.manning.com/freebook and follow the instructions to complete your pBook registration.

That's it!
Thanks from Manning!

Learn Amazon Web Services in a Month of Lunches

DAVID CLINTON

MANNING
SHELTER ISLAND

For online information and ordering of this and other Manning books, please visit
www.manning.com. The publisher offers discounts on this book when ordered in quantity.
For more information, please contact

> Special Sales Department
> Manning Publications Co.
> 20 Baldwin Road
> PO Box 761
> Shelter Island, NY 11964
> Email: orders@manning.com

Manning Publications Co.
20 Baldwin Road
PO Box 761
Shelter Island, NY 11964

Development editor:	Frances Lefkowitz
Technical development editor:	Al Scherer
Review editor:	Aleksandar Dragosavljević
Project editor:	Tiffany Taylor
Copyeditor:	Tiffany Taylor
Proofreader:	Katie Tennant
Technical proofreader:	Luis Carlos Sanchez Gonzalez
Typesetter:	Dottie Marsico
Cover designer:	Leslie Haimes

ISBN 9781617294440
Printed and bound by CPI Group (UK) Ltd, Croydon, CR0 4YY

brief contents

    1 ▪ Before you begin   1

PART 1   THE CORE AWS TOOLS..13

    2 ▪ The 10-minute EC2 web server   15

    3 ▪ Provisioning a more robust EC2 website   33

    4 ▪ Databases on AWS   51

    5 ▪ DNS: what's in a name?   68

    6 ▪ S3: cheap, fast file storage   83

    7 ▪ S3: cheap, fast system backups   97

    8 ▪ AWS security: working with IAM users, groups, and roles   112

    9 ▪ Managing growth   127

   10 ▪ Pushing back against the chaos: using resource tags   136

   11 ▪ CloudWatch: monitoring AWS resources for fun and profit   147

   12 ▪ Another way to play: the command-line interface   159

PART 2   THE AWS POWER USER: OPTIMIZING YOUR INFRASTRUCTURE...171

   13 ▪ Keeping ahead of user demand   173

   14 ▪ High availability: working with AWS networking tools   180

v

15 ▪ High availability: load balancing   199

16 ▪ High availability: auto scaling   212

17 ▪ High availability: content-delivery networks   225

PART 3   FOOD FOR THOUGHT: WHAT ELSE CAN AWS
         DO FOR YOU? 239

18 ▪ Building hybrid infrastructure   241

19 ▪ Cloud automation: working with Elastic Beanstalk,
      Docker, and Lambda   253

20 ▪ Everything else (nearly)   266

21 ▪ Never the end   284

contents

preface   xv
acknowledgments   xvii
about this book   xix

1 Before you begin   1

1.1 Is this book for you?   2

1.2 Using this book   3

The main chapters   3 ▪ Hands-on labs   4 ▪ Try it now   4

1.3 Being immediately effective   5

1.4 Setting up your lab environment   5

1.5 Finding help   8

1.6 How AWS does it   8

The big picture   10

PART 1 THE CORE AWS TOOLS 13

2 The 10-minute EC2 web server   15

2.1 What is EC2, and what does it do?   16

2.2 Launching an AWS instance   17

2.3 Accessing your AWS instance   23

2.4 Building an Ubuntu Linux web server   24

Installing the software   25 ▪ Creating the website   28

2.5   Troubleshooting   30

2.6   Lab   31

3   *Provisioning a more robust EC2 website*   **33**

3.1   Calculating capacity needs   33

3.2   Getting the measure of EC2's core compute services   34

vCPU   34 ▪ EBS   34 ▪ Memory   35 ▪ Bandwidth   35

3.3   Assessing your application   35

3.4   Choosing the right instance for your project   38

3.5   Adding WordPress   41

*Preparing the server   42 ▪ Preparing MySQL   42
Downloading and configuring WordPress   43
Setting up the WordPress filesystem   46 ▪ Testing your
application   47 ▪ What next?   48*

3.6   Lab   49

4   *Databases on AWS*   **51**

4.1   The database   51

4.2   Choosing the right database model   52

*Relational databases   52 ▪ NoSQL databases   53
How to choose   53*

4.3   Infrastructure design: where does
your database belong?   54

4.4   Estimating costs   56

4.5   Migrating your database to RDS   57

Creating a MySQL dump   58

4.6   Building an Amazon RDS instance   58

4.7   Configuring security group settings   63

4.8   Populating the new database   64

4.9   Lab   66

5   *DNS: what's in a name?*   **68**

5.1   Adding a name to public indexes   70

5.2   Configuring your hosted zone   71

Configuring record sets   72 ▪ Elastic IP addresses   75

5.3   Routing policies   76

Creating a health check   77 ▪ Create a routing policy   79

5.4   Lab   82

6   *S3: cheap, fast file storage   83*

6.1   How does S3 work?   84

Creating an S3 bucket   85 ▪ Uploading files to an S3 bucket   86

6.2   Integrating S3 resources into an EC2-based website   91

6.3   Using S3 to create a simple static website   93

6.4   Lab   96

7   *S3: cheap, fast system backups   97*

7.1   Why back up?   98

Your AWS account: what might go wrong?   98

7.2   Backing up to S3: snapshots   100

*Creating a snapshot   101 ▪ Creating an image   103
Using an image to re-create an instance   105*

7.3   Backing up to S3: manual process   105

*Choosing what to back up   106 ▪ Generating a
compressed archive   106 ▪ Installing the AWS CLI   107*

7.4   Lab   110

8   *AWS security: working with IAM users, groups,
and roles   112*

8.1   Defining the pieces of the IAM picture   113

*Policies   113 ▪ Users   113 ▪ Groups   115
Roles   115 ▪ Best practices   116*

8.2   IAM-ifying an AWS account   118

*Creating an admin user   118 ▪ Signing in as an IAM
user   122 ▪ Locking down the root   123 ▪ Creating and
configuring a group   124*

8.3   Lab   126

9   *Managing growth   127*

9.1   Estimating the true costs of your cloud project   128

9.2   Working with the TCO Calculator   131

10   *Pushing back against the chaos:
       using resource tags   136*

      10.1   What are resource tags?   136

      10.2   Working with resource tags   137
             *Creating and applying a tag   137 ▪ Designing a
             naming scheme   140 ▪ Searching your tagged resources   141*

      10.3   Working with resource groups   143
             Using tags to track costs   146

      10.4   Lab   146

11   *CloudWatch: monitoring AWS resources for fun
       and profit   147*

      11.1   AWS Budgets   147
             *Creating a budget   148
             Using tags with your budgets   150*

      11.2   CloudWatch   153
             *CloudWatch billing alerts   154
             CloudWatch usage alerts   157*

      11.3   Lab   158

12   *Another way to play: the command-line interface   159*

      12.1   What is the AWS CLI?   159

      12.2   Why use a CLI?   160

      12.3   Installing the AWS CLI   161
             *Installing with a Windows MSI file   161 ▪ Installing on
             Linux   162 ▪ Using a bundled installer (Linux and
             macOS)   162 ▪ Installing using Python pip (all OSs)   163*

      12.4   Configuring the AWS CLI   164
             *Choosing a region   164 ▪ Choosing an output
             format   165 ▪ Working with multiple AWS profiles   166*

      12.5   Using the help system   166

      12.6   Using the CLI to administer your
             AWS account resources   167
             Launching a new EC2 instance using the CLI   167

      12.7   Lab   169

PART 2 THE AWS POWER USER:
        OPTIMIZING YOUR INFRASTRUCTURE 171

13 *Keeping ahead of user demand 173*
    13.1 Automating high availability 175
    13.2 Cloud computing 177
    13.3 Elasticity vs. scalability 177

14 *High availability: working with AWS
       networking tools 180*
    14.1 Organizing AWS resources in VPCs 181
          Creating a new VPC 185
    14.2 Availability zones and network subnets 189
          *Network design 189 ▪ TCP/IP addressing 190
          NAT addressing 191*
    14.3 Deploying a website across two availability zones 195
    14.4 Lab 197

15 *High availability: load balancing 199*
    15.1 What is load balancing? 199
    15.2 Building a multizone load balancer 201
          *Launching four instances 202 ▪ Creating a target
          group 204 ▪ Registering instances in a target
          group 206 ▪ Creating a load balancer, and
          associating it with a security group 208
          Associating the target with the load balancer 210*
    15.3 Testing the cluster 210
    15.4 Lab 211

16 *High availability: auto scaling 212*
    16.1 Creating a launch configuration 214
    16.2 Creating an auto scaling group 218
          *Integrating a load balancer 219 ▪ Configuring
          scaling policies 220*
    16.3 Cleaning up after yourself 224
    16.4 Lab 224

17   *High availability: content-delivery networks*   **225**

17.1   How does Amazon CloudFront work?   226

17.2   Creating a CloudFront distribution   228

*SSL/TLS encryption   230 ▪ Other settings   230
CloudFront costs   232 ▪ SSL/TLS certificates   234
Wrapping it all up   235*

17.3   Lab   236

PART 3   FOOD FOR THOUGHT: WHAT ELSE CAN
AWS DO FOR YOU? 239

18   *Building hybrid infrastructure*   **241**

18.1   Why go hybrid?   242

18.2   Hybrid storage solutions   243

*S3 and Glacier   243 ▪ AWS Storage Gateway   244
AWS Snowball   245*

18.3   Hybrid connectivity   246

*AWS Direct Connect   246 ▪ The hardware virtual
private gateway   246 ▪ AWS Directory Service   248*

18.4   Disaster recovery   249

18.5   The Amazon EC2 Systems Manager   250

18.6   VMware integration   252

19   *Cloud automation: working with Elastic Beanstalk,
Docker, and Lambda*   **253**

19.1   AWS Elastic Beanstalk: what you don't see won't
hurt you   254

19.2   AWS EC2 Container Service: running Docker
in the cloud   258

19.3   AWS Lambda: going serverless   261

The server is dead; long live serverless—?   264

20   *Everything else (nearly)*   **266**

20.1   Databases   268

DynamoDB   268 ▪ Redshift   268 ▪ ElastiCache   269

20.2 Developer tools 270

*CodeCommit 270 ▪ CodeBuild 272 ▪ CodeDeploy 272
CodePipeline 274 ▪ API Gateway 274
CloudFormation 275*

20.3 Security and authentication 276

AWS WAF and AWS Shield 276 ▪ Cognito 278

20.4 Messaging 279

SNS 279 ▪ SQS 280 ▪ SES 281

20.5 Shortcuts 281

AWS Quick Starts 282 ▪ Migration shortcuts 283

21 **Never the end 284**

21.1 Keeping up 284

21.2 Where to turn for help 285

21.3 Certifications 286

21.4 Lab: the steroid overdose edition 286

appendix Connecting to your EC2 instance 289

index 293

preface

If you've ever struggled to learn a new technology, you'll feel my pain. My first AWS experience, close to a decade ago, was ultimately successful, but the process was deeply frustrating. I was looking for a way to run some remote interactive classes for a group of my former high school students. None of the video-conferencing hosting platforms at the time matched our needs or budget, but there was (and still is) an attractive open source package called BigBlueButton. A bit of research suggested that dropping BigBlueButton into an Amazon Web Services EC2 instance might be the way to make it all happen.

It worked—but not before leading me down one conceptual rabbit hole after another as I struggled to figure out how to bring together all the many moving parts. A smarter guy would have been quicker to grasp the grand structure. Not me. I did it through sheer force of will. Hard work? You bet. But very satisfying.

So I know exactly how hard mastering a big, complex new platform can be. More to the point: because I've been through this before (many times), I've become pretty good at breaking down complex technologies and organizing all the parts. Once I've got a comprehensible structure, I can then present the ideas in a way that's practical and useful.

In a way, this book is the record of how I wished my learning had progressed all those years ago. Having the schematic diagrams, context-rich sidebars, and layer-by-layer buildup of skills would have made my life easier.

Think this might be a plan for you, too? Then feel free to dive in. I hope we'll get to spend some fun and rewarding time together.

acknowledgments

This book has only one author (that would be me), but it's the product of a team effort. To be honest, the sheer size of this team has been nothing short of alarming. A wise and cynical man once wrote that "a committee is a creature with six or more legs and no brain"—and that's pretty much been my thinking since my teen years.

Until now, that is. Because the Manning team has proven to be the most efficient, capable, and whip-smart multilegged creature I've ever encountered. Don't believe me? You've got all the proof you'll need resting in your hands—or on your screen.

This book is the product of hours of long editorial board meetings and conversations with Marjan Bace, Bert Bates, Michael Stephens, and Greg Wild, who struggled mightily to shape a training experience that could benefit the greatest number of readers in the most effective possible way. Those individuals know the technology publishing business inside and out; and, more important, they understand the best ways to teach technology.

Learn Amazon Web Services in a Month of Lunches is also a far better book for the work of its peer reviewers, each one of whose valuable observations were carefully noted, weighed, and, where possible, applied: Pierre-Michel Ansel, Jérôme Baton, Michael Bright, Randy Coffland, Martin Dehnert, Jose Estefania, Alexey Galiulin, Paul Grebenc, Tim

Kane, Jens Christian Bredahl Madsen, Miguel Paraz, Peter Perlepes, Prabhuti Prakash, Pethuru Raj, Conor Redmond, Sergey Royz, Shawn Smith, Robert Thyne, Ruslan Verbelchuk, and Jan Vinterberg.

Greater still was the influence of my development editor, Frances Lefkowitz, and senior technical development editor Al Scherer. There wasn't a paragraph, a diagram, or an image that escaped their scrutiny, nor was there a concept that wasn't closely tested for clarity and purpose. Granted, Frances has now made certain parts of my life unlivable—I can't eat breakfast without hearing her voice in my head saying, "Too fast. Explain *why* you should want to eat breakfast and *what* your readers will gain when they eat breakfast. And how can the principle be applied to lunch?"

I never understood how references to the marketing department could possibly make it into a book. After all, they don't do anything until after it's in print, right? Another myth shot down in flames. Candace Gillhoolley and Christopher Kaufmann have already been both busy and effective getting this book in front of every eye that needs to see it. And I mustn't forget Kyle Jackson, who has always been there when an image wouldn't transform the way it should or GitLab "broke." Although they arrived late in the process, the efforts of Janet Vail, Tiffany Taylor, Katie Tennant, Dottie Marsico, and other members of the production team proved significant.

Finally, although technology and technical editing aren't among my wife's many remarkable talents, her hand invisibly graces each of the many pages and paragraphs you'll read in this book. None of this would be remotely possible without her.

about this book

AWS certainly isn't the only cloud provider on earth, and there's no single service it offers that can't be replicated elsewhere at a comparable or sometimes lower price. But although Microsoft Azure and Google Cloud Platform offer some serious products, AWS is by all measures the biggest player in this market.

You've probably already heard this old joke: no one ever got fired for choosing IBM. The idea was that IBM's size and history made choosing its products and services the safe choice. These days? AWS is probably getting close to IBM status.

Of course, that's only a joke. Sometimes, safe choices can lead to disaster. And there's still plenty of risk to be found in AWS: finding yourself so heavily invested in uniquely AWS technologies that you're effectively unable to move your resources elsewhere is one significant example. But AWS's reputation for innovation and product reliability is well earned. When it comes to talking about the cloud, AWS is the elephant in every room.

Learn Amazon Web Services in a Month of Lunches is designed to give you the insights and skills you'll need to quickly move from being a raw beginner to someone who's able to safely and effectively launch and manage a wide range of AWS resources. The book encourages you to get your hands dirty with real infrastructure projects pretty much right away. The skills you'll use in the early chapters will serve as a foundation for everything that comes after.

The book's chapters more or less follow a small company's intrepid efforts to create a public-facing web application. You'll watch them as, one step at a time, they add security, resilience, high availability, and elasticity. The topics mostly follow a realistic upward curve of technical sophistication.

As you'll soon see, I don't try to cover all the 100+ services that are currently part of the AWS platform. Any book that tried to do so would be so big, it would probably break your e-book reader. Rather, I've limited the book's primary focus to the dozen or so services that form the core of most of the action on AWS. If you understand how those 12 work, most of the rest will eventually make sense to you.

Finally, AWS—like cloud computing as a whole—is a moving target. In addition to new services and features constantly being introduced, visual elements of the browser interface change from time to time. Practically, this means by the time you read this book, some of the images and specific instructions may be outdated. Unfortunately, that's how life is in the fast lane. But keep in mind that this book is primarily about the principles and processes of AWS deployments rather than exactly where on a page you're supposed to click. When you're finished reading the book, I expect you'll have drawn the greatest value from those principles and processes.

Who should read this book

This book isn't about creating an application, a website, or a project. That's your job. So at the very least, I expect that you have some idea of what you'd like to accomplish: perhaps migrating an existing multi-tiered local infrastructure or building an e-commerce WordPress website. With that in mind, you probably already have some experience with the way basic application-support tools like databases, networking, and filesystems work.

My first job is to help you deploy the project in the AWS cloud. My other job is to skillfully take the ideas behind the principles, processes, and functionality of the AWS cloud and park them neatly in your mind so that your imagination and creativity can take over.

Roadmap

As you can see from the table of contents, I've divided the book's chapters into three sections: the core toolset (chapters 2–12), high availability (chapters 13–17), and brief introductions to some of the AWS services and functionality that didn't fit into the book's other sections (chapters 18–20):

- Chapter 1 introduces the cloud, the space within it that AWS inhabits, and, in broad terms, the kinds of things you can accomplish there.
- Chapter 2 is a quick-start project in which you'll launch an actual virtual machine on AWS EC2, serving a simple web server to the internet.
- Chapter 3 demonstrates capacity-analysis techniques and adds WordPress to your EC2 server.
- Chapter 4 introduces managed-database hosting on Amazon's Relational Database Service (RDS).
- Chapter 5 shows you how to register and administer DNS domains and routing policies using Route 53.
- Chapter 6 addresses cheap, reliable, fast data storage using Simple Storage Service (S3).
- Chapter 7 demonstrates a couple of approaches to using S3 for system and archive backups.
- Chapter 8 turns your attention to security through the IAM service.
- Chapter 9 shows how you can (and must) work with AWS tools to estimate and model the true costs of your projects.
- Chapter 10 demonstrates the far-reaching value of applying resource tags.
- Chapter 11 promotes regular, smart monitoring of your resources through CloudWatch.
- Chapter 12 introduces you to administering AWS resources through the AWS command-line interface (CLI).
- Chapter 13 discusses elasticity and scalability as they relate to virtual servers.
- Chapter 14 addresses organizing your infrastructure within VPCs and availability zones to enhance their reliability.

- Chapter 15 covers load balancing as a tool for intelligently directing client traffic among multiple servers.
- Chapter 16 shows how auto scaling can be used to automatically manage changes in user demand and server health.
- Chapter 17 describes how the CloudFront content-delivery network can be used to reduce latency for geographically dispersed users.
- Chapter 18 illustrates the use of various tools to permit hybrid local/cloud solutions.
- Chapter 19 discusses some AWS cloud-automation tools (specifically, Elastic Beanstalk, ECS, and Lambda).
- Chapter 20 briefly surveys some of the AWS tools I couldn't properly cover in the book.
- Chapter 21 says, "Goodbye—it's been great spending time with you!"

Source code

This book contains examples of source code both in numbered listings and in line with normal text; the code is formatted in a `fixed-width font like this` to separate it from ordinary text. All of the book's code is available at https://www.manning.com/books/learn-amazon-web-services-in-a-month-of-lunches.

In many cases, the original source code has been reformatted; we've added line breaks and reworked indentation to accommodate the available page space in the book. Occasionally, even this was not enough, and listings include line-continuation markers (➥). Code annotations accompany some listings, highlighting important concepts.

About the author

David Clinton is a system administrator, teacher, and writer. He has administered, written about, and created training materials for many important technology subjects including Linux systems, cloud computing (AWS in particular), and container technologies like Docker. Many of his video training courses can be found on Pluralsight.com, and links to his other books (on Linux administration and server virtualization) can be found at https://bootstrap-it.com.

Book forum

Purchase of *Learn Amazon Web Services in a Month of Lunches* includes free access to a private web forum run by Manning Publications where you can make comments about the book, ask technical questions, and receive help from the author and from other users. To access the forum, go to https://forums.manning.com/forums/learn-amazon-web-services-in-a-month-of-lunches. You can also learn more about Manning's forums and the rules of conduct at https://forums.manning.com/forums/about.

Manning's commitment to our readers is to provide a venue where a meaningful dialogue between individual readers and between readers and the author can take place. It is not a commitment to any specific amount of participation on the part of the author, whose contribution to the forum remains voluntary (and unpaid). We suggest you try asking the author some challenging questions lest his interest stray! The forum and the archives of previous discussions will be accessible from the publisher's website as long as the book is in print.

Before you begin

1

Welcome to the cloud: the brave new world where "here" doesn't matter, and where anything is possible. Right now.

Let me explain. Cloud computing is the provision of on-demand (that is, self-service) compute, memory, and storage resources remotely over a network. In addition to its many built-in service efficiencies, the model is most cost effective for the widest range of projects when usage charges are calculated and billed in very small increments (often in fractions of a penny).

I'll try that again. Suppose you didn't want to purchase, build, and house all the expensive hardware you'd need to properly support your new e-commerce website. Perhaps you're not sure how successful the project will be, so investing heavily in server, cooling, and routing equipment doesn't make sense. But if you could rent just enough of *someone else's* equipment to match the fast-changing ups and downs in demand on your site and pay only for what you actually used, then your new venture might work.

Is there anyone out there who might rent you this kind of stuff? Yup. They're called *cloud computing providers*. And Amazon Web Services (AWS) is by far the most feature-rich and (generating nearly $12 billion in revenue in 2016) successful player in the market.

> **Above and beyond: just how big is AWS?**
>
> According to the research firm Gartner (http://mng.bz/31dr), "[AWS] has the largest share of compute capacity in use by paying customers—many times the aggregate size of all other providers in the market…. It has the richest array of IaaS and PaaS capabilities. It provides the deepest capabilities for governing a large number of users and resources. It continues to rapidly expand its service offerings and to offer higher-level solutions."
>
> AWS has proven itself capable of providing a secure and reliable hosting platform for both mission-critical (e-commerce, enterprise intranets) and compute-intensive (big data analytics, development environments) applications. Given its depth, if your project can be virtualized in one form or another then, according to Gartner, AWS is "the safe choice."

That's not to say that there aren't projects that still make more sense to host on traditional local server setups—there are times when key technical or regulatory requirements can make alternatives impossible. Deploying infrastructure using a hybrid half-local, half-cloud design can also be a valuable compromise option. And it would be foolish not to consider competing cloud providers like Microsoft Azure and Google Cloud Platform. But AWS is big and does a lot of things really well. You definitely can't ignore it.

The bottom line: most of the time, neither you nor your customers care where the physical hardware running your application lives. "Somewhere else" is just as good as "here." And you don't have to allow weeks for your IT team to spec, purchase, test, and deploy a new server. You can literally have an entire infrastructure up and running in a few minutes.

1.1 *Is this book for you?*

Is AWS a good match for your project? Without knowing all the dependencies and functionality you need, I can't say. But reading this book and becoming familiar with the AWS system—the tools AWS offers and the way it charges for services—should help you answer that question for yourself.

Looking to build a secure, scalable, and cost-effective e-commerce site? Many thousands already have. Need a platform for an off-site data-backup solution? Say the word, and AWS is on it. Got data—lots and lots of data—that could use real-time analysis? AWS has you covered. Have a popular mobile-optimized game that could use some help managing authentication and traffic control? You guessed it: AWS has been there and done that. If you're looking for ideas and examples of how other businesses have incorporated the cloud into their workflows, you may find it worthwhile to spend time browsing some of the case studies created by AWS: https://aws.amazon.com/solutions/case-studies/all.

In addition to giving you practical, hands-on AWS skills that will allow you to build your own simple, reliable, secure web service, a primary role of this book is to introduce you to the way AWS tools work. If you can at least identify the value and function of the 30 or so most common AWS services, then you'll be much better able to see for yourself exactly how the AWS universe can be applied to serve your needs.

1.2 Using this book

Let's do lunch. Or breakfast.

Whichever slice of your busy schedule presents itself as "available," there's a great deal you can accomplish in a single month. The idea is for you to read just one chapter a day. Lunch works, but so does a long, boring commute (where someone else is doing the driving). Each chapter should take you around 40 minutes to read, plus another 20 minutes practicing what the chapter showed you. Try to work on just one chapter a day. Focus on it. Let your brain absorb it. Then, the next day, you'll be prepared for the next chapter, refreshed and ready to learn more.

1.2.1 The main chapters

To make this happen, the book is divided into three parts. Part 1, covering the first dozen chapters, loosely traces the step-by-step construction of a WordPress-based website for an imaginary business by focusing mostly on Amazon's core compute (EC2), database (RDS), storage (S3), security (IAM), and cost-management tools. You should definitely follow along at home (or wherever your "here" happens to be). Parts 2 and 3 of the book dig deeper into key cloud architecture concepts like these:

- *Scalability*—The ability to accommodate greater demands on compute infrastructure
- *Elasticity*—The ability to quickly and dynamically incorporate new virtual resources into existing infrastructure to meet demand
- *High availability*—The ability of a service to remain reliably available despite unpredictable events

It's difficult to imagine any AWS project that won't demand all the skills you'll learn in part 1; but for simpler projects, you might never need to directly address the topics covered in parts 2 and 3. Feel free to pick and choose from whatever you need from those later chapters. I won't be in the least insulted. No, really.

One more thing. Each of you has a unique background and experience. But since it's impossible to custom-tailor a book to fit everyone's exact needs, some of the skills I'll need to cover to ensure that no one is left behind may already be obvious to you. Keep an eye on the chapter and section headings and feel free to skim through any topics you've already covered on your own.

1.2.2   Hands-on labs

Just reading about complicated environments like AWS has limited value. If you really want to learn how to get things done the right way, there's no alternative to rolling up your sleeves and experimenting on your own. One of the things I love the most about AWS is the way it makes it easy to pick up skills through its Free Tier. The Free Tier provides free access to lighter versions of just about every service AWS offers for the first 12 months after you open a new account.

Most chapters conclude with at least one lab exercise, allowing you to put what you've learned into practice in your own account. Just about anything I'll ask you to do in those labs will fall into the Free Tier.

Read the chapter. Build the infrastructure. This ain't your grandmother's technology textbook.

1.2.3   Try it now

Doing is more effective than reading. (Not that reading isn't effective, mind you.) From time to time, I'll highlight particularly useful reasons to log in to your own AWS account so you can quickly try out some key skill you've been exploring. If at all possible, grab the opportunity. The truth is, though, that the way AWS works means "doing" is more likely to happen with larger processes than with

Above and beyond

As you move through the chapters, you'll notice a few "Above and beyond" sidebars. These indicate additional information that you might find interesting but that isn't essential to your understanding of this book. If you're pressed for time—or just can't say no to that second donut—feel free to skip those sections or make a mental note to return to them later.

quick, one-off exercises. So the practical try-it-yourself stuff in this book will more often take the form of longer, hands-on labs.

1.3 *Being immediately effective*

I want you launching your own AWS Hello World resources by the time you're done with the next chapter, and capable of deploying simple real-world production services soon after that. This means each chapter teaches practical skills that can be useful right away, requiring nothing that you won't already have seen in a previous chapter. Keeping my word on this may sometimes mean I'll show you how to use an AWS tool in an early chapter in a basic way, leaving many important configuration or feature details for later. But it's all for a good cause.

1.4 *Setting up your lab environment*

Of course, by *lab environment* I mean AWS *account*. If you haven't already, you'll need to create one. Don't worry: as long as you don't fire up a resource, just having an account won't cost you anything. When you're logged in, the Console page (http://console.aws.amazon.com) is the hub through which you can get stuff done. As you can see in figure 1.1, links to 50 or so core AWS services are arranged by category, such as Compute, Storage, and Database. Clicking a link for the first time will

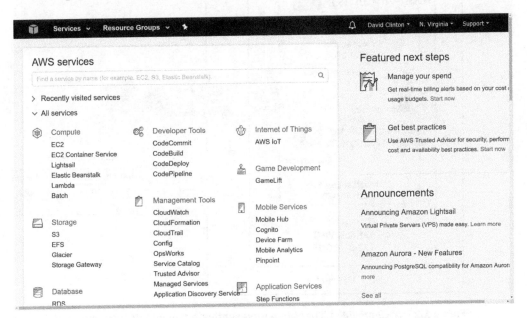

Figure 1.1   The AWS main Console: each item links to a complete AWS service.

take you to a page with a product overview, links to documentation and demos, and a Get Started button via which you can, well, get started. Feel free to try one for yourself.

Getting a head start visualizing how AWS resources are organized can make your transition into the AWS universe a bit smoother. Anything you launch will, in nearly all cases, be placed in a single virtual private cloud (VPC) that, in turn, is hosted in a physical data center in one of Amazon's dozen or so geographic regions. What, exactly, is a VPC? I suppose you could say it's a virtual TCP/IP network that, by default, is designed to permit easy communication between compute and database instances in the VPC while restricting external communication. Naturally, all accessibility configurations can be edited to meet your needs. Figure 1.2 (from docs.aws.amazon.com/AmazonVPC/latest/UserGuide/VPC_ Introduction.html) shows a schematic diagram from AWS's documentation site that illustrates a typical VPC and its contents.

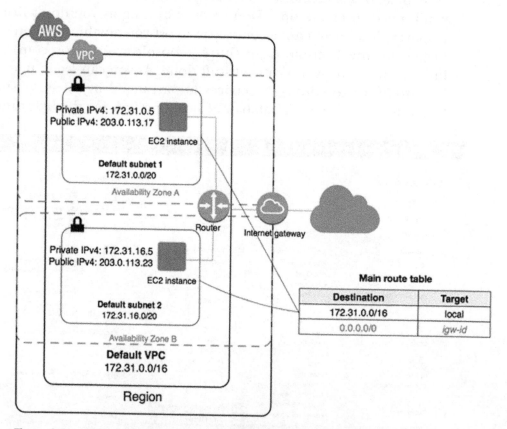

Figure 1.2　AWS-provided illustration representing a typical VPC configuration

Try it now

Why not head over to your AWS account and, from any Console page, change your selected region? Then visit one or two service pages like Elastic Compute Cloud (EC2) or Relational Database Service (RDS). If you already happen to have a live EC2 instance in, say, N. Virginia, you won't see any sign of it on the EC2 dashboard while you're set for EU Ireland.

Creating multiple VPCs—into which compute and database instances and stored data can be placed—can help you organize and, where necessary for security purposes (to ensure that sensitive data isn't exposed any more than absolutely necessary), isolate the elements of your deployment. You can also, as shown in figure 1.3, easily switch between geographic regions. Remember: whichever region name is currently displayed at upper right in your Console is the region into which resources will be launched.

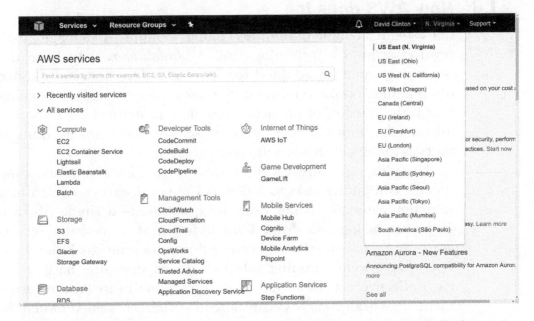

Figure 1.3 Drop-down menu (found near the upper-right corner of the Console) allowing you to switch your base geographic region

1.5   *Finding help*

AWS is an enormous universe with its own language, standards, and rules. And it's growing at a pace that's almost frightening. So it shouldn't come as a surprise if, from time to time, you find yourself in need of help finding your way around. Fortunately, AWS has invested heroic efforts in maintaining an excellent documentation system. You can access well-written, consistent help pages—complete with practical examples and tips—through the main documentation hub at https://aws.amazon.com/documentation or through links on the home page of each individual service. You can also join the support forum or purchase paid support through the Support Center.

1.6   *How AWS does it*

Let's spend a couple of minutes talking about the AWS magic. It all revolves around a technology called *virtualization* that, from the beginning, Amazon adopted for its own online bookstore (once upon a time, books were the only things Amazon sold). Virtualization is the division of physical compute and networking resources into smaller, more flexible units, presenting these smaller units to users as though each was a discrete resource.

The idea (as figure 1.4 illustrates) is that, instead of assigning specific computing tasks to individual physical servers—which may sometimes end up being over- or underused—a single physical server can be logically divided into as few or as many virtual servers as needed. That means there can be dozens of individually installed operating systems running side by side on the same hard drive, each effectively unaware that it isn't all alone in its local environment. Practically, each OS instance can be accessed remotely by both administrators and customers in exactly the same ways as any other server.

In this kind of environment, as soon as your virtual server completes its task or becomes unnecessary, you can instantly delete it, freeing up the resources it was using for the next task in the queue. And there's no need to over-provision virtual servers to anticipate

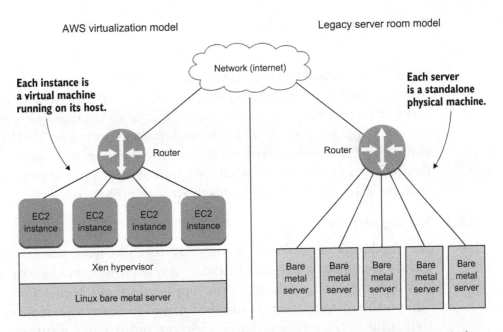

Figure 1.4   An illustration of the way compute instances are virtualized within a single physical server on AWS versus the use of individual physical machines in the legacy model

possible future needs, because future needs can be easily met whenever they arrive. In fact, today's virtual server might only live a few minutes or even seconds before, having completed its task, being shut down for good to make room for whatever's next. All this allows for far more efficient use of expensive hardware and the ability to provision and launch new servers at will, either to test new configurations or add fresh power to your production services.

A server by any other name

I should note that by *server* I mean any compute device that exists to provide digital services of any kind to either individual users (of the human variety) or other computers. A virtual server is exactly the same as its traditional cousin, except that its OS only *thinks* it's running directly on the underlying hardware. In fact, it's running on top of some kind of software layer that interprets hardware-software communication for it.

And don't be confused: terms like *instance*, *node*, *host*, *droplet*, *virtual machine* (VM), and even plain *computer* are also often used to refer to virtual servers, but they're all pretty much the same kind of thing.

In addition, virtual network interfaces, routing devices, and security firewalls could be defined creating entire virtual environments within which virtual computers could interact. Amazon saw a great business opportunity in renting out capacity to anyone looking to run publicly accessible virtual servers for their own projects. The flexibility and reliability of what AWS had to offer proved so popular that, by 2015, AWS was Amazon's most profitable product.

1.6.1 *The big picture*

For the kinds of projects that interest us right now, the center of gravity is definitely the EC2 instance. As you'll discover as you work through the book, although your application will be installed and run on the instance/server just as it would in your own data center, that application will be fed and sheltered by an army of support services. As you can see from the illustration of a typical AWS infrastructure in figure 1.5, there's at least as much going on *around* the server as on it.

Note the following:

- The security group controls the movement of data between your AWS resources and the big, bad internet beyond (chapter 2).
- The EC2 Amazon Machine Image (AMI) acts as a template for replicating precise OS environments (chapters 2 and 7).
- The Simple Storage Service (S3) bucket stores and delivers data for both backup and delivery to users (chapter 6).
- The EBS volumes act as data volumes (like hard drives) for an instance (chapter 2).

That's the game plan. I hope this book will give you a solid start as you take your important first steps into the world of Amazon Web Services. Let's learn.

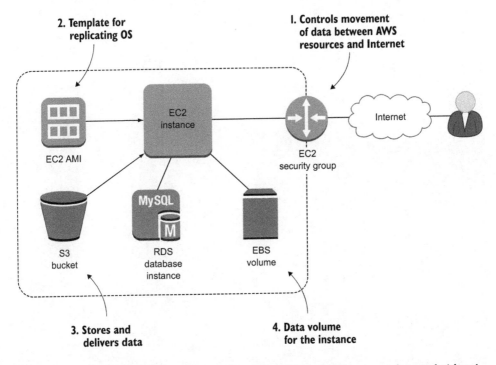

2. Template for replicating OS

I. Controls movement of data between AWS resources and Internet

EC2 instance

EC2 AMI

Internet

EC2 security group

S3 bucket

RDS database instance

EBS volume

3. Stores and delivers data

4. Data volume for the instance

Figure 1.5   The kind of deployment you should be able to build once you've read at least the first 12 chapters of this book

Definitions

- *Virtualization*—The virtual division of physical compute, storage, or network resources into smaller, virtual parts
- *Instance*—The term used to describe a single virtual machine running on AWS's EC2 cloud
- *Node*—Another common term used to describe a single virtual machine
- *Droplet*—A third common term used to describe a single virtual machine (most commonly within the DigitalOcean platform)
- *VM*—Acronym for *virtual machine*
- *Elasticity*—The ability to dynamically increase or decrease virtual compute resources according to demand
- *Scalability*—The ability to quickly and dynamically incorporate new virtual resources into existing infrastructure to meet demand
- *High availability*—The ability to maintain service levels despite unexpected events
- *Virtual private cloud (VPC)*—AWS's primary organizational grouping of virtual resources

Part 1

The core AWS tools

In this part of the book, I present the most basic Amazon infrastructure services including compute, database, storage, security, and networking tools. Even if you eventually end up spending most of your AWS time using serverless (like Lambda) or server-abstracted (like Elastic Beanstalk) services, you'll need to understand how all the key underlying pieces fit together. You'll probably want to read all of chapters 2–12.

The 10-minute EC2 web server

Here's where the real work of the book starts. So, technically speaking, now would be a good time to talk about whether AWS is right for you in the first place. In fact, AWS has a great tool called the Total Cost of Ownership (TCO) Calculator (http://awstcocalculator.com) that lets you make apples-to-apples cost comparisons between your existing physical or locally hosted deployment and similar infrastructure running on the AWS cloud. But if we got into that discussion, this 10-minute EC2 web server would stretch out to at least a half an hour. Can't have that, can we?

So I pushed the TCO Calculator back to chapter 9; feel free to jump ahead if you like. The rest of us will fearlessly dive right in and get the first simple version of the example company's website up and running. Using nothing besides the Free Tier resources AWS makes available during an account's first year, the goal is to have a functional HTML page all set to greet your global customers.

Although the website you're going to build may be basic, the infrastructure you'll put in place to support it could be used as the foundation for just about everything else you'll do throughout the rest of this book. In other words, there's nothing "junior varsity" about the tools you're using now. Here's what you'll accomplish through the rest of this chapter:

- Launch an EC2 Ubuntu Linux server instance
- Use SSH to connect with your instance
- Use the Ubuntu package manager to install the software packages it will need to run as a web server
- Create a simple Welcome page for your site

In just a few minutes, Amazon's EC2 service will place some serious, industrial-grade resources at your disposal, and your deployment journey will begin.

Set your watch: 10 minutes. (Not including the time it takes you to read this chapter. Some restrictions may apply. Offer void where prohibited by law.)

2.1 What is EC2, and what does it do?

Elastic Compute Cloud (EC2) is a hugely successful service at the core of the AWS platform that allows you to effectively rent units of compute power (EC2 instances), storage space (Elastic Block Store [EBS] volumes, which work like a PC's hard drive), and network connectivity running in AWS's vast infrastructure. If you need to provide a web-based service to your customers, users, or readers—anything from a community wiki to a fully integrated, multilevel, commercial mobile application—you can use those resources to create a virtual machine that, to the outside world, acts and feels just like the real thing. For you, as you take your first steps in the AWS cloud, what's nice is that the servers require little time and effort to launch, so if you make a mistake or somehow mess up some important configuration files, you can easily pull the plug on an instance and have a replacement up and running, usually in less than a minute.

If you don't already have an AWS account, head over to www.aws.amazon.com right now and sign up. You'll have to give them your credit card information, but you won't be charged anything unless you actively launch resources; by default, nothing is running on a new account—you're only responsible for the services you activate. Not only that, but all the resources you'll launch in this chapter—and, unless I specify otherwise, throughout the entire book—fall into Amazon's generous Free Tier, which is available to all accounts in their first year. So don't worry about charges: this one's on the house.

NOTE   Because this AWS account will be associated with your credit card, you should exercise normal precautions, including using a good password made up of both uppercase and lowercase characters, at least one number, and one non-alphanumeric character. Adding multifactor authentication using your smartphone or a dedicated device is also highly recommended (see https://aws.amazon.com/iam/details/mfa for details).

2.2   *Launching an AWS instance*

Let's begin the process of starting up a new virtual Linux server. Why Linux? Because it can be easily adapted to fill just about any role, and, in most cases, the OS is available for free. And besides, the last time I checked with The Cloud Market (thecloudmarket.com/stats#/totals), more than 92% of all EC2 instances launched were running one flavor or another of Linux (the OS and user data live on the attached EBS volume). You wouldn't want to be antisocial, would you?

TIP   Don't be concerned if you haven't got any previous Linux experience. It'll be a pretty shallow learning curve. Having said that, although we'll be focusing on accessing and managing AWS-based Linux instances (along with all the Linux-specific skills you'll need to keep up), there's nothing to prevent you from running Windows in your EC2 instance, even in the Free Tier.

Once your account has been activated, point your web browser to the AWS Console (http://console.aws.amazon.com), and click the EC2 icon (see figure 2.1). You may first need to click All Services to expand the displayed links.

The GUI Console

AWS-land is a fast-changing place. New services are constantly being introduced, and there are frequent updates to the ways the older ones work. Keep that in mind as you make your way through the click-here-click-there parts of this book: as time goes on, some of those options will change.

The AWS command-line interface is far more stable. Once I introduce you to it in chapter 12, it will gradually come to replace the Console for most of your interactions.

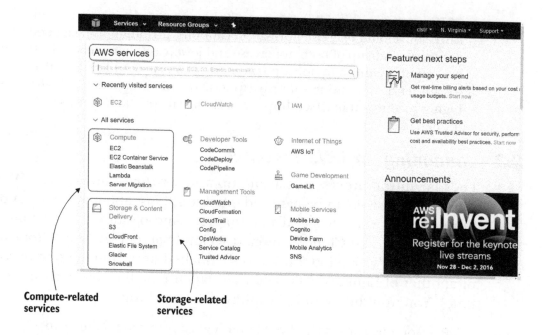

Figure 2.1   **Part of the AWS Console displaying key services grouped by theme, with compute and storage services highlighted**

There's a big, blue, Launch Instance button on the EC2 dashboard. Click it. Scroll down a bit until you see an Ubuntu Server 16.04 LTS Amazon Machine Image (AMI; see figure 2.2), and click the blue Select button to the right. That 16.04 version will probably be replaced by Ubuntu Server 18.04 some time late in 2018. Mostly because of its popularity in relation to other Linux distributions, I work with Ubuntu for many of the demos in the book. With a few minor variations, though, everything you do here will work just as well using any flavor of Linux.

Amazon Machine Images

An Amazon Machine Image (AMI) is effectively a template that defines the OS, application, and storage environment for an EC2 instance. AWS provides a couple of dozen official and supported Quick Start AMIs you can use (including the Ubuntu 16.04 AMI you just selected).

But there are also many hundreds of specialty AMIs available in the AWS Marketplace. Beyond that, you can easily build your own AMI out of any instance that you've customized to fit your specific needs. I'll talk a bit about how that works in chapter 12.

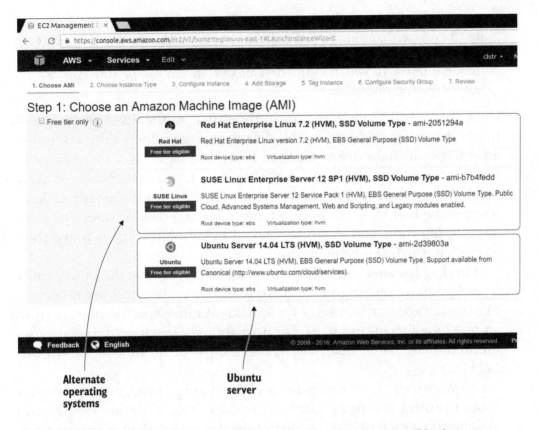

Figure 2.2 Select an Ubuntu AMI. Note also some of the many alternative OSs that are available as AMIs.

On the Choose an Instance Type page that follows, the General Purpose t2.micro Free Tier-eligible type will probably be preselected. Because your server will be exposed to only very light use, that option will give you plenty of power and cost you the least, so select it if it isn't already. For an instance profile called "micro," the t2 packs quite a wallop; you may not want to use a computer built with such specs for high-end gaming, but I was pleasantly surprised by how well this little fellow can handle the demands of a relatively light website workload.

Now click the Next: Configure Instance Details button at lower right. The Configure Instance Details page lets you customize the network neighborhood in which your instance will live. Edits will be necessary for some of the more advanced scenarios we'll play with later in the book; but for now, the preset values for settings like VPC, subnet, and shutdown will work well.

TIP If you've already been actively using your AWS account, there may be more than one virtual private cloud available in the Network pull-down menu on this page. Make sure the VPC you've selected has usable subnets, or switch to the default VPC so you can be sure you've got everything you need.

Click Next: Add Storage to add storage (that is, the EBS volume you'll use as the instance's drive). The default storage value you're offered—an 8 GB solid state drive (SSD) to host your base OS—is also fine. In fact, all the software that will make up your Linux server will probably use less than half of the space you've given it. And, unless you later make some bad choices about retaining old log data or where to store large application and database files, 8 GB should remain more than enough in the foreseeable future.

The Tag Instance page that comes up next gives you the opportunity to assign an identifying name to your instance. As you'll learn later in the book, tags can be useful for quickly finding specific objects from among long lists of resources. For now, though, feel free to type any useful identifying name (like, say, MyInstance)—or nothing at all—in this field.

Now comes the Configure Security Group page, whose settings should protect you from attack or, in other words, define exactly who gets access to each of your project's resources. AWS security groups work much the same way as the various kinds of network firewalls with which you may already be familiar, but you can also think of them as filters that only allow objects of just the right size and weight through to the other side.

I'll illustrate how this works with a simple—and important—example. The way things are set by default, anyone with a copy of your private authentication key (which I'll discuss soon) can get into your server from anywhere in the world. Assuming you're careful not to carelessly expose your private key, that's not quite as scary as it sounds. But restricting SSH access to only requests coming from behind the unique public IP address used by your own desktop PC is a good idea and something AWS strongly recommends.

One solution is to click the drop-down menu under the Source column, currently set to Anywhere, and select My IP instead. AWS will automatically populate the field with the public IP address that was given to you by your ISP. You could also specify a custom IP address if, say, you wanted to give access to members of your team toiling away in a remote office.

> **TIP** If you need access from machines using more than one IP address, you can create multiple security-group rules, one for each address. Also, many local ISPs provide *dynamic* IP addresses that change from time to time (after a power outage, for instance). So remember: after an update, you won't be able to log in to your instances until you update the address in the security group.

You need to make one more edit to the security group. Because you're building a web server—whose purpose is, after all, to serve pages using the HTTP protocol—you need to create a new rule to open the default HTTP port: 80, the port used by most unencrypted browser-based web traffic. Click Add Rule once, and then click the Custom TCP Rule drop-down menu. Select HTTP from the list that appears. Notice in figure 2.3 how the value of Port Range for this rule is automatically set to 80, and Source is Anywhere: that is, 0.0.0.0/0, meaning any users anywhere on the internet will have access to your content. In addition to HTTP, you

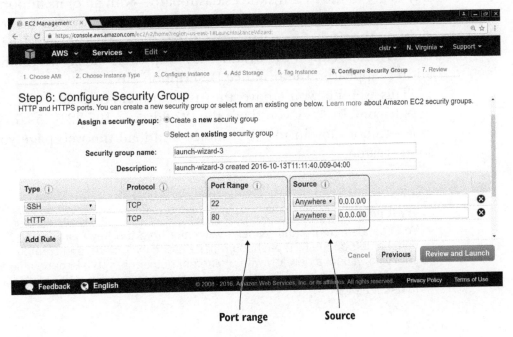

Port range   Source

Figure 2.3   AWS security group configuration page

can choose from a long list of common protocols, including various email and database standards.

Click Review and Launch and then Launch—although, technically, nothing will happen until after one final step: choosing a key pair. If you can contain your curiosity for just a paragraph or two, I'll explain what that's all about. In the meantime, select Create a New Key Pair, and give it a name—perhaps something that reflects the project, like, say, `book-sales-site-key`. I used `keyname`. Click Download Key Pair to download the key to your local computer; a dialog will pop up, asking where you want to save your new file. So that you'll have easy access to it right away whenever you open your terminal, I suggest saving it to the default home folder where your files are normally saved. Note that the new key has a .pem extension.

When you're done with that, click Launch Instance, and you're finished. Your first EC2 instance! It will take a minute or two before the instance will be ready for action; in the meantime, the quickest way to get to the EC2 Instances dashboard—with all of its important login information—is to click the View Instances button at lower-right on the page. Once you're on the Instances dashboard (see figure 2.4), you'll know the instance is ready when you see its public IP address appear in the Instance Description tab.

This website won't have the usual human-readable URL, like google.com. Instead, you'll use the IP address—107.22.95.59, in this case—to both log in to the instance and load the web page you'll soon create.

> **Try it now**
>
> You can also create and manage key pairs from the Key Pairs link in the panel at left on the EC2 dashboard page. Head over there, and create (and safely download) a new key with a different name that you'll later be able to select for use with new EC2 instances. Feel free to delete it if you don't plan to use it again.

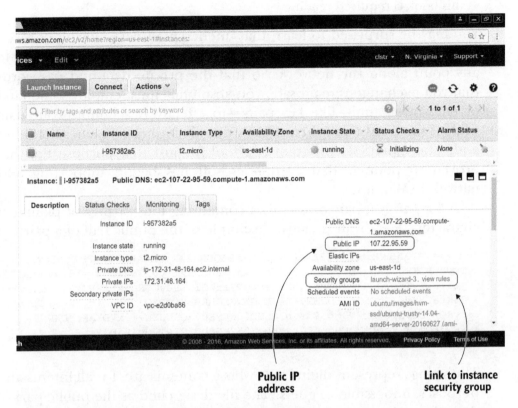

Figure 2.4 EC2 Instance details page, which displays important information—including the instance's public IP address—and links to instance-related resources

2.3 Accessing your AWS instance

Although your instance is now active and running, it's not doing much on behalf of humankind. If you want to get it working for you, you'll have to log in and configure some software. The way you gain access to a remote server like those on AWS depends on two main factors: what OS is running on the server, and what OS is running on your local desktop machine.

Because your EC2 server is using Linux, it expects you to visit using the SSH secure remote management tool. Clicking the Connect button on the Instances dashboard will provide you with specific information.

NOTE   If you're not sure how to access a remote Linux server from your Windows, macOS, or Linux PC, then the appendix at the end of this book is required reading.

You may be surprised to learn that unencrypted data moving between computers is easily visible to just about anyone with physical access to any point along the network. So that the private data and passwords that you exchange remain safe, you absolutely must employ some kind of encryption tool—like key pairs—to effectively scramble your data while it's in transit and then reliably decode it once it reaches the other end. The OpenSSH program is a tool for just that purpose that has proven so popular that even Microsoft has begun supporting SSH natively in Windows.

A *key pair* is a pair of text files containing long strings of plain-text characters. Here's an (inactive) example of the public half of a pair:

```
ssh-rsa AAAAB3NzaC1yc2EAAAADAQABAAAABAQDKu2XRjOEtABbkat1PS7/3CkqSo
➥5tdhuMOKVgJGRpgIBe/riiby6PCTc53maT28hD5AfM1yV1lba1iUEZyh3yvaoCuC3
➥jZ3+kiTyTYm/dpZ5eInMMAAj5DFhev4sTFfzWClo3BuvOS2U9/5fRPTz8YPYuuYnTr+
➥84Kta28Yd6/IqDb7hz6UaMNv+Z36MhG0NOXJhRBBYiyPYQFd9nxE+cyMZ+FmGjMz
➥6y8Q8dS4v5f6cnz8V3mbSFdZyn3OSMD0DxDxEu47GRNUYw+i9x7DkAKc/DKNN94
➥RPD3bQm1W9koNL0MQNHgp4LJfvMKbo1852FNBbd1OIPTVBvlLjH39wbF
➥root@container
```

The strings represent digital keys whose contents are, for all intents and purposes, impossible to guess. The file designated as the public part of the pair can be copied to the remote computer you'd like to later log in to. The existence of both halves of the pair on the two computers assures OpenSSH (and its users) that it's safe to allow the session to begin.

For Amazon instances, AWS will embed the public half of a pair on your instance as it starts up. You'll only need to safely download and store the private key on any computer from which you'd like to connect. Assuming you don't already have one, AWS will also help you create a new key pair. Note, however, that there will be no way for you to access and retrieve the private key once you close the dashboard dialog box. If you lose your copy, it's gone.

2.4 *Building an Ubuntu Linux web server*

Once you're connected to your instance, you only need to do a little preparation to turn it into a fully qualified, fire-breathing web server. To be precise, it will be a fully qualified, fire-breathing *Linux* web server.

Although nothing is stopping you from creating a fire-breathing Windows web server on AWS, I'll focus my attention specifically on Linux. Why? Because that's where the vast majority of AWS action will be happening for the foreseeable future, and a bit of experience with the Linux command line can take you a long way down that street.

2.4.1 Installing the software

If everything went as planned, your terminal should now be connected to your Amazon Ubuntu server instance, and you're all set to begin getting things ready to host your website. That means it's time to start installing the software you'll be using. First, you'll update the software repository. Type `sudo apt update`. Here's a sample of the output you'll get:

```
$ sudo apt update
Ign http://us-east-1.ec2.archive.ubuntu.com trusty InRelease
Get:1 http://us-east-1.ec2.archive.ubuntu.com trusty-updates
➥InRelease[65.9 kB]
Get:2 http://us-east-1.ec2.archive.ubuntu.com trusty-backports
➥InRelease [65.9 kB]
Hit http://us-east-1.ec2.archive.ubuntu.com trusty Release.gpg
Hit http://us-east-1.ec2.archive.ubuntu.com trusty Release
Get:3 http://security.ubuntu.com trusty-security InRelease [65.9 kB]
Get:4 http://us-east-1.ec2.archive.ubuntu.com trusty-updates/main
➥Sources [383 kB]
Get:5 http://us-east-1.ec2.archive.ubuntu.com trusty-updates/
➥restricted Sources [5,360 B]
[...]
Get:36 http://us-east-1.ec2.archive.ubuntu.com trusty/universe
➥Sources [6,399 kB]
Get:37 http://us-east-1.ec2.archive.ubuntu.com trusty/multiverse
➥Sources [174 kB]
Hit http://us-east-1.ec2.archive.ubuntu.com trusty/main amd64
➥Packages
Hit http://us-east-1.ec2.archive.ubuntu.com trusty/restricted amd64
➥Packages
[...]
Hit http://us-east-1.ec2.archive.ubuntu.com trusty/universe
➥Translation-en
Ign http://us-east-1.ec2.archive.ubuntu.com trusty/main
➥Translation-en_US
[...]
Ign http://us-east-1.ec2.archive.ubuntu.com trusty/universe
➥Translation-en_US
Fetched 11.7 MB in 4s (2,720 kB/s)
Reading package lists... Done
```

What is a software repository, and why does it need to be updated?

Most of the tens of thousands of free programs that help make Linux as secure, efficient, and useful as it is are curated and managed by one of two groups of trusted administrators. The online software archives run by these administrators are known as *repositories*.

So that your copy of Linux knows what software is available and how it can be found, from time to time (ideally, before each software installation) you need to update the local version of the repository information that's kept in an index on your computer. Ubuntu, as part of the Debian family of distributions, uses the *apt* command-line interface to manage packages.

That one hardly hurt at all. Now you'll install the three software packages that will power your website. These packages in particular are used together with Linux so often that the combination has been given its own acronym—LAMP (*L*inux, *A*pache, *M*ySQL, and *P*HP):

- Apache web server management tool, to point inbound internet visitors to your website resources
- MySQL database, so any software you'll use later—including WordPress—will have a platform on which to build the databases it needs
- PHP scripting language, also necessary for many applications, including WordPress

Here's how the command (and a very small selection of the output) will look. Don't leave out the caret (^) character at the end of the command. Note how you're prompted to confirm the installation by typing y (for *yes*):

```
$ sudo apt install lamp-server^
Reading package lists... Done
Building dependency tree
Reading state information... Done
Note, selecting 'mysql-server-core-5.5' for task 'lamp-server'
Note, selecting 'mysql-server-5.5' for task 'lamp-server'
[...]
0 upgraded, 27 newly installed, 0 to remove and 49 not upgraded.
Need to get 15.2 MB of archives.
After this operation, 123 MB of additional disk space will be used.
*Do you want to continue? [Y/n]*
[...]
```

```
apache2_switch_mpm Switch to prefork
 * Restarting web server apache2

                          [ OK ]
apache2_invoke: Enable module php5
 * Restarting web server apache2

                          [ OK ]
Setting up php5-json (1.3.2-2build1) ...
php5_invoke: Enable module json for cli SAPI
php5_invoke: Enable module json for apache2 SAPI
Processing triggers for libc-bin (2.19-0ubuntu6.9) ...
```

What? No password?

Doesn't sudo always require you to enter your password? Another question: just what *is* your password on this AWS instance?

The short answer: for security reasons, you don't have a password. The (slightly) longer answer: if you managed to log in using your unique and highly secure key pair, you're assumed to be who you claim.

During the installation process, you'll be asked to create a password for your MySQL database. Make sure you don't lose it, because you'll need it later.

So that you can begin setting up your new website, you need to visit your new web root directory—which, by default, is where all the files accessed by visitors to your site will be kept. By *web root directory* I mean the directory in your Linux filesystem where Apache will look to find the files that will make up your website. On an Ubuntu machine, this is normally /var/www/html/, but you can configure Apache to expect it just about anywhere you like. Here's the command:

```
$ cd /var/www/html
```

Type ls to list the current directory contents:

```
$ ls
```

As you can see in figure 2.5, the only file there right now is index.html. Web browsers generally load this file first whenever visiting a site.

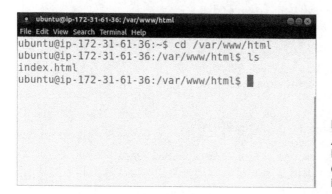

Figure 2.5   Contents of the
/var/www/html directory.
Note the ls command, which
displays the existing
index.html file.

2.4.2 Creating the website

To see what the index.html file produces, type the IP address AWS assigned your server—it's the same four-part numeric address you used to open the SSH shell session from your terminal—into the browser URL field. As you can see in figure 2.6, the current index.html displays the Apache-Ubuntu welcome and orientation page.

Now run back to your terminal's command line to do some customization. Let's use the mv (move) command to rename the default index.html file to index.html.backup. This way, you'll be free to create a new index.html file while preserving the old one in its original state for future reference. When working with configuration files on servers, it's always a good idea to make backup copies of older versions rather than overwrite them. Note that because you're working on resources owned by system users rather than your own user, you need to use sudo to elevate your authority:

```
sudo mv index.html index.html.backup
```

You're now ready to write a simple HTML page of your own, using your favorite text editor. Mine is nano, so the command is as follows:

```
sudo nano index.html
```

Type whatever you want into the editor. Just so you can see how it works, try adding a little HTML formatting, perhaps something like this:

```
<h1>Welcome!</h1>
We hope you <i>really</i> enjoy your stay here.
```

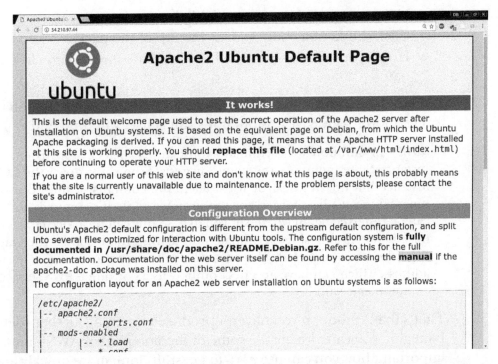

Figure 2.6   The default Apache welcome page, which includes important information about how Apache is run from an Ubuntu server

When you're done, press Ctrl-X and then Y to save the file and close nano. To view your new page, click the refresh button on the browser tab that, until now, had displayed your site's Apache page.

That's it. Your very own web server.

9:58 … 9:59 … 10:00 minutes!

If you're planning to continue working through the next few chapters right away, then—because you'll be using it again—you may want to keep this instance running. But if you think you're ready for a break— or if you'd prefer the opportunity to practice launching more instances—then, once you've finished admiring it from all angles, you can shut this one down. It's never a good idea to leave unused AWS instances running; they'll eventually start to cost you a lot of money, and doing so can be a security risk.

If you decide to shut down, here's how it works:

1 Go back to the EC2 Console (http://console.aws.amazon .com/ec2).

2 Make sure your instance is highlighted.

3 Click the Actions button near the top of the page.

4 Hover your mouse over the Instance State menu, and click Terminate.

You'll be warned that your EBS volume and all of its contents will be lost forevermore. Your SSH session, if it's still active, will then end.

> **NOTE** In addition to Terminate, you can also select Stop from the Instance State menu. As the name suggests, Stop shuts down the EC2 instance but doesn't destroy it or delete the contents of the EBS volume. You won't be charged for the instance while it's stopped, and it can be restarted again whenever you like, so this can be a nice compromise between choosing Terminate and leaving the instance running. But when it's restarted, the instance will be using a different IP address, which can have an effect on how users or other AWS services communicate with it.

That's that. Although you haven't produced anything all that useful yet, I imagine you can already see some of the potential of AWS—and, more important, how you can use AWS to get stuff done more quickly and better than ever before. Stay tuned.

2.5 *Troubleshooting*

What if something didn't work? I can tell you from personal experience that, sooner or later, that'll definitely happen. Here are some basic troubleshooting suggestions you can apply to your EC2 mishaps or any other AWS adventure that's gone off the rails:

- If you can't connect to your instance through either SSH or your browser, double-check that your security groups aren't blocking you. Remember, every communication protocol requires an open port.

- Ditto for any restrictive rules in a network access control list (NACL) associated with your VPC (see chapter 14) that may be active. By default, ACLs are wide open.

- It's also possible that your instance (or other resource) hasn't had enough time to fully launch or to reload if you've made a configuration change. The dashboard for a particular status usually has information about the current status.

- Does Amazon do logs? You bet it does. For EC2, select your instance, and then click Actions > Instance Settings > Get System Log. That'll give you something interesting to read.
- If the connection or lifecycle status depends on authentication, make sure the credentials you gave were current and accurately entered.
- If (almost) all else fails, try an internet search, including any error messages you've seen. AWS documentation will often prove useful at this stage.

2.6 Lab

If you've been following along with the demos and still have a LAMP server humming along happily, I suggest that you throw caution to the wind, shut it all down, and build it again from scratch. With a little luck, you'll encounter one or two different frustrating problems and will be forced to troubleshoot your way out. You can't lose!

Definitions
- *EC2*—AWS's Elastic Compute Cloud virtual cloud computing service.
- *Free Tier*—The free AWS service level offered to new customers for their first year.
- *Tag*—A name identifying a single AWS resource.
- *Security group*—A collection of rules controlling access to an AWS resource.
- *IP address*—A numeric address identifying an object's location on a network.
- *URL*—Uniform resource locator. A network address through which a network client (like a web browser) is identified.
- *Key pair*—Matched private and public files used to secure connections over insecure networks.
- *SSH*—The Secure Shell protocol for communication over insecure networks.
- sudo—A command prefix used when you want to temporarily elevate your account status to that of administrator.
- *Apache*—An open source web server software package.
- *MySQL*—An open source database package.
- *PHP*—PHP: Hypertext Preprocessor. A popular scripting and programming language.
- *nano*—A lightweight, terminal-based text editor.
- *MySQL*—An open source database package.

(continued)

- *PHP*—PHP: Hypertext Preprocessor. A popular scripting and programming language.
- *nano*—A lightweight, terminal-based text editor.

Command-line review

- Limit access to a private key—`chmod 400 keyname.pem`
- SSH to a remote server—`ssh -i keyname.pem ubuntu @54.152.9.184`
- Install the OpenSSH Server package—`apt install openssh-server`
- Start the OpenSSH server—`systemctl start ssh`
- Give a file a new name (location)—`mv index.html index.html.backup`

Provisioning a more robust EC2 website

3

Creating the previous chapter's simple Hello World web page was all very well; but considering what's on display, do you suppose anyone will drop by for a visit? Adding the kind of killer content that'll have people falling over each other to get a good look at your site is your department. But assuming the hordes are on their way, what's next?

In this chapter, you'll learn how to prepare for those hordes by choosing the right blend of AWS resources to meet your unique needs. Then, using your new and improved web server, you'll install and launch a WordPress site to take your project to the next level.

3.1 Calculating capacity needs

How can you be sure that your humble AWS server has everything it needs to handle the expected load? What *is* the expected load?

I'll start with some basic assumptions about the nature of happiness:

- Your users will be happiest when their browser requests are answered quickly and accurately.
- Your virtual server will be happiest when it doesn't have to strain to get its job done.
- You'll be happiest when you can be confident that your users' needs are being served, your server has things under control,

and you're not spending any more money on your AWS resources than is absolutely necessary.

Let's dig a bit deeper. To make sure your server won't have to strain its poor, delicate self, you need to give it enough of these things:

- *Processing power*—CPU capacity
- *Storage space*—Hard drive capacity
- *System memory*—RAM
- *Network bandwidth*—Maximum amount of data that can be transferred into and out of your infrastructure at a given time

I'll translate these into AWS-friendly terms so you'll know we're speaking the same language.

3.2 Getting the measure of EC2's core compute services

Let's see how AWS packages virtual versions of each of the four basic categories of compute services:

3.2.1 vCPU

In the Amazon universe, processing power is measured in virtual central processing units (vCPUs). AWS tells you that a single AWS vCPU is roughly the equivalent of a "1.0-1.2 GHz 2007 Opteron or 2007 Xeon processor." Modern consumer PCs often come with four cores, each running at 2.5 GHz; so, in simplified terms, your PC will deliver approximately eight times the processing power of a single vCPU. Having said that, because a virtual server doesn't have to devote resources to most of the thirsty stuff running on your laptop—like a high-resolution video interface or a web browser with 10 or 15 tabs open—it can get a lot more serious work done with a lot less power.

3.2.2 EBS

The AWS storage that's most comparable to the physical hard drive inside your PC is the EBS volume. Elastic Block Store (EBS) is a vast collection of hundreds of thousands of storage drives kept running in AWS's data centers. An EBS *volume* is a logically defined amount of storage space carved out of that vast storage system that's been set aside for an EC2 customer—which would be you.

Relatively speaking, renting space on an EBS volume is expensive, so you'll generally want to keep application data (data generated either for or by your applications) elsewhere. More often than not, that "elsewhere" will mean AWS's S3 storage service. I'll talk a lot about how S3 works in later chapters.

EBS volumes are generally used for your OS, your application code, and sometimes your database, but nothing more. That's why, unlike the 500–1,000 GB drives you'll see on bargain-basement home PCs, an 8 GB volume is often more than enough for Linux cloud servers. After all, who (besides YouTube) stores hundreds of cute cat videos on a server?

3.2.3 Memory

Memory is memory, no matter where it lives. Because RAM memory is much more instantly accessible than any other widely available option, it's usually used to temporarily store as much system-process and application data as possible. If, for example, serving a single web page to a single customer requires one tenth of a megabyte (100 KB) of RAM, you'll want to make sure you have at least 100 KB times n of the stuff available, where n is the maximum number of pages you might need to serve at a single time. Naturally, you can run this calculation using your own page size and traffic volumes.

3.2.4 Bandwidth

The quality of an EC2 instance's connectivity to its network is described as its *network performance*. For most instance types, the value is Low, Moderate, or High.

The real-world performance you'll experience will depend on a wide variety of factors, but it's been estimated that you'll get anywhere from 2 to 100 Mbps for Low, 10 to 250 Mbps for Moderate, and 95 to 1000 Mbps for High. Compare those numbers with the amount of data you expect you'll need to transfer in and out of your server to keep your customers happy, to determine what level of network performance to select.

3.3 Assessing your application

In order for all that information to be useful, you'll need to get a sense of how much computing power your application will need. By far the most reliable approach is to try it out for yourself. From within an SSH

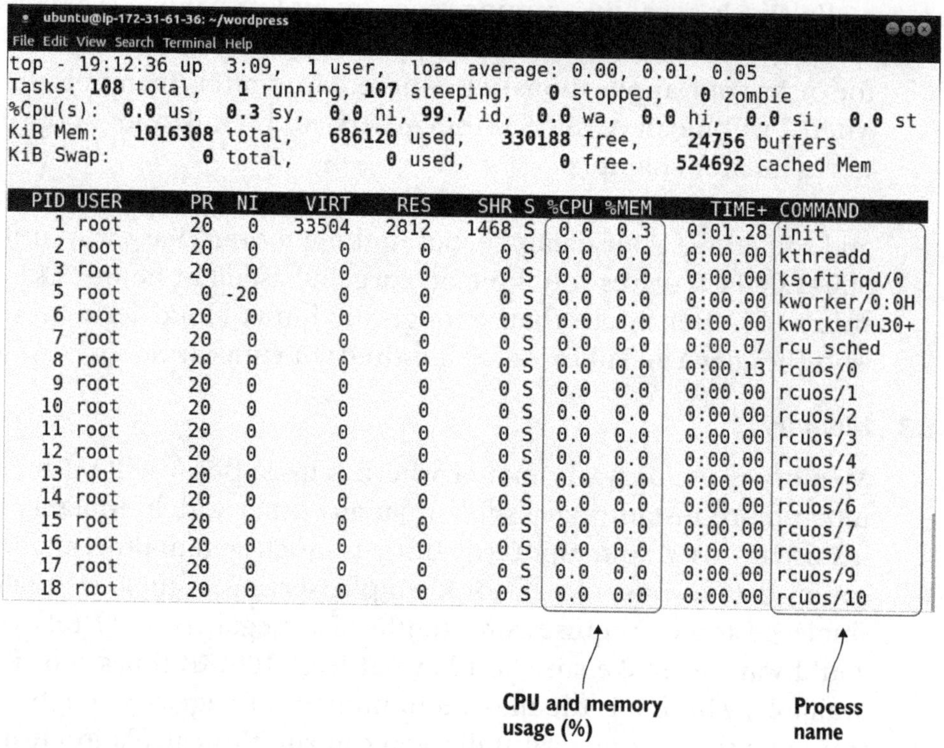

```
  ●  ubuntu@ip-172-31-61-36: ~/wordpress                              ● ● ⊗
 File Edit View Search Terminal Help
top - 19:12:36 up  3:09,  1 user,  load average: 0.00, 0.01, 0.05
Tasks: 108 total,   1 running, 107 sleeping,   0 stopped,   0 zombie
%Cpu(s):  0.0 us,  0.3 sy,  0.0 ni, 99.7 id,  0.0 wa,  0.0 hi,  0.0 si,  0.0 st
KiB Mem:   1016308 total,   686120 used,   330188 free,    24756 buffers
KiB Swap:        0 total,        0 used,        0 free.   524692 cached Mem

 PID USER      PR  NI    VIRT    RES    SHR S %CPU %MEM     TIME+ COMMAND
   1 root      20   0   33504   2812   1468 S  0.0  0.3   0:01.28 init
   2 root      20   0       0      0      0 S  0.0  0.0   0:00.00 kthreadd
   3 root      20   0       0      0      0 S  0.0  0.0   0:00.00 ksoftirqd/0
   5 root       0 -20       0      0      0 S  0.0  0.0   0:00.00 kworker/0:0H
   6 root      20   0       0      0      0 S  0.0  0.0   0:00.00 kworker/u30+
   7 root      20   0       0      0      0 S  0.0  0.0   0:00.07 rcu_sched
   8 root      20   0       0      0      0 S  0.0  0.0   0:00.13 rcuos/0
   9 root      20   0       0      0      0 S  0.0  0.0   0:00.00 rcuos/1
  10 root      20   0       0      0      0 S  0.0  0.0   0:00.00 rcuos/2
  11 root      20   0       0      0      0 S  0.0  0.0   0:00.00 rcuos/3
  12 root      20   0       0      0      0 S  0.0  0.0   0:00.00 rcuos/4
  13 root      20   0       0      0      0 S  0.0  0.0   0:00.00 rcuos/5
  14 root      20   0       0      0      0 S  0.0  0.0   0:00.00 rcuos/6
  15 root      20   0       0      0      0 S  0.0  0.0   0:00.00 rcuos/7
  16 root      20   0       0      0      0 S  0.0  0.0   0:00.00 rcuos/8
  17 root      20   0       0      0      0 S  0.0  0.0   0:00.00 rcuos/9
  18 root      20   0       0      0      0 S  0.0  0.0   0:00.00 rcuos/10
```

CPU and memory usage (%)   Process name

Figure 3.1 A quiet EC2 web server, as measured by `top`

session on an AWS Ubuntu instance, figure 3.1 shows the output of the
`top` command with the system at rest.

   `top` is a Unix/Linux program that reports on the processes that are
currently using the most system resources; it can be a great way to
quickly assess the state of your instance. The two columns of most interest are %CPU, which indicates the percentage of total CPU capacity
taken up by the most active processes; and %MEM, which tells you the
percentage of system memory used by the most active processes. In this
case, very little of either resource is currently being used.

   But figure 3.2 shows the same `top` command run immediately after I
loaded a web page served by this instance in my browser. This time, the
Command column at far right shows that the two most active processes
are associated with the Apache web server software and MySQL:
between them, they account for 4% of the CPU and around 7.5% of
memory.

CPU and memory usage (%)   Process name

```
● ubuntu@ip-172-31-61-36: ~/wordpress                                    ●●●
File Edit View Search Terminal Help
top - 19:20:28 up  3:17,  1 user,  load average: 0.01, 0.03, 0.05
Tasks: 109 total,   2 running, 107 sleeping,   0 stopped,   0 zombie
%Cpu(s):  3.3 us,  0.3 sy,  0.0 ni, 96.3 id,  0.0 wa,  0.0 hi,  0.0 si,  0.0 st
KiB Mem:   1016308 total,   694848 used,   321460 free,    24936 buffers
KiB Swap:        0 total,        0 used,        0 free.   528872 cached Mem

  PID USER      PR  NI    VIRT    RES    SHR S %CPU %MEM     TIME+ COMMAND
 5628 www-data  20   0  277676  22584  15612 S  3.0  2.2   0:00.09 apache2
 3186 mysql     20   0  623920  53604   7296 S  1.0  5.3   0:03.19 mysqld
    1 root      20   0   33504   2812   1468 S  0.0  0.3   0:01.28 init
    2 root      20   0       0      0      0 S  0.0  0.0   0:00.00 kthreadd
    3 root      20   0       0      0      0 S  0.0  0.0   0:00.00 ksoftirqd/0
    5 root       0 -20       0      0      0 S  0.0  0.0   0:00.00 kworker/0:0H
    6 root      20   0       0      0      0 S  0.0  0.0   0:00.00 kworker/u30+
    7 root      20   0       0      0      0 S  0.0  0.0   0:00.07 rcu_sched
    8 root      20   0       0      0      0 R  0.0  0.0   0:00.14 rcuos/0
    9 root      20   0       0      0      0 S  0.0  0.0   0:00.00 rcuos/1
   10 root      20   0       0      0      0 S  0.0  0.0   0:00.00 rcuos/2
   11 root      20   0       0      0      0 S  0.0  0.0   0:00.00 rcuos/3
   12 root      20   0       0      0      0 S  0.0  0.0   0:00.00 rcuos/4
   13 root      20   0       0      0      0 S  0.0  0.0   0:00.00 rcuos/5
   14 root      20   0       0      0      0 S  0.0  0.0   0:00.00 rcuos/6
   15 root      20   0       0      0      0 S  0.0  0.0   0:00.00 rcuos/7
   16 root      20   0       0      0      0 S  0.0  0.0   0:00.00 rcuos/8
```

Figure 3.2 `top` **output illustrating a busier web server. Note the MySQL and Apache activity.**

At this rate, you could certainly handle a dozen or so users launching requests within a short time; but after that, assuming you're not using some clever optimization program, you'll be pretty much hitting the limit. In other words, if you're expecting serious traffic to head your way, you'd better select a more robust instance type. Having said that, the virtualization underlying AWS makes it simple to upgrade resources later if your needs change.

Naturally, you'll also want to experiment with the quality of network response times and keep an eye on available storage on your EBS volume. Need a good tool to monitor network capacity? Look no further than EC2. With your instance selected in the EC2 Instances dashboard, select the Monitoring tab and scroll down through the data charts. You'll find accurate, up-to-date representations of network activity displayed, based on a number of metrics.

> **Try it now**
>
> Why not take some time right now and see if you can use these methods to work out the kind of resource levels you'll need for your project? How much traffic can your server handle before it will choke?

3.4   Choosing the right instance for your project

In addition to storage—which is a separate decision—the CPU, memory, and network-performance capacity you get will all depend on the instance type you choose. You probably remember seeing the Choose an Instance Type page (figure 3.3) in the previous chapter.

Keeping in mind what you've just learned about these values, spend some time looking through the vCPUs, Memory, and Network Performance columns and thinking about which type you're likely to need. To

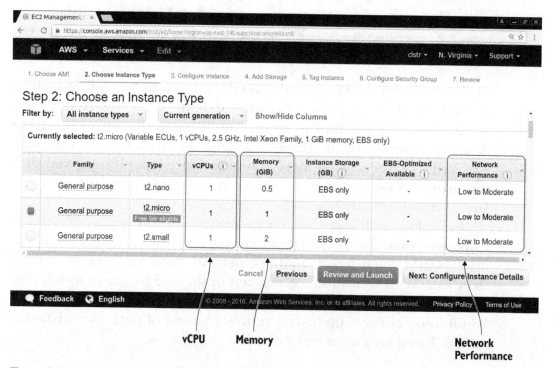

Figure 3.3   The EC2 Choose an Instance Type page

help you through that process, I'll give you an overview of AWS's instance type families.

Because AWS knows that the specific needs of individual users' projects are wildly different, it offers various categories of instance types, known as *families*, each focusing on a specific profile range. The general overview in this section should help you interpret what might otherwise feel a bit overwhelming.

As listed in table 3.1, AWS currently organizes its instance types into 10 families, each designated by a single letter: T, M, and so on. The identifying name of a particular type within a family consists of its family letter along with a number to differentiate it from any other types that exist in the family. The missing numbers (where's T1, for instance?) are probably older types that have since been deprecated. The Focus column describes the particular strength peculiar to each family.

Table 3.1 EC2 instance type families

Type family	Member types	Focus
T	T2	Baseline general purpose (*burstable performance*)[a]
M	M3, M4	General purpose: balance between compute, memory, and network
C	C3, C4	Computer optimized: high-performance processors
X	X1	Memory optimized for enterprise-class, in-memory applications
R	R3, R4	Memory optimized for memory-intensive applications
P	P2	Graphics accelerated for GPU-intensive applications
G	G2	Graphics-heavy processing
F	F1	Hardware acceleration with field-programmable arrays (FPGAs)
I	I2, I3	Storage optimized: very fast storage volumes for efficient I/O operations
D	D2	Storage optimized: high disk throughput for very large data stores

[a] *Burstable* means the vCPU of a T2 instance is capable of spending *CPU credits* to achieve brief bursts of higher performance to meet periods of higher demand. An instance acquires these credits during stretches of sub-baseline activity.

Each member type, such as M4, is generally available in a number of variations: M4.large, M4.xlarge, M4.2xlarge, and so on.

Suppose it's your job to keep Netflix.com's customer account database running smoothly. Based on all this information, if you're going to be running that sort of large, high-performance database operation, you'll want to choose a flavor of R3 instance—or, more accurately, many hundreds of them. But what if you're responsible for a busy multitiered web server, such as a popular blog that attracts more than 100,000 unique users each month? Then M4, or even C3, instances might work better. The good news is that AWS has a profile to match your needs. The better news is that if you choose badly or your needs evolve, updating your profile later isn't difficult.

That wasn't so complicated, was it? Maybe not, but only because I left out some stuff. Take another look at the AWS Console, and let your eyes wander toward the upper-right corner and the drop-down menu to the right of your account name. In my case (as you can see in figure 3.4), N. Virginia is the menu's current title, but clicking the menu shows a long list of other geographic areas.

> **NOTE** *N. Virginia* isn't short for North Virginia. Last time I looked, there was no such state in the United States. The AWS folk probably mean northern Virginia.

The area (or region) you select will determine where in the world the resources you subsequently launch will be physically based. This is important for many reasons, including the fact that you may prefer to host your virtual servers on hardware that's as close as possible to your customers. But it's also significant because not every instance type is available in every region.

Try it now

Take a few minutes to browse through the instance types that are available in your region and—bearing in mind their specific attributes like vCPU count, memory, and storage—try to imagine which will work best for your needs. When you're finished, you should have a decent idea of which type you'll choose.

Whether you're going to use the same instance you created in the previous chapter or launch a new one, you'll need to log in to it again using

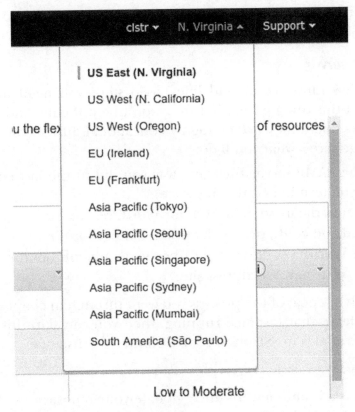

Figure 3.4 Select an AWS region.

SSH or PuTTY. While you're configuring a new instance, if AWS complains that no existing keys are found, check to make sure you're still using the same AWS geographic region as when you created the keys in the first place.

3.5 Adding WordPress

What is WordPress? Nothing much, really. Just the content management system (CMS) and website-creation tool used to build more than a quarter of all the internet's websites, as measured by the technology-usage trackers at w3techs.com (https://w3techs.com/technologies/overview/content_management/all).

Why should you use WordPress for a privately hosted site? Of course, you don't need to use WordPress if you don't want to, and I promise not to take it badly. But because WordPress makes it a lot easier to produce a professional-looking, reliable, secure website of just about any kind without needing a strong web development background, I think it's a good way to illustrate how your website might evolve. So here we go.

3.5.1   *Preparing the server*

There are a few Linux command line–based steps you need to walk through to get this thing going, but they won't be difficult. And if you keep your eyes open, they *will* be highly educational. Just so you know what's coming, here's what you'll do:

1   Install the LAMP server the same way you did in the last chapter (before you terminated that instance).
2   Create a new database in MySQL for WordPress to use.
3   Download and configure the latest version of WordPress.
4   Copy the WordPress files to your Apache document root directory.
5   Log in to your new WordPress site.

The first step is a repeat of the process you went through in chapter 2. If you chose to leave that instance running, then you can skip this part. Either way, the goal is to SSH in to your Ubuntu AWS instance:

```
$ ssh -i keyname.pem ubuntu@<your-instance-IP-address>
```

Assuming this is a brand-new instance, update your repositories. Then, once again, install the LAMP server package:

```
$ sudo apt update
$ sudo apt install lamp-server^
```

Don't forget to open port 80 (HTTP) in the AWS security group used by your instance; otherwise, your users will be unable to reach your site.

3.5.2   *Preparing MySQL*

You'll have to create a new user account and database for WordPress to use. Technically, you could use the MySQL root user for this purpose, but it's always best to use root accounts sparingly; they possess more power than they need, and using them more than absolutely necessary exposes you to an unnecessary security risk.

Use the root user (and the root password that you created and didn't forget during the MySQL installation) to log in to the MySQL shell. -u tells MySQL that you'll assume the root user, and -p says that you want to be prompted for your password:

```
$ mysql -u root -p
```

Once in the shell, you need to create a new database—I call it wordpressdb, but the name makes no difference. Then create a new user (which I call wpuser), assign a password, and grant the user privileges on the new database. Remember to end each MySQL command with a semicolon, or the shell will have absolutely no idea what you're trying to tell it. Finally, exit the shell:

```
mysql> CREATE DATABASE wordpressdb;
Query OK, 1 row affected (0.00 sec)
mysql> CREATE USER 'wpuser'@'localhost' IDENTIFIED BY 'mypassword';
Query OK, 0 rows affected (0.00 sec)
mysql> GRANT ALL PRIVILEGES ON wordpressdb.* To 'wpuser'@'localhost';
Query OK, 0 rows affected (0.00 sec)
mysql> FLUSH PRIVILEGES;
Query OK, 0 rows affected (0.00 sec)
mysql> exit
```

3.5.3 Downloading and configuring WordPress

In your browser, visit the WordPress download page (http://wordpress .org/download) to get the address of the package you're after. You don't want to download the package directly to your personal computer, because that's not where you're going to be installing WordPress. You could right-click the Download WordPress button and select Copy Link (or some variation) from the menu that appears. That option points to a .zip file, which would work fine but would require an extra step on your Ubuntu instance to install the unzip program. Instead, right-click Download .tar.gz to get the same package, but archived in the more Linux-friendly tar format.

Back in the SSH terminal session, use the wget program to download WordPress, using the address you copied from the WordPress website:

```
$ wget https://wordpress.org/latest.tar.gz
--2017-03-21 19:47:20--  https://wordpress.org/latest.tar.gz
Resolving wordpress.org (wordpress.org)... 66.155.40.249, 66.155.40.250
Connecting to wordpress.org (wordpress.org)|66.155.40.249|:443... connected.
HTTP request sent, awaiting response... 200 OK
Length: 8008833 (7.6M) [application/octet-stream]
Saving to: 'latest.tar.gz.1'

latest.tar.gz.1     100%[====================>]   7.64M  1.35MB/s   in 6.6s

2017-03-21 19:47:27 (1.16 MB/s) - 'latest.tar.gz.1' saved [8008833/8008833]
```

Once that's finished (and it shouldn't take more than a few seconds), use the `tar` program to decompress and unpack the file. The x tells `tar` to extract the archived contents, z means it's going to need decompression as well, and f points to the filename:

```
$ tar xzf latest.tar.gz
```

Run `ls` to list the current contents of your directory. You'll see that, in addition to the latest.tar.gz file you just downloaded, there's a new subdirectory called wordpress. Use `cd` to change to that directory and `ls` again to list its contents:

```
ls
cd wordpress
ls
```

See the file called wp-config-sample.php? That's a template you can use to manage your WordPress configuration. You'll use `cp` to create a copy of that file named wp-config.php (so WordPress will know that this is the configuration file you want it to use) and then edit its contents:

```
$ cp wp-config-sample.php wp-config.php
```

You can use the nano text editor to work with the config file:

```
$ nano wp-config.php
```

This (as you can see in figure 3.5) is where you tell WordPress about its new neighborhood. Replace `database_name_here` with the name you'd like to give your database, `username_here` with the wpuser you created for MySQL, and `password_here` with that user's new password, so that WordPress can successfully log in and manage its database. For the values I used, those lines now look like this:

```
/** The name of the database for WordPress */
define('DB_NAME', 'wordpressdb');

/** MySQL database username */
define('DB_USER', 'wpuser');

/** MySQL database password */
define('DB_PASSWORD', 'mypassword');
```

> **TIP** Using *mypassword* (or any remotely similar variation) for a password on any working server is nuts. Don't try it.

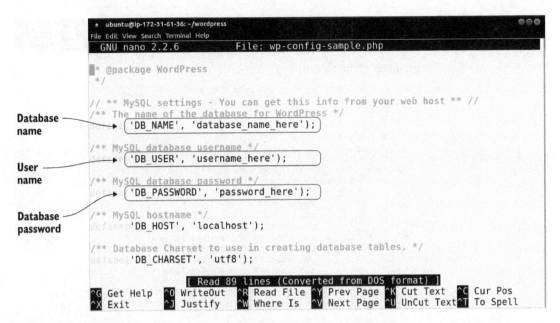

Figure 3.5 Lines from the wp-config.php file that require your attention

You can quickly generate a unique set of keys and salts—character strings used by WordPress to allow secure authentication with the database, as shown in figure 3.6—by loading the WordPress secret-key page (https://api.wordpress.org/secret-key/1.1/salt) in your browser, copying the text that's displayed, and then using that text to replace the existing sample text.

> **TIP** When using nano, rather than pressing the Delete key over and over again to remove the hundreds of characters making up the sample salts lines, move your cursor to anywhere on a line you want to delete and press Ctrl-K. The entire line will magically disappear. Repeat to taste. To save the file and exit, press Ctrl-X.

That's it for the configuration. All that's left is to copy the contents of the wordpress directory to wherever you'd like your WordPress site to live.

> **TIP** The only absolutely reliable way to know if you've configured the file properly is to try it out and see whether you can load the page in your browser (more about that later). If something goes wrong, you should look for any error messages that appear. Consulting system logs like those at /var/log/apache2 and /var/log/mysql can also be helpful.

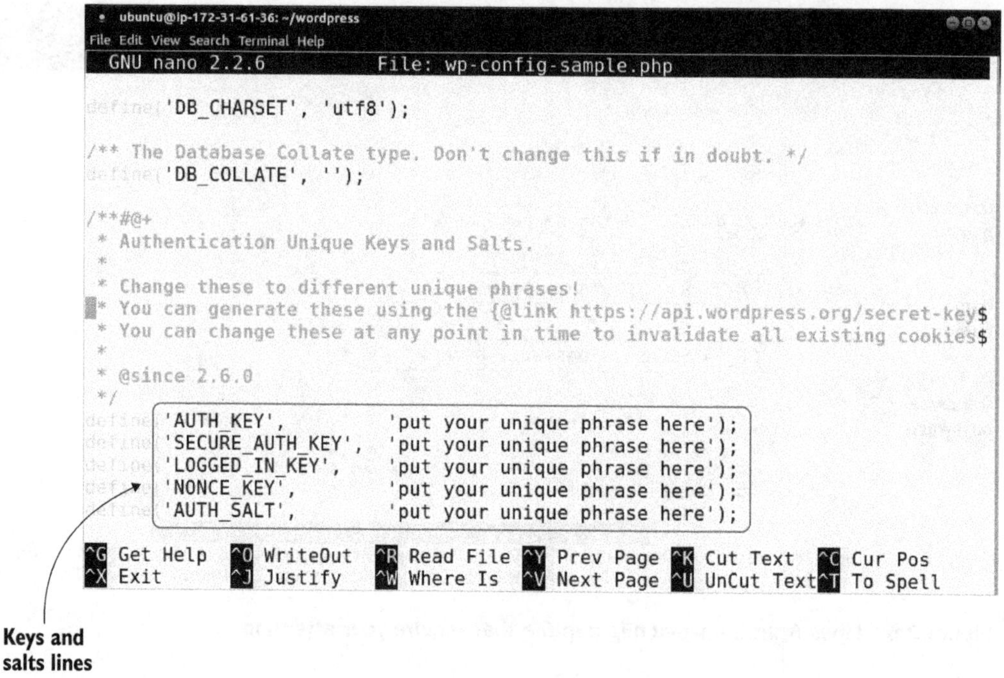

Figure 3.6 Lines from the wp-config.php file reserved for authentication keys

3.5.4 *Setting up the WordPress filesystem*

If you want to use WordPress to manage all the content on your domain—perhaps you like the fact that the WordPress ecosystem includes so many resources for closely integrating content and transaction processing—you should copy all the files in the wordpress directory to Apache's document root directory. On Ubuntu machines, you'll recall, this is /var/www/html/. If you do this and your domain is, for instance, bootstrap-it.com, visitors will see the contents of WordPress's main page. But if you're already using bootstrap-it.com to host other content, and you'd prefer to use WordPress, say, only as a blog, then you might create a directory called blog within /var/www/html/. Visitors to bootstrap-it.com/blog will then see that content.

Copying files along with subdirectories and their contents requires the -r flag along with the cp command, invoking the recursive feature. When run from within the wordpress directory, the following example copies all the files in the directory to the document root:

```
$ sudo cp -r * /var/www/html
```

3.5.5 *Testing your application*

When that's done, it's time to head back to your browser and point it to your instance's public IP address (the one you used to SSH in). Just this once, add the route to the install.php file, where you can create a Word-Press admin account. The address will look something like this:

```
54.218.241.9/wp-admin/install.php
```

As you can see in figure 3.7, you're off to the races!

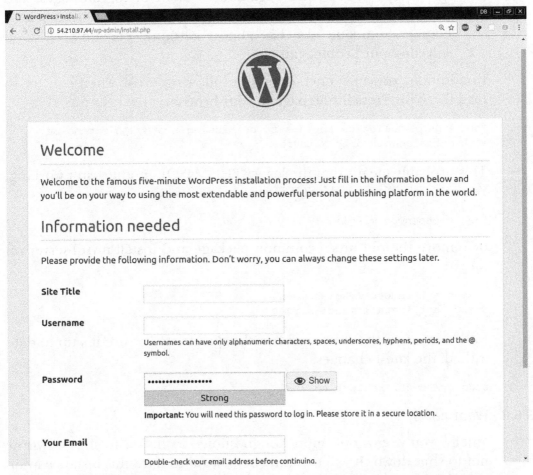

Figure 3.7   The setup screen that will welcome you to your new WordPress site (accessed using *your-ip-or-sitename*/wp-admin/install.php)

Of course, it's possible that you won't be off to the races and the page will fail to load. There's a long list of things that may have gone wrong, but these three troubleshooting steps are nearly always helpful:

1 Note any error messages that are displayed.
2 Look for log messages. On an Ubuntu system, you'll find useful log files in the /var/log/apache2/ and /var/log/mysql/ directories. Remember that although log files can be long, each entry usually has a timestamp.
3 Copy important-looking segments of error or log messages, and paste them into the search bar of your favorite internet search engine. Someone else has almost certainly encountered—and solved—your problem already.

In addition, you may encounter the following error when you try to load the WordPress install page in your browser:

```
Your PHP installation appears to be missing the MySQL extension
which is required by WordPress.
```

This probably means that the legacy PHP MySQL module isn't working. You can either enable MySQLi using

```
$ sudo phpenmod mysqli
```

or remove the old mysql-common package and install mysql-server on top:

```
$ sudo apt remove mysql-common
$ sudo apt install mysql-server
```

Either way, you should restart Apache, just to make sure it's up to date with all the latest changes:

```
sudo systemctl restart apache2
```

3.5.6 *What next?*

Finally, you've got one more tough choice to make: to shut down or not to shut down. It will certainly be helpful to have this instance available for coming chapters, so leaving it running would be nice. But if there's a good chance that you'll put the book aside for some weeks—your boss cancelled your lunch break, for instance—then you may want to terminate the instance and build it again from scratch when you're ready to continue.

If you decide to shut down, remember that you can do so from the EC2 Instances dashboard. Make sure this instance is selected, and click Actions > Instance State > Terminate. Rather than terminate it, you can also click Stop to stop your instance and restart it at a later time. One thing to keep in mind about Stop, though, is that the IP address you've been using to access the instance will no longer be available when you restart.

If that might be a problem (and it often will), you can associate a permanent elastic IP address to the instance. This will be useful later as your AWS resources become more dependent on each other. You can read more about elastic IPs in chapter 5.

3.6 *Lab*

With a live EC2 instance running WordPress—build it again, if you've shut down the one from the demo—use a number of browsers to load its pages. From inside the instance (via SSH), use `top` (or similar tools) to measure how close you get to your system capacity.

Definitions

- *vCPU*—Virtual central processing units
- *Network bandwidth*—The rate (or volume of data) at which data can travel through a network
- *Instance type*—A standard measure of an AWS EC2 virtual machine
- *AWS region*—A collection of physical AWS data center server farms located within a specific geographic area
- *PuTTY*—A Windows client used to access remote resources through SSH servers.
- *Root account*—The main administration user account for an operating system or database
- *tar*—The Unix/Linux file-archiving program
- *Keys and salts*—WordPress authentication keys

Command-line review

- *Create a database in MySQL*—`mysql> CREATE DATABASE wordpressdb;`
- *Extract an archive using* `tar`—`tar xzf latest.tar.gz`
- *Make a working copy of the sample config file*—`cp wp-config-sample.php wp-config.php`
- *Delete a complete line of text (in nano)*—Ctrl-K
- *Copy the current directory contents to the web root*—`sudo cp -r * /var /www/html`

Databases on AWS

As you saw in the previous chapter, WordPress stores in a database all the bits and pieces that make up your website. But of course, this approach isn't limited to WordPress: it would be hard to imagine any public-facing application of even minimal complexity that didn't rely on structured data of one sort or another. Working on an application? Learn to love databases. The coming pages explore how to choose a database architecture and how (and why) to move your database away from the WordPress instance to run independently in its own environment.

4.1 The database

Just in case you haven't yet been formally introduced, I'll take a moment to explain what a database does. A *database* is software that's good at reading digital information and then reliably storing it in a structured format so that the information can later be efficiently retrieved in useful formats and combinations.

Imagine that your business keeps records of all your customers, including their names, addresses, and previous purchases. From time to time, you'll probably want access to that information. Perhaps you need an address so you can mail an invoice, or maybe you'd like to analyze your data to look for correlations between street addresses and purchasing patterns.

4.2   *Choosing the right database model*

The data world can get really complex, really fast. In practical terms, though, it's fair to say that most projects can be successfully served by one of two database models: relational (SQL) and NoSQL.

4.2.1   *Relational databases*

If you need your data organized in ways that carefully define how various categories of information relate to each other, then a relational database may be what you're after. Think of it in terms of a business that, say, has to manage its employees in the context of the jobs they do, the way they're paid, and their health insurance status. Data related to each employee appears in each of those categories but, at the same time, may not be accessible to other users beyond what's individually necessary.

Relational databases are often managed by one flavor or another of the SQL standard. SQL stands for *Structured Query Language,* and the "structured" part of that tells most of the story. An SQL-type database (leading examples of which include Oracle, MySQL, PostgreSQL, Microsoft's SQL Server, and, more recently, Amazon's Aurora) is made up of *tables,* which, in turn, contain *records* (or, as some call them, *rows*). Records are made up of individual values known as *fields.* Thus, the contents of a database of customer information could be represented this way:

ID	Name	Address	City	# of purchases
1	John Doe	123 Any St.	Yourtown	5
2	Jane Smith	321 Yna Ave.	Hertown	2

Here, the database has records identified by the numbers 1 and 2, and each record contains fields made up of a name, an address, and a number of purchases.

Perhaps the key benefit of this kind of strong structure is that it allows high levels of predictability and reliability, because carefully defined rules can be applied to all transactions affecting your data. You can, for example, apply constraints to the way users of an application can access the database, to ensure that two users aren't trying to write changes to a single record at one time (which could lead to data corruption).

4.2.2 NoSQL databases

Times change. Across all segments of the IT world, data is being produced, consumed, and analyzed in volumes and at speeds that weren't anticipated when the first relational database was designed more than a generation ago. Imagine, for instance, that you're building a wholesale business that needs to handle constantly changing product descriptions and inventory information for tens of thousands of items; that data, in turn, must be integrated with sales, shipping, and customer service operations.

In such a case, you'll likely want to use a NoSQL database (such as AWS's DynamoDB): highly flexible relationships between NoSQL data elements allow much simpler integration of data stored across multiple clients and in different formats. This makes it possible to easily accommodate fast-growing data sources.

Despite what you may think, some people argue that NoSQL stands not for *No SQL* or *Not SQL*, but rather for *Not Only SQL*. That's because these databases can sometimes support SQL-like operations. In other words, you can sometimes trick a NoSQL database into providing functionality similar to what you might expect from a relational database.

If you'd like more complete insights into NoSQL and how it fits into the larger spectrum of database models, the AWS document "What Is NoSQL?" should be helpful: http://aws.amazon.com/nosql.

4.2.3 How to choose

The database architecture you choose for a project will often depend on the specific needs of your application. For instance, if you're running financial transactions, and, because of the overriding need for absolute accuracy and consistency, it's critical that a single record can never have more than one value, you'll probably opt for a relational platform. Just imagine the chaos that would result if all the money in a particular account was withdrawn by two concurrent client sessions.

On the other hand, suppose you host a popular online multiplayer game. If being able to quickly update data points can make all the difference for player experience, and the occasional write failure won't cause a zombie apocalypse, you'll definitely want to consider NoSQL.

4.3 *Infrastructure design: where does your database belong?*

The WordPress project you created in chapter 3 was built on top of a LAMP server. As you no doubt remember, that means WordPress stored all of its data on the MySQL database you installed on the same EC2 instance you used for WordPress itself. That's a common way to do things for a lighter, less mission-critical deployment like a temporary demo website or a hobby blog. But although such single-machine arrangements can be simpler and inexpensive, simplicity and short-term cost savings aren't always the only goals.

Here are some reasons you might want to install and run a database *off-instance* (on its own dedicated server):

- *Security*—Although you usually want the contents of a website or application to be open to anyone out for a stroll on the internet, that won't be the case for your database. Wherever possible, it should be protected from outside access. Think what might happen if everything Google knows about its billions of customers was exposed to the public eye (it's scary enough that Google knows those things). Isolating your various resources from each other on completely separate machines can make it a lot easier to open up what needs to be open and close off the rest. Databases usually have significantly different access profiles than applications, so they're perfect candidates for this kind of separation.

- *Data accessibility*—It's common to launch more than one server as part of a single application. This can be because each provides a unique service, but it's usually either so you can duplicate your content to protect against the failure of any single server, or to accommodate growing user demand. In any case, when you have multiple application servers using the same data, it's often a good idea to keep your database separate.

- *Hardware*—Web or application servers often consume compute resources differently than databases. The former may rely heavily on the power of a strong, multicore CPU, whereas the latter may thrive on super-fast, solid-state drives. It's always nice to let everyone play with their favorite toys.

- *Software*—Suppose you have an application that requires a Windows server, but you want your data kept on a Linux machine. Even if, technically, it can be done using the magic of virtualization, you may want to avoid the extra complications involved in running both OSs on a single server.
- *AWS RDS*—We're back at last to the *AWS* in *Learn AWS in a Month of Lunches*. Amazon Relational Database Service (RDS) provides a fully managed database solution that can be easily integrated into EC2-based applications. *Managed* means that Amazon takes care of all the hardware and administrative worries and gives you a single internet address (called an *endpoint*) through which to access the resource. AWS provides you with a database (MySQL, Oracle, Aurora, and so on) that's guaranteed to be available, replicated (backed up to protect against data loss through failure), and patched (the software is the latest and greatest available). You can only get these features by off-loading your database.

Figure 4.1 is a simple illustration of how an on-instance versus a managed RDS arrangement might work.

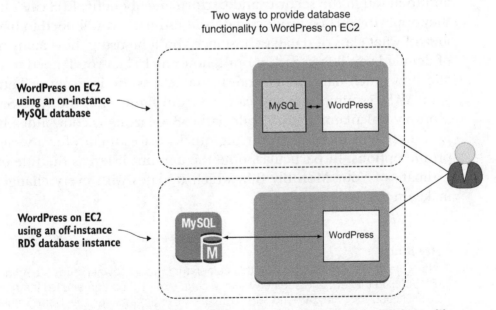

Figure 4.1 WordPress running on an EC2 instance and accessing a database either on-instance or from a managed RDS instance

4.4   *Estimating costs*

Before I show you how to migrate the MySQL database of your existing WordPress deployment to RDS, we should have a frank discussion about money. Running your database on RDS rather than sharing your application instance will, obviously, incur some extra costs. In fact, even selecting a light database instance like db.t2.small that will be used 100% of the time will come with a monthly bill of around $25 US at current rates. Swapping that for a db.m3.xlarge instance (which you'll need to handle higher demand loads) will increase those costs by about 10 times. Running a second instance to greatly enhance reliability using Amazon's Multi-AZ feature will, of course, double your costs.

On the other hand, maintaining a busy database on your EC2 instance may require more computing horsepower to keep up without placing a possible drain on application performance. Moving from a t2.medium EC2 instance to m4.large, for instance, could add nearly $50 per month to your bill.

When planning your deployment, your job is to accurately estimate the kind of usage you'll encounter and what that will cost you on RDS, and then weigh the security and performance benefits RDS can offer as they apply to you. To produce a decent estimate, you'll need to have an idea of what class of database instance you'll be using, how many hours of demand you'll face each month, how much data you'll need to store, and how much data will be transferred across the internet or between your AWS resources. As you can see from figure 4.2, the AWS Simple Monthly Calculator (http://calculator.s3.amazonaws.com/index.html) is an excellent tool for producing quick cost estimates for a variety of profile options. In particular, note the amount listed as the title of the Estimate of Your Monthly Bill, which updates with every change you make on the Services tab.

Try it now

Navigate to the AWS Simple Monthly Calculator in your browser, click the Amazon RDS tab on the left, and see how much a couple of RDS on-demand DB instances would cost you. Play around with a range of estimates for the Data Transfer fields, and see what kind of difference that can make.

Total current monthly estimate

Enter database usage parameters.

amazon
webservices SIMPLE MONTHLY CALCULATOR

Need Help? Watch the

Get Started with AWS: Learn more about our Free Tier or Sign Up for an AWS Account »

FREE USAGE TIER: New Customers get free usage tier for first 12 months

Reset All

| Services | Estimate of your Monthly Bill ($ 695.19) |

Choose region: US-East / US Standard (Virginia) ▼   Inbound Data Transfer is Free and Outbound Data Transfer is 1 GB free per

Amazon RDS is a web service that makes it easier to set up, operate, and scale a relational database in the cloud. Cost calculation for Amazon Aurora soon. Please check the pricing page for Amazon Aurora pricing details.

Amazon EC2
Amazon S3
Amazon Route 53
Amazon CloudFront
Amazon RDS
Amazon DynamoDB
Amazon ElastiCache
Amazon CloudWatch
Amazon SES
Amazon SNS
Amazon

Amazon RDS On-Demand DB Instances:

	Description	DB Instances	Usage		DB Engine and License	Class and Deployment	Storage	I/O	
⊝		1	100	% Utilized/Mo ▼	MySQL ▼	db.r3.2xlarge ▼ Standard (Single-AZ) ▼	General Pu ▼ 50 GB	Provisioned IOPS:	0
⊕	Add New Row								

Additional Backup Storage (Free backup storage up to 100% of provisioned Storage):

	Backup Type	Backup Storage
⊕	Add New Row	

Amazon RDS Reserved DB Instances:

	Description	DB Instances	Usage		DB Engine and License	Class and Deployment	Offering and Term	Storage	I/O
⊕	Add New Row								

Figure 4.2   The RDS section of the AWS Simple Monthly Calculator lets you quickly try out alternative profiles.

To give you a sense of the instance you should choose, AWS offers three type families, each with its own set of member instance classes: *burst capable class type* (db.t2) are the cheapest instances, but despite their relatively weak specs, they can provide brief bursts of higher performance. These make sense for applications that face only intermittent spikes in usage. *Standard* (db.m4) instances are cost effective for sustained usage, but their balance of resources may not give you enough to hold up against extreme demand. And I'll bet you can figure out the use case for *memory optimized* (db.r3) instances all on your own.

I'll talk more about the Simple Monthly Calculator later, in chapter 9.

4.5   *Migrating your database to RDS*

Assuming you've decided a managed RDS-based relational database is what you've always wanted for your birthday, you have to figure out how to build one—or, in this case, how to take the database you've already built for your WordPress project and migrate it to RDS without having to rebuild it. Here's what you're going to do to make this work:

1 Make a usable copy of your existing database, which, by default, is already populated and active. This is known as a *database dump*.
2 Head over to the AWS Console to create an RDS instance. Make sure a secure connection between it and your EC2 instance is possible.
3 Upload your saved database dump to the RDS database server.

NOTE If your database is currently active and you don't want any ongoing transactions to be lost, then you'll need to add some careful preparation to this process—which would go far beyond the scope of this book. One excellent tool to consider using to help ease the transition is the AWS Database Migration Service (https://aws.amazon.com/dms/).

4.5.1 Creating a MySQL dump

You're ready to start the dump of the database. From an SSH session in your EC2 instance, which you set up according to the instructions in chapter 3, run this single command:

```
mysqldump -u wpuser -p wordpressdb > /home/ubuntu/mybackup.sql
```

This example assumes that the name of your MySQL user (identified by -u) is *wpuser*, you want to be prompted for that user's password (-p), the name of the database to be dumped is wordpressdb, and you want the output saved to a file called mybackup.sql in your user's home directory. We'll come back to this file once you've got an RDS instance to host it.

TIP Forgot your username and password? This time you're in luck. Both should be available in plain text in the wp-config.php file you created in chapter 3.

NOTE If you're working with the instance from chapter 3 after having stopped and restarted it, it may have a new IP address. This may require you to update values pointing to your site's old IP address in the wp_options table of your MySQL database. WordPress has directions at https://codex.wordpress.org/Changing_The_Site_URL. If you're not comfortable working with databases, these edits might cost you more time and trouble than firing up a brand-new instance.

4.6 Building an Amazon RDS instance

For now, it's back to the AWS Console (http://console.aws.amazon .com) to launch an RDS instance. As long as your account is eligible for the Free Tier, this won't cost you anything. Click the RDS link in the

Database part of the Console page, and you'll be taken to the RDS dashboard. Assuming you don't already have an RDS instance running, you'll see a blue Get Started Now button.

Go ahead—click it. You know you want to.

As you can see in figure 4.3, you need to select a database engine. Your choice will, to some degree, depend on your specific needs. For instance, older companies with existing Oracle or Microsoft SQL Server databases will probably want to go with those engines for the sake of compatibility. MariaDB is a community version of MySQL that, by some accounts, boasts stronger security and far better support. And Aurora was built by AWS and optimized for use in that environment. It's your call; but considering that your original EC2-based database uses MySQL, going with MySQL here should keep things as simple as possible.

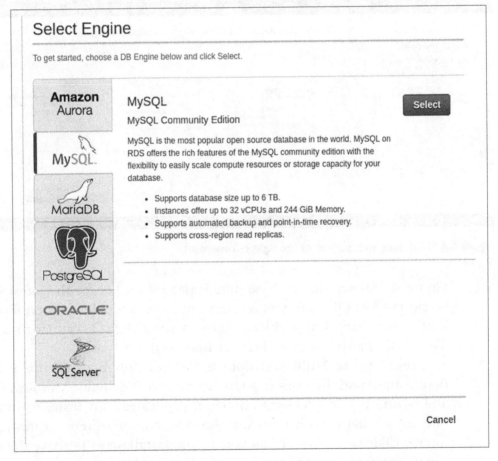

Figure 4.3   AWS currently supports these six powerful relational database engines.

Once you've selected your database engine, the next screen (see figure 4.4) allows you to choose an environment that best fits your needs:

- *Production*—An instance that will handle real customers or users
- *Dev/Test*—Something lighter-weight, to let you try out a possible setup

Because this is Amazon, you're given one more chance to select its Aurora engine. If you're trying RDS for the first time, you should definitely choose the test version, because by default, the profile you're given is available under the Free Tier. As you'll soon see, you're given only 5 GB of storage, but that's usually more than enough for a test database.

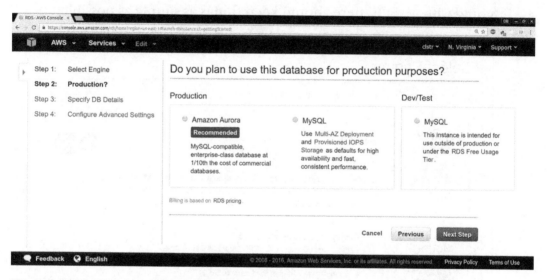

Figure 4.4 Matching your project to the right environment

Figure 4.5 shows the database details page. I settled for the latest stable version of MySQL—but you might want to use an older version if you're having compatibility problems with existing data. I went with a Free Tier db.t2.micro instance class because, well, it's free.

I said "no" to Multi-AZ Deployment, but only because this is a test deployment and the option carries extra cost. Normally, Multi-AZ (availability zone) is an excellent choice: it replicates your instance in a second AZ so that even if one Amazon data center suffers a catastrophic failure (like a total power blackout), your database will survive thanks to the instance running in the second. Because AWS manages the service,

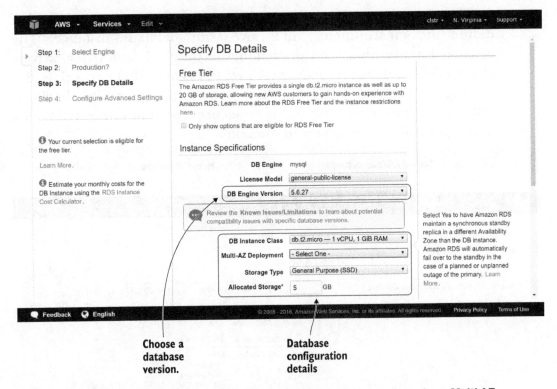

Choose a database version.

Database configuration details

Figure 4.5 Defining your database configuration (release version, instance class, Multi-AZ, authentication, and so on)

the transition or *failover* between a dying instance and its live replacement is pretty much instantaneous, and your users will probably never know anything happened.

A provisioned IOPS (input/output operations per second) drive—available through the Storage Type drop-down—may be an attractive option if you're looking for extra-fast access to your data. You can enter the maximum amount of allocated storage you'll need, in gigabytes. For this example, your needs are minimal, so the General Purpose option is fine.

The name you choose for DB Instance Identifier in the Settings section will be the official name given to the database; you'll use this database name later, in the wp-config.php file, when you're ready to connect. You don't have to use the same database name you used in your original, local configuration, but you may find it convenient. Master Username and Password, on the other hand, *must* match the values you used in the wp-config.php file on your EC2 instance.

The next screen (figure 4.6) contains some important settings that define the environment you'll give your database instance. The instance is currently set to launch in my account's default virtual private cloud (VPC), which is exactly what I want, because that network is also hosting my EC2 server. Having them both in the same VPC allows for faster and (more important) more-secure communications. I'll talk much more about VPCs later in the book.

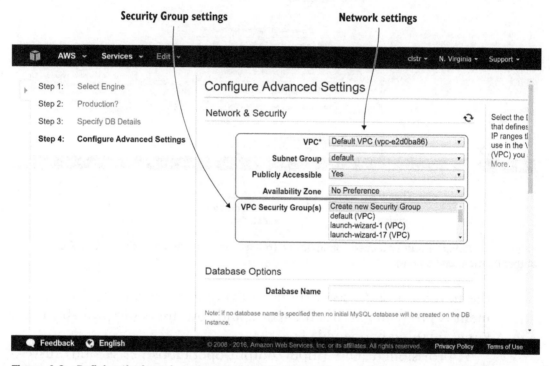

Figure 4.6   Defining the launch environment details (network, security group, port, and so on)

In the case of the MySQL database on your WordPress site—whose only legitimate user is the WordPress instance—there's no reason to provide access to your database to anyone or anything besides your EC2 server. So, set Publicly Accessible to No. One of the cardinal rules of IT administration security is to open the fewest possible system resources to the fewest possible users. That way, you limit your exposure to risk.

RDS instances have network-traffic-filtering security groups, just as EC2 instances do. Choose Create New Security Group; later, you'll edit this to permit traffic between the WordPress instance and the database. Provide a name for an empty database that RDS will create on your new instance (an RDS instance can have more than one database, by the way). This isn't the same as the instance identifier you created on the previous screen, which is used to identify the RDS instance. For simplicity, you can give this database the same name you gave the original database on your EC2 instance.

The remaining settings on this page are well documented, so I'll leave you to explore them on your own. For now, click Launch DB Instance, and wait for the instance to come to life.

4.7 Configuring security group settings

In the meantime, you can return to the EC2 dashboard to edit your security group to allow traffic between your EC2 and RDS instances. Click Security Groups in the left panel. Depending on how you've been using your AWS account, you may see many groups, but in any case you should see at least three: Default VPC Security Group, the group being used by your EC2 instance, and one whose description is Created from the RDS Management Console. The last choice is the one used by your RDS instance, so select it and then click its Inbound tab.

If you've already been experimenting with RDS instances, you may see more than one Created from the RDS Management Console security group. How do you know which one you're after? Here are three possible approaches:

- If you expand the Description column associated with a security group—you may need to scroll to the right and then drag the vertical column separator over a bit—there might be a Created On date stamp. Go with the date that makes the most sense.
- Visit the RDS dashboard, select your instance, and note the ID of the security group that's displayed on the bottom half of the page.
- Give your security groups (and other AWS resources) descriptive tags. See chapter 10 for more on tagging.

Now that you're sure you've got the right security group, click Edit. As shown in figure 4.7, you should see a single rule of the MYSQL/Aurora type that uses port 3306 (the default MySQL port) and allows traffic from the IP address listed in the Source box. That's probably the public IP address of your local computer, which AWS assumes is the one you want to use. Instead, because this is an AWS deployment, you're going to connect directly to the Security Group of your *EC2 instance*: select

Custom from the drop-down menu, and type the letter *s* in the box. AWS will understand that *s* is the start of a security group ID (they always begin with the letters *sg*) and offer you a choice of all the groups currently available in your account. One of those is the group used by the EC2 WordPress server, which you can confirm by checking the EC2 instance dashboard. Select it, and then save the rule.

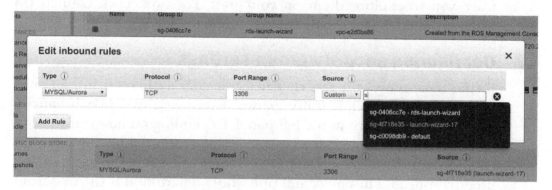

Figure 4.7   Allow network traffic between your database and EC2 instances.

With that done, return to the RDS dashboard. Click the Instances link in the left panel, and details about your now-running database instance will be displayed. The one that interests you the most right now is the endpoint instance (see figure 4.8). Copy that endpoint, leaving out the *:3306* at the end; MySQL won't require that when you connect to the database from EC2.

4.8   *Populating the new database*

Now, from the SSH session on the EC2 server, move to the directory to which you saved your MySQL dump:

```
cd /home/ubuntu
```

The next command connects to the RDS MySQL database at the host address, logs in using the *wpuser* name and password, and then, using the < character, streams the contents of the mybackup.sql file into the wordpressdb database:

```
mysql -u wpuser -p --database=wordpressdb \
--host=wpdatabase.co7swtzbtfg6.us-east-1.rds.amazonaws.com \
< mybackup.sql
```

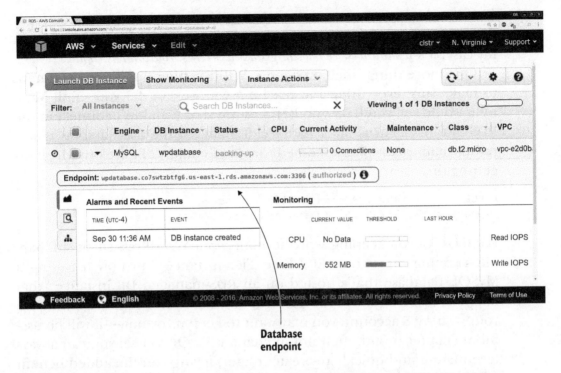

Figure 4.8 The instance details dashboard for your MySQL database, including the database endpoint

Troubleshooting

That's a long command, and any out-of-place character will throw the whole thing off. Adding a space after a single or double dash, using two dashes rather than one or one instead of two, getting the username or password wrong, adding a space after the backslash line-break character, or even forgetting to substitute your RDS endpoint for my example as the value for host will cause the command to fail.

Didn't work on your first try? You're in good company. Carefully go through the command again from scratch. And don't forget to do an internet search for the error message you receive—you'll be surprised how many others have already been there.

All that's left is to enter the new endpoint into the WordPress wp-config .php file in the /var/www/html/ directory on your EC2 server:

```
sudo nano /var/www/html/wp-config.php
```

Check to be sure the DB_USER and DB_PASSWORD values are correct, and then edit the hostname DB_HOST value to equal your RDS endpoint. In my case, it's *wpdatabase.co7swtzbtfg6.us-east-1.rds.amazonaws.com.*

One more thing: spelling counts. While setting up this environment to make sure everything I'm teaching you works (did you think Manning would sell you flaky goods?), I found that I couldn't connect to the RDS instance. Turns out I had accidentally set the username as *wbuser* rather than *wpuser*. For a moment or two, I couldn't figure out why I was getting this error:

```
ERROR 1045 (28000): Access denied for user
'wpuser'@'172.31.59.16' (using password: YES)
```

For those of you keeping score at home, your WordPress site is still happily running on its own EC2 Free Tier instance, but now it's using a MySQL database that's hosted on an RDS-managed DB instance (that happens to be equally Free Tier). If you have an instance running on your own AWS account, you may want to keep it for now—it will be useful in chapter 6 (although not in chapter 5). Of course, you can always terminate it and quickly re-create it later, giving you the added benefit of a helpful review.

4.9   *Lab*

Launch your RDS MySQL database, and then connect to it using a MySQL client on a remote computer. It may take a few attempts before you get the syntax quite right, but it's worth it to see the triumphant smile on your face when you succeed. Even if you don't see the smile (after all, your eyes aren't well positioned for the job), feel free to send me a picture.

Definitions
- *Relational database*—Highly structured database that uses the Structured Query Language (SQL) standard.
- *Relational database elements*—Tables, records, and fields.
- *NoSQL*—Not Only SQL. Databases that feature less structure but, in some cases, far greater speed than SQL.

- *Managed services*—Services provided by AWS (including RDS and Dynamo-DB), for which it takes full responsibility for the underlying hardware, leaving users to focus on their data.
- *RDS instance class types*—Burst capable, standard, and memory optimized.
- *Database dump*—Making an accurate copy of a database and its contents to allow it to be archived or migrated.
- *Multi-AZ*—An RDS deployment replicated over more than on availability zone to increase reliability.
- *Endpoint*—Public address through which an RDS database can be accessed.

DNS: what's in a name?

As your website grows and more people discover it, I'm sure you won't be satisfied with having to identify it by its IP address indefinitely. A nice, easy-to-remember name like, say, best-site-ever.com will work much better. Let's make that upgrade right now.

Under all those bright, cheerful web pages with external links displayed as softly chiseled 3D boxes and identified by catchy, easy-to-remember names, it's all about numbers. There's no real place called google.com or wikipedia.org; rather, they're 172.217.3.142 and 208.80.154.224. The software that does all the work connecting us to the websites we know and love recognizes only numeric IP addresses.

The tool that translates back and forth between text-mad humans and our more digitally oriented machines is called the *domain name system* (DNS). *Domain* is a word often used to describe a distinct group of networked resources—in particular, resources identified by a unique name like, oh, I don't know, manning.com. As shown in figure 5.1, whenever you enter a text address in your browser, the services of a DNS server are invariably—and invisibly—sought.

The first stop is usually a local index of names and their associated IP addresses, stored in a file that's automatically created by the OS on your computer. If that local index has no answer for this particular translation question, it forwards the request to a designated public

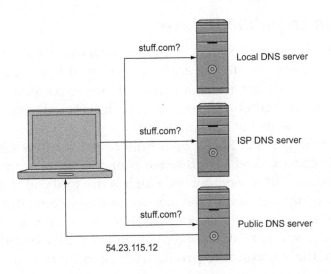

stuff.com? — Local DNS server

stuff.com? — ISP DNS server

stuff.com? — Public DNS server

54.23.115.12

Figure 5.1 DNS address query for stuff.com, and the reply containing a (fictional) IP address

DNS server that maintains a much more complete index and can connect you to the site you're after. Well-known public DNS servers include those provided by Google—which uses the deliciously simple 8.8.8.8 and 8.8.4.4 addresses—and OpenDNS.

Until something breaks, you normally won't spend a lot of time thinking about DNS servers—unless, of course, you want your customers to be able to access your website by its plain-text name. For that to happen, you'll have to reserve the name you'd like with a domain name registrar. The job of a registrar is to update the indexes used by the big DNS servers so that translation requests from anyone on the internet can be quickly satisfied. Once you're over that critical hurdle, you can go back to ignoring DNS.

In this chapter, you'll use Amazon's Route 53 service to register a domain name and associate that name with the IP address being used by your website. This will tell name servers where to send traffic aimed at your domain. You may eventually want to add instances of your server to allow for more efficient and individualized service; to do this, you'll also learn how to use Route 53 to set up traffic redirection among a pool of multiple servers.

> **NOTE** Even if you don't have any real domains to manage, you can still work through all the exercises in this chapter.

5.1   Adding a name to public indexes

If you don't yet have any domain-related resources on this AWS account, clicking the Route 53 link in the Networking section of the main AWS Console (assuming the All Services control is already expanded) takes you to an introductory screen. If you've already created resources, you're instead sent to the Route 53 dashboard.

As you can see in figure 5.2, Route 53 is built to deliver four distinct but closely related services: *domain registration* (Amazon, it turns out, is a domain name registrar); *DNS management*, which is the tool you'll use to direct traffic to your domain; *traffic management*, to handle traffic redirection; and *availability monitoring*, to confirm that your target resources are performing the way they're supposed to. A bit later, I'll explain how you can use each of these features to productively manage the way users experience your website.

First, though, you need to identify the domain name of your dreams: something short, easy to remember, suggestive of what you do, and, most of all, not already taken by someone else. Route 53 will tell you if your choice is still available. Click the Get Started Now button beneath Domain Registration, and then click Register Domain. Type the main part of the name—for example, the *bootstrap-it* part of my own

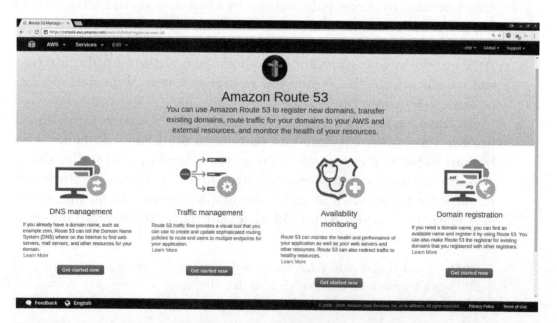

Figure 5.2   Amazon Route 53 introduction page showing the service's four distinct elements

bootstrap-it.com—into the data field. A drop-down menu displays domains including .com, .org, .net, and so on, with their annual registration cost; select one, and click Check. Route 53 will search online records to see if that combination is currently available.

When you find a domain name that fits your needs, add it to your cart, and go through the checkout process to submit payment for your first year's registration fee. Domain registrations usually cost between $10 and $15 US per year and aren't included in Free Tier usage. In a short time, your new domain will appear in the Route 53 dashboard.

> **NOTE** Nothing forces you to use Route 53 for your domain registration. In fact, you may find that other providers offer cheaper alternatives. You can use Route 53's other features even for domains registered through other companies.

5.2 Configuring your hosted zone

Your domain is now registered, but you haven't told it what to do with incoming requests. So, from the dashboard, click Hosted Zones and then Create Hosted Zone. Fill in your domain name, and, assuming you want your domain to be publicly available, select Public Hosted Zone in the pull-down menu shown in figure 5.3.

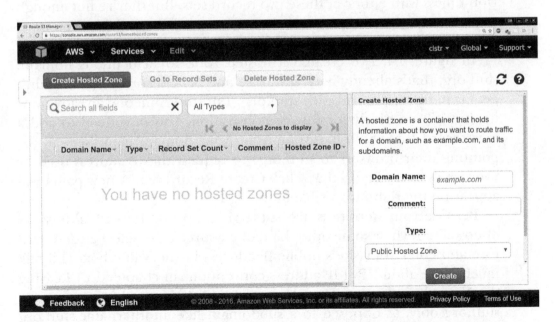

Figure 5.3   The Create Hosted Zone page where you supply the basic data for your domain

> **DEFINITION** *Hosted zone*—The way AWS describes the information you provide to define how traffic aimed at your domain name will be managed.

5.2.1 Configuring record sets

Click the link to your new hosted zone, and you'll find yourself on a page with two pre-created record sets:

- *Start of authority (SOA)*—Identifies your domain's basic DNS configuration information
- *NS*—List of authoritative name servers that can be queried about your domain host. These are the public services that provide answers to domain-name translation requests.

> **DEFINITION** *Record set*—A set of data records that defines a particular aspect of domain behavior.

> **TIP** If you're going to use a domain that's been registered with another provider, you need to copy the four NS records you see here and import them into the appropriate interface page of your provider's account-management site. Doing so will tell internet routers to direct any traffic aimed at your domain name to Route 53's name servers.

Don't mess with either of these two record sets. But they're not enough on their own to make your new domain name fully available. You need to add at least one more record.

In figure 5.4, I've created a hosted zone for a fictitious domain, stuff.org, that's already been given NS and SOA records. You wouldn't get far in the real world with stuff.org (I'm sure someone already owns it), but it'll do nicely for this demonstration. You now need to add a new record that will tell anyone using your domain name servers (by pointing their browsers to stuff.org) to request the IP address used by your web server. To do that, click Create Record Set. A new panel will appear on the right; it's visible in the figure.

Because your website is accessible via a normal IPv4 IP address, as opposed to IPv6 or some other kind of resource type, select an A record type and enter your site's public IP address in the Value box. (I'll talk much more about IPv4 IP address conventions in chapter 15.) Leaving the Name box empty will apply the rules of this record to requests for stuff.org only, as opposed to a subdomain like anothername.stuff.org or, as you'll soon see, www.stuff.org.

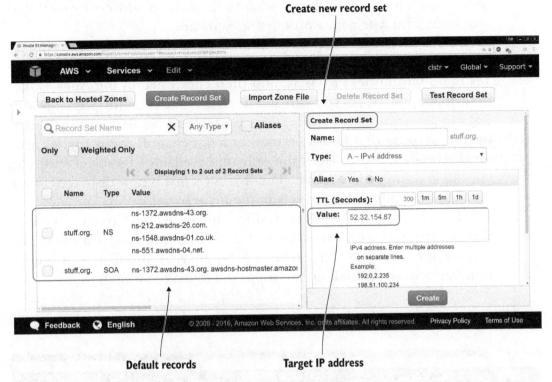

Figure 5.4   The Record Set administration page. Here's where you add or edit the resource record sets for your hosted zone.

The time to live (TTL) rule determines how long a target value such as the value of a DNS record provided by a name server will remain valid before it's automatically refreshed. The higher the value, the more time you allow between refreshes, and the lower your cost. But that also means changes to records (updates between pages) will take longer to be noticed by end users.

It may take a few hours for the new rules to propagate through enough public records to reliably direct traffic to your site. You can always test this by pointing your browser to your domain name to see what happens.

RECORD SETS: OTHER USE CASES

You may be surprised to know that as things sit right now, only browser requests using the stuff.org address will be successful. Requests with www.stuff.org won't work! That's because *www* doesn't play a significant role in internet addressing; it's treated like a separate subdomain. Thus, unless you tell your DNS server what to do with an address formed that way, users who type *www* won't get to your site.

To fix that, you need to create an *alias* record set. Click Create Record Set again, and this time, enter www in the Name field. Click the Yes radio button next to Alias, and then click once in the Alias Target field that appears. As you can see in figure 5.5, a menu pops up with links to any existing record sets based on resources that currently exist in your account that could be used as a target. stuff.org is the last one on the list—or, in this case, the only one available. To select stuff.org, click it, and then click Create. The first A record is now displayed along with the other active record sets in the main panel.

If you need to redirect traffic aimed at one name, such as vids.stuff.com, to a different name, like videos.stuff.com, you can create a *canonical name* (CNAME) record. This may be useful if you have a number of domains that are all supposed to lead to a single site.

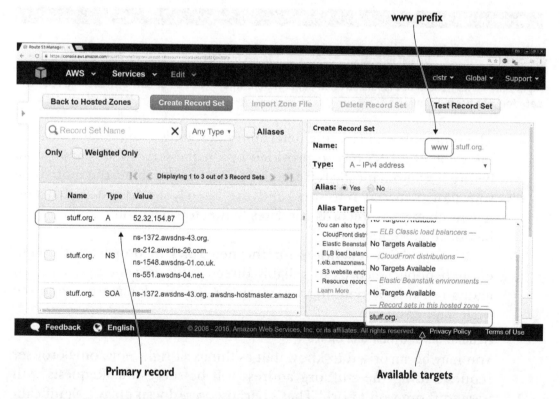

Figure 5.5   Creating a new alias record set, this time to accommodate www URL prefixes

> ### A record? CNAME record?
>
> It's not as complicated as it may seem. An *A record* contains instructions to route requests for a particular domain like stuff.com to a specified IPv4 address. You use AAAA records for IPv6 addresses.
>
> A *CNAME record*, on the other hand, allows one domain name (such as stuff.com) to act as an alias for a second domain (such as mystuff.stuff.com). Requests to the first are redirected to the second.

All of this is possible even though the IP address I used in this example (54.32.154.87) doesn't exist and I have no control over the domain stuff.org. Without access to its name servers, I'd have no way to point visitors to my IP address. Route 53 provides the platform to create as many hosted zones and record sets as your heart desires, while leaving practical details—like their authenticity—in your hands.

In this case, I'd be charged a fee of $0.50 for every month I left my stuff.org hosted zone active, regardless of how much work it was actually doing. To allow for experiments and testing, AWS doesn't charge for zones that are deleted within 12 hours.

5.2.2 Elastic IP addresses

Which IP address should you use for this hosted zone? The public IP that you were assigned when you created your WordPress site on EC2 will work, but using it would be a terrible idea. That's because there's no guarantee that the address will be persistently associated with your EC2 instance. If, say, your instance ever crashes, it will probably receive a new IP address when it starts up again, thereby breaking all existing links to your site. At some point, you may also want the power to transfer an existing IP address from one instance to another, but you can't do that with the IP you have now.

Associating an *Amazon Elastic IP* address to your instance can solve these problems by giving you a single, static address that you can closely control. And doing so is dead easy.

From the EC2 dashboard, click the Elastic IPs link in the left panel and then click Allocate New Address. Confirm that this is what you want to do, and, within a few minutes at most, the new Elastic IP will appear in the dashboard. Once it's there, you can associate your new IP with any existing instance (or network interface) in your account. Select

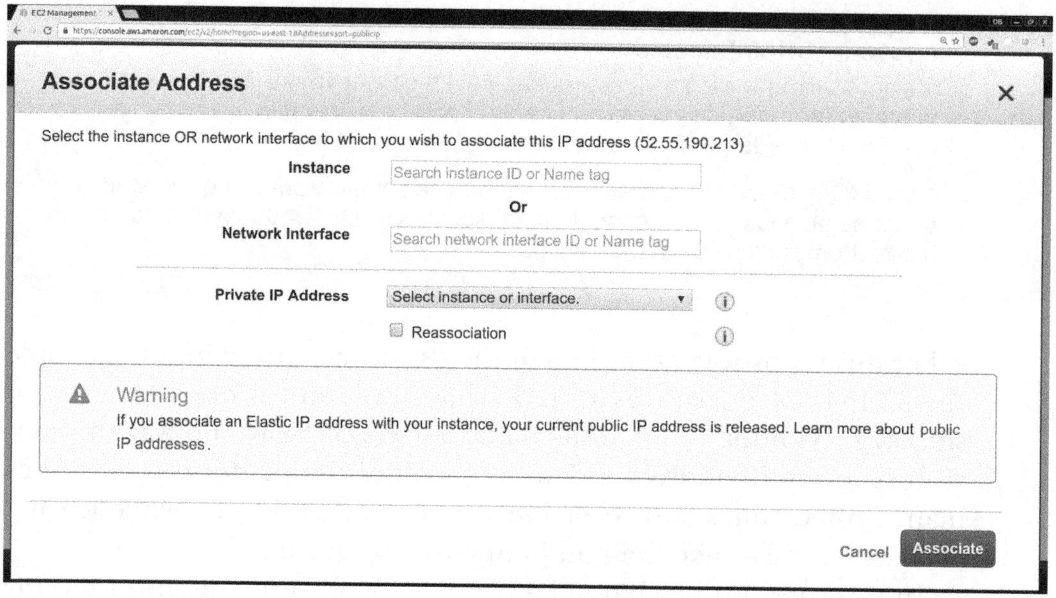

Figure 5.6   You use the Associate Address pop-up box to apply an Amazon Elastic IP address to your EC2 instance.

your IP, click Actions, click Associate Address, and then, as shown in figure 5.6, click once in the Instance field to see a list of available instances. When you click Associate, that instance will be publicly accessible through the Elastic IP.

> **TIP**   Once you're no longer using an Elastic IP—for instance, if you've shut down the instance with which it was associated—you should release it by selecting Release Address from the Actions drop-down. Leaving an *unused* Elastic IP in your account will accrue charges.

5.3   *Routing policies*

The busier your website gets, the more likely it is that you'll choose to incorporate multiple servers into the overall design. You may do this to make your content more highly available so that, even if one server fails, traffic can be shifted to another one that's still healthy. Or perhaps you want the ability to improve your users' experience by efficiently distributing workloads across multiple resources so that no one server slows down due to overwork. You can apply health checks and routing policies through Route 53 to simplify the configuration and management of such designs:

- A *health check* is usually an automated, server-based process that periodically tries to load a specified remote web page to confirm that it's still available. If the web page fails to load, a predetermined action like an email notification or an update of a routing configuration setting is triggered.
- A *routing policy* configures your networking software to base traffic-routing decisions on the contents or characteristics of the moving data, or on network conditions.

Suppose you're running two servers that provide the same content but are configured with significantly different capacities. You don't want to send an equal volume of traffic to each of the servers, because doing so may overload the weaker instance and leave the stronger one underutilized. To prevent that, you can create a *weighted rule,* where a higher proportion of total visits are directed to a particular instance. You can also set up one of the following:

- *Failover rule*—Redirects traffic to a backup in the event your primary server fails a health check
- *Geolocation rule*—Serves specialized content to visitors, tailored to their country or region of origin
- *Latency rule*—Directs users to the servers located geographically closest to them

TIP There's overlap between some of what Route 53 does and Amazon's Elastic Load Balancer (ELB) service, which I'll discuss at length in chapter 16. In fact, ELB excels at intelligently directing traffic between resources and is a critical, high-availability tool. But if you're looking to more finely tune your routing using closely defined rules, then you should consider Route 53 first.

5.3.1 Creating a health check

You can create a simple health check and set it to notify you in the event of a failure by clicking the Health Checks link in the left panel of the Route 53 dashboard and then clicking Create Health Check (or Availability Monitoring, if you find yourself back at the Route 53 intro page). As figure 5.7 shows, in this example I named my health check Bootstrap-health-check. You can click the Domain name radio button to search by domain name rather than IP address (the IP address option is useful for sites without DNS names). Type your domain name into the appropriate

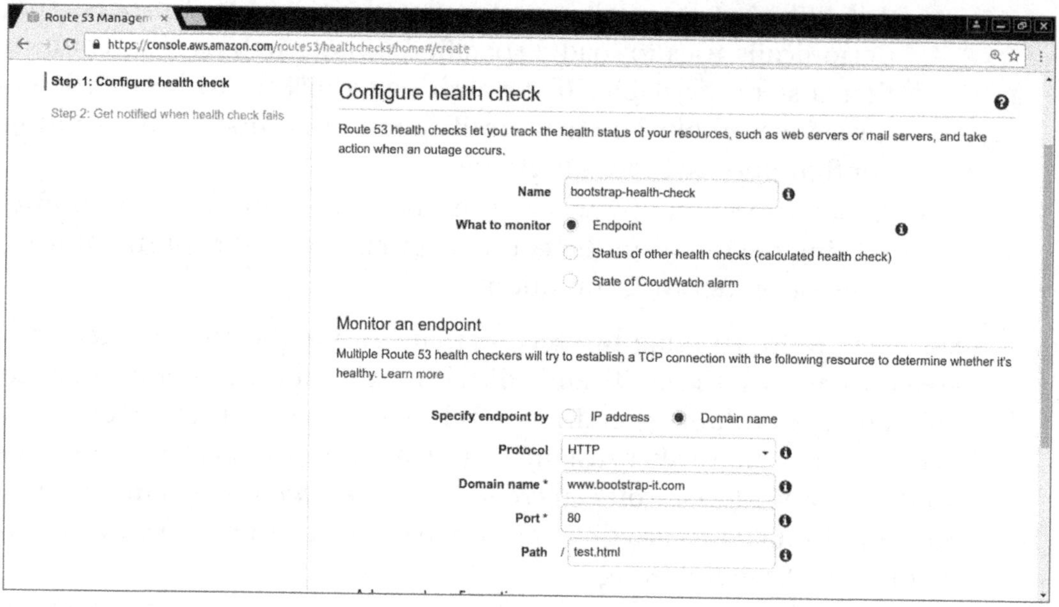

Figure 5.7   Use the Configure Health Check page to define what constitutes a healthy/unhealthy domain.

field, and then add test.html to the Path; the health check will try to load a web page of that name in the website root directory. Naturally, for this to work, you must already have created such a file—although it needn't have any contents.

Click Next to move on to the next step, where you can set up an alert for when things go wrong (see figure 5.8). Right now, you don't have any AWS Simple Notification Service (SNS) topics, so select New SNS Topic; add a topic name and at least one email address to which alerts will be sent. Click Create Health Check, and you're done.

From here on, if you get an email alert, be sure to check your instance right away.

Try it now

Even without an actual registered domain, you can quickly fire up an EC2 instance as an Apache web server, add a test.html file to the /var/www/html directory, and point your health check to it following the steps in this section. Configure it to send an email to your address on failure. Then, to test it, shut down the instance from the EC2 Console, and wait to see what happens.

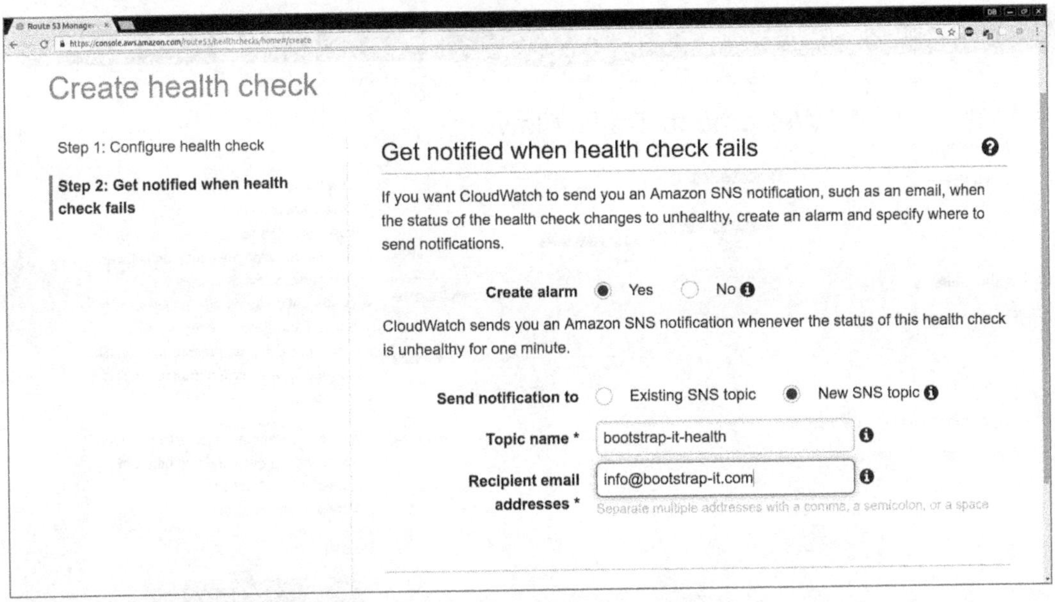

Figure 5.8   Set up alert notifications using email or SNS-based text messages.

5.3.2   *Create a routing policy*

Although not every deployment will require this, sometimes you'll want to route (that is, redirect) customer traffic among multiple servers. Route 53 provides routing policies as a tool for managing that situation.

I'm sure you know the drill by now. Click the Traffic Policies link in the Route 53 dashboard; then, as shown in figure 5.9, click Create Traffic Policy. Isn't website standardization nice, especially when executed as well as it is on the AWS website?

Give your policy a name, and click Next. You'll see a user-friendly GUI that first asks you to specify the DNS type you'll be using: that is, which kind of DNS host you'll be working with for this rule. Because this rule will be used to service your website, which uses an IPv4 address, stick with the default A: IP Address value.

When you click the Connect To box, you're first asked to choose the kind of rule you want. Choose Failover. If you've been following along up to this point in the book, you probably have only one EC2 instance running, so the second instance required to justify using most of these rules is going to require a bit of imagination. We'll all smile and nod

Figure 5.9   The Traffic Policies dashboard has a Create Traffic Policy button and a Learn More link that leads to useful documentation.

and pretend this is going to work! For now, here's a brief overview of the policies AWS makes available:

- *Simple Routing Policy*—Follows the values in a resource record set pointing to a single server.
- *Weighted Routing Policy*—Allows you to direct higher or lower proportions of your total traffic to specified servers. Useful for cases where one server has greater capabilities than another.
- *Latency Routing Policy*—Directs users to the specific server that will be able to respond with the lowest latency (that is, delay).
- *Failover Routing Policy*—Redirects traffic away from a server that's failed to a backup server.
- *Geolocation Routing Policy*—Directs users to the server that's located in the AZ geographically closest to them.

In this case, select the Failover rule, which launches a dialog box with two panels: one for a primary server and one for its secondary backup. Note how the primary server being targeted by the rule is subject to health checks by default. Figure 5.10 shows that clicking the Connect To box associated with the primary server displays the same list of

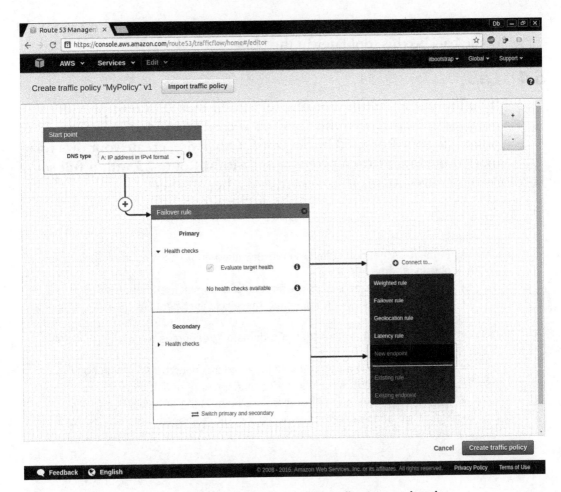

Figure 5.10 Use the GUI to configure and apply a routing policy to your domain.

rules—but this time, because you're ready to apply your rule to a resource, click New Endpoint. Then, assign your primary EC2 instance's IP address as its value. This tells Route 53 which of your instances it should treat as primary. Now, click the Connect To box next to the Secondary panel, and enter the IP address of the instance you want to use as a failover. Click Create Traffic Policy, and you'll be sent to the Traffic Policies page. There, click Create Policy Records, choose your hosted zone from the drop-down menu, and click the new Create Policy Records button, and you're finished.

As I'm sure you can imagine, this tool allows for plenty more permutations and combinations of rules, but this is a good start—and knowing how to configure server failover is quite an accomplishment. We'll come back to this tool later in the book.

5.4   Lab

If you've got an actual domain registered by a different provider that needs some work, use the four NS records provided by Route 53 to point it to your Route 53 hosted zone. Otherwise, create your own imaginary domain and then a record set within Route 53 with a full set of records, subdomains (like www.), and a health check.

Definitions

- *Domain*—A defined collection of networked compute resources (roughly synonymous with *website*)
- *Route 53*—Amazon's DNS registration and administration service
- *Domain registration*—Purchasing the exclusive right to use a particular domain name
- *Health check*—A remote test of a domain's resources to confirm that they're running properly
- *Routing policy*—The way you've configured incoming traffic redirection
- *Hosted zone*—AWS's domain traffic management definition profile
- *Record type*—Kinds of DNS record, including A, AAAA, CNAME, and MX
- *Elastic IP address*—Permanent (static) IP addresses issued by AWS on request

S3: cheap, fast file storage

As you saw way back in chapter 3, an EC2-based server's core filesystem is kept on a relatively small Elastic Block Store (EBS) volume. In that case, the volume had only 8 GB to start with, which proved to be more than enough for the example WordPress site. But once they're running in the real world, most applications—generating, as they often do, fast-growing databases, directories filled with videos, and reams of logs—require far more storage space than an 8 GB or even an 80 GB drive can provide.

Why didn't we provision a larger EBS volume? Because, relatively speaking, doing so is expensive. A 100 GB general-purpose, solid state drive from EBS will cost you around $10 per month. If there's a better alternative, you'll want to know about it. You've already seen how large databases can be moved off-site to Amazon's RDS (although, gigabyte for gigabyte, I'm not sure that will always be cheaper); but what about, say, the media files needed by an application? More often than not, your first choice will be Amazon's Simple Storage Service (S3). The cost? S3's most expensive storage option will set you back less than $0.025/month for a gigabyte of data, or less than $2.50/month for 100 GB. So, if your EC2 WordPress server deployment includes providing larger media files for a lot of users, S3 can make a big difference.

In this chapter, you'll learn how S3 works, how you can both gain and control access to it, how to quickly integrate the resources you store on S3 into your applications, and, finally, how you can use S3 to create a super-cheap, super-simple static website. Sound like fun?

6.1   *How does S3 work?*

S3 provides fast, inexpensive object storage. But what exactly is object storage? As you can see in figure 6.1, unlike block storage, which organizes data in blocks directly on a physical medium, or filesystems, which provide hierarchical representations of files and directories to make very large groups of files easier to work with, *object storage* systems are organized around data objects that can contain files. No matter how large or small a single object may be, an object storage system will write it to a single location. The system will also add metadata to identify the object's basic vital information and assign it a URL (a network-friendly address) through which it can be accessed.

We'll get back to the steady growth of your website in just a bit. First, let's look at how S3 works in its natural habitat.

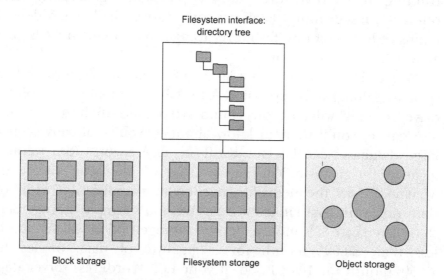

Figure 6.1   Differences in design between block storage, filesystem storage, and object storage

6.1.1 *Creating an S3 bucket*

Clicking the S3 link in the main AWS Console takes you to a page with a big blue Create Bucket button. If nothing else, that tells you that S3 uses buckets as its metaphor to describe the way it stores the files you upload. Click Create Bucket to open the Create Bucket wizard. First, you'll need to choose a bucket name. Because the name you choose will become an important part of the bucket's URL, it must be completely unique among all S3 buckets across the system. And because there are probably millions of S3 buckets already in existence, a name like mys3bucket probably won't be available. The odds are that you'll have to intersperse numbers in your bucket name—something like 100my67s3bucket67—to find one you can use.

> **TIP** To ensure that the bucket name you choose is compliant with DNS services and will work in all AWS regions, use only lowercase letters and avoid using periods.

As shown in figure 6.2, you can host your bucket in any of Amazon's geographic regions. If your users all happen to live near each other—for example, if your website is run by a municipal government for the exclusive benefit of its citizens—it makes sense to locate your files as close to home as possible. You can also save yourself some time by copying the settings from an existing bucket.

The next two pages of the wizard throw five more categories of settings at you, all of which are optional and can also be accessed later from the S3 dashboard:

- *Versioning*—When enabled, versioning saves copies of files even when newer versions with the exact same name are uploaded. Rather than being overwritten and lost, files stored in versioned buckets remain available for later retrieval. By default, versioning is disabled.
- *Logging*—Logging tracks all access requests against the bucket. If you may be subject to audits or security regulations—or if you're just plain curious about who's using your resources—then you'll want such an activity record.
- *Tags*—Chapter 10 discusses using resource tags to manage a busy AWS account. If you expect to create dozens or hundreds of S3

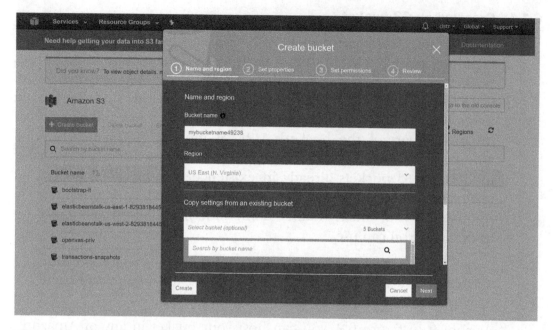

Figure 6.2   The Create Bucket wizard prompts you for a unique name, the geographic region in which you want your bucket files stored, and any preexisting settings you want applied.

buckets, then applying an intelligent system of tagging can make your data much more usable. This is where it's done.

- *User management*—You can provide varying levels of access to the contents of a bucket to other users, to allow resource sharing.
- *Permission management*—You can open access to your bucket contents to either all authenticated AWS users or anyone on the internet.

Finally, you'll get the chance to review your settings and then create your new bucket. As long as you don't upload any files, it won't cost you anything (and remember: a full gigabyte of data will cost you less than $0.025/month—sometimes a lot less, depending on the way you use it).

6.1.2   *Uploading files to an S3 bucket*

To get a good feel for how S3 handles data, try creating your own bucket and uploading a file—any file will do. You'll see your new bucket in the main S3 Console. Clicking your new bucket's name in the left panel will take you to a page (figure 6.3) with tabs along the top pointing to configuration categories like Properties (see the previous

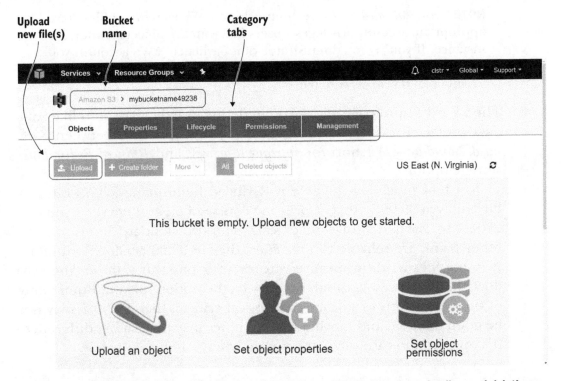

Figure 6.3 The Objects settings page for an S3 bucket. Note the links for uploading and deleting objects and creating new folders.

descriptions of versioning and logging) and Permissions (see the descriptions of user management and permission management). Right now, though, you're interested in the Objects tab and, in particular, the Upload button. Click it.

Once again, you're confronted with a four-part wizard. On the first page, click Add Files to select a file or files from your local system. The second page lets you manage users and public permissions just as you did when you created the bucket. The difference is that this time, your choices will affect only specific files, not the entire bucket.

You could, for instance, permit any authenticated AWS user to open a file and both view and edit its permissions. That would give such users the power to permit (or deny) access to others. Granting everyone in the entire universe the right to open and download the file would be a reasonable setting for files that were, say, meant to be part of a public website.

NOTE   *Authenticated users* are users whose AWS sign-in profiles have appropriate account privileges—users like you, the object's owner, for instance. If you're an administrator of a particular AWS account, you can permit authenticated access to resources like this file to any user or automated process you like.

The wizard's third page allows you to define exactly how you'd like your data protected. As shown in figure 6.4, you can choose between *Standard*, *Standard—IA* (short for *infrequent access*), and *Reduced Redundancy* storage options.

Just how much less reliable is Reduced Redundancy? AWS rates its durability at 99.99%: that is, over the course of an average year, you can expect to *lose* 0.01% of your objects. The two standard levels, on the other hand, are reliable to *nine nines*: they're 99.999999999% durable. If losing files wouldn't inspire you (or your boss) to leap out the window, then Reduced Redundancy may be the option for you. But if many of the objects you're storing are mission critical, then 99.99% may not be good enough, and moving to nine nines may make a big difference. It's up to you to carefully assess your current and future needs.

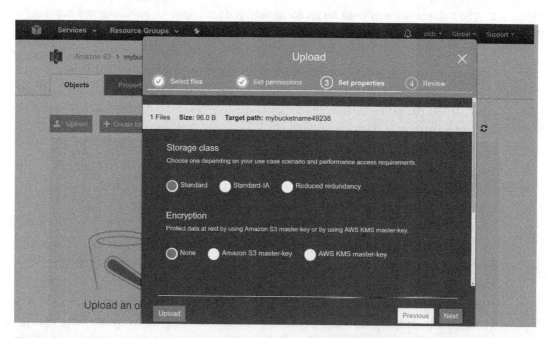

Figure 6.4   Tell S3 what kind of storage you want for your files and whether they should be encrypted.

NOTE You might think that Reduced Redundancy storage would be cheaper than Standard storage because it's backed up using a slightly less robust process—which is another way of saying there's an incrementally higher chance of your data being lost. Surprisingly, however, recent price drops to Standard storage haven't been matched for Reduced Redundancy, suggesting that AWS is no longer seriously promoting the service. It may be best to avoid Reduced Redundancy for now.

The difference between Standard and Standard-IA is their level of guaranteed *availability*: that is, the chances of you not being able to retrieve a file at a given time (even if it will eventually become available again). Standard promises 99.99% availability, as opposed to 99.9% for Standard-IA. Standard-IA is the least expensive of all S3 levels, costing only $0.0125/month per GB. It's your call. Table 6.1 presents all the numbers.

Table 6.1 S3 storage service levels

Value	Standard	Standard-IA	Reduced Redundancy
Durability	99.999999999%	99.999999999%	99.99%
Availability	99.99%	99.9%	99.99%

You can also select from a number of encryption options to encrypt the file you're uploading using AWS's encryption keys. This way, even if an unauthorized user gets to your account data—assuming they don't somehow log in to the account itself—the data will be worthless to them.

What's encryption?

The problem with data is that it's designed to be readable. If you've ever lost a USB thumb drive with sensitive personal information on it and worried about where it ended up, you know what I mean. To protect the privacy of data even if a host device falls into the wrong hands, security software can use an *encryption key*: a small file containing a random sequence of characters, which can be applied as part of an encryption algorithm to convert plain-text readable data into what amounts to total gibberish.

At least, that's how it will appear until the key is applied against the encrypted file—via a reverse application of the same algorithm—to convert the gibberish back to its original form. As long as you and your trusted friends are the only people in possession of the key, no one else should be able to read the file's contents, even if they're intercepted.

Again, you're given the chance to review your choices and, finally, start the upload. Once your file is uploaded, return to the S3 Console to see how it's settling in to its new home. Click the Amazon S3 link at the top to go to the main S3 page, and click the link to your new bucket. Let's see what S3 has to tell you about your file.

The Overview tab displays the file's important metadata, including the public link URL through which it can be accessed from the internet (see figure 6.5). The Properties and Permissions tabs allow you to revisit or update the storage and access values you set before uploading the file. As is the case with most modern OSs, there are usually multiple ways of performing an administrative task.

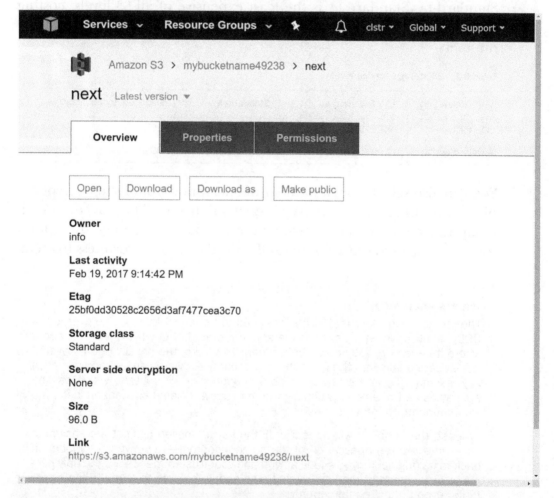

Figure 6.5   File properties as displayed by the S3 Properties interface. Note the Version drop-down at the top and the internet-facing link URL at the bottom.

Make a note of how S3 displays the object's URL, because your immediate goal is to incorporate S3 data into your website. The link is the file's address (URL), available for use by both humans and machines. You'll soon use this address from within your website server to connect with stored files.

Try it now

Take a moment and test this for yourself. Copy the URL of an object you've uploaded to your S3 bucket, and then paste it into your browser. Are you able to open and view the file properly? If you leave the object's permissions at their default value (accessible only to the object's owner—you), does your experience match the permissions? What happens if you try the same thing from a different browser that isn't logged in to your AWS account?

6.2 *Integrating S3 resources into an EC2-based website*

Finally, we're ready to get down to business. I'm sure you've enjoyed this introduction to the wonders of S3 storage as much as I have, but how will all this improve your EC2 WordPress site? The answer is so simple that it's almost embarrassing.

Suppose you'd like to embed an S3-hosted video into a WordPress page or blog post, so visitors can view the video inline on the page. Here's how to do it. On the Edit Post page of the WordPress admin interface, click the spot on the page where you want to insert the video, and paste the URL link of an S3-hosted video (see figure 6.6).

That's it! WordPress can take it from here.

TIP Adding *wp-admin* to the address of your blog or WordPress site and entering that into your browser's URL box will take you to the WordPress administration interface. If your site uses a plain IP address, you'll enter something like 54.78.131.45/wp-admin. If you've got a DNS address (like my imaginary stuff.com), you can try a variation of stuff.com/blog/wp-admin.

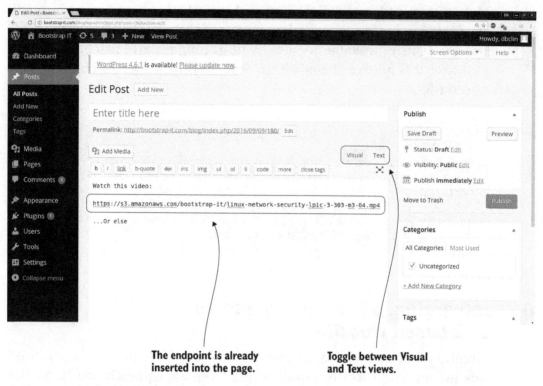

**The endpoint is already
inserted into the page.**

**Toggle between Visual
and Text views.**

Figure 6.6   The Edit Post page of a WordPress post, including a link to a video hosted on S3

What will the page look like to visitors? Figure 6.7 leaves nothing to the
imagination. That's a screen from a video I created for one of my Plu-
ralsight courses, playing within a page on a WordPress site.

That's WordPress. But what if your project involves normal HTML
pages? How can you add an S3 link? The answer is only slightly less obvious. Here's some HTML code that centers all objects, prints a couple of
horizontal lines, and, most important, uses your S3 URL to call a video
as a media resource:

```
<div align="center">
<br><br>
<hr>
<b>
<video width="640" height="480" controls>
  <source src="https://s3.amazonaws.com/bootstrap-it/linux-network-
    security-
  ➥lpic-3-303-m3-04.mp4" type="video/mp4">
</video>
<hr>
```

Figure 6.8 shows the result in a browser.

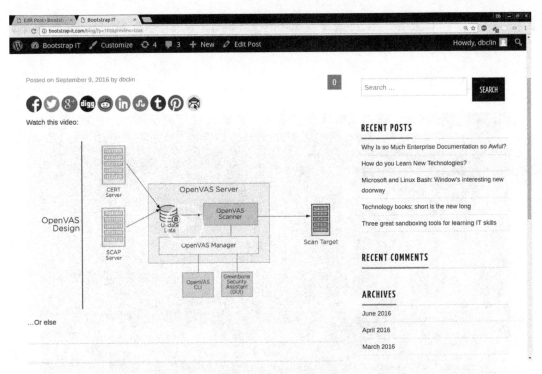

Figure 6.7　This blog post includes an embedded, running video.

6.3　*Using S3 to create a simple static website*

Until now, you've seen how S3 storage can be used in support of websites or other external deployments. But you can also use S3 as a host for an entire website, avoiding the expense and complexity of EC2 servers. The only caveat is that this works only for static sites.

A *static website* is a site whose content doesn't rely on a server-side scripting language like Java or PHP or on calls to a database. That means you can't run a WordPress instance directly on S3. But if your site is made up of straightforward HTML pages—even if they incorporate images or videos—then you're a candidate in good standing. And at less than $0.03/month per GB for storage—plus as much as $0.090/GB of data transferred out to the internet (in other words, downloaded by users)—this could be cost effective.

Practically speaking, this makes it easy to put up something like a brochure site to display information about an organization's services and contact data, or to quickly make short-term news widely available.

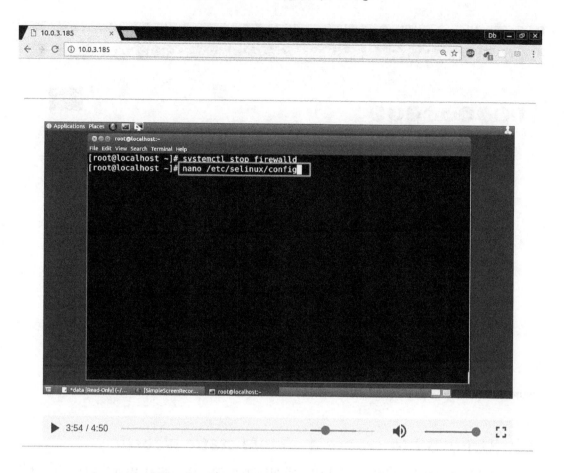

Figure 6.8   An S3-hosted video embedded in an HTML web page

I've been running a lightly used site out of S3 for a few years now, and the total cost has yet to hit $10.00.

How do you set up a static site? It's easy. On the main S3 page, click the name of the bucket you want to use. Doing so takes you to the page with all the settings tabs. This time, click the Properties tab. One of the tiles you'll see is Static Website Hosting: click it to go to the hosting setup form (see figure 6.9). Tell S3 which document in the bucket should be loaded by default when a user visits (by convention, usually index.html) and how redirects and errors should be handled. Note the site's URL (actual URL) at the top.

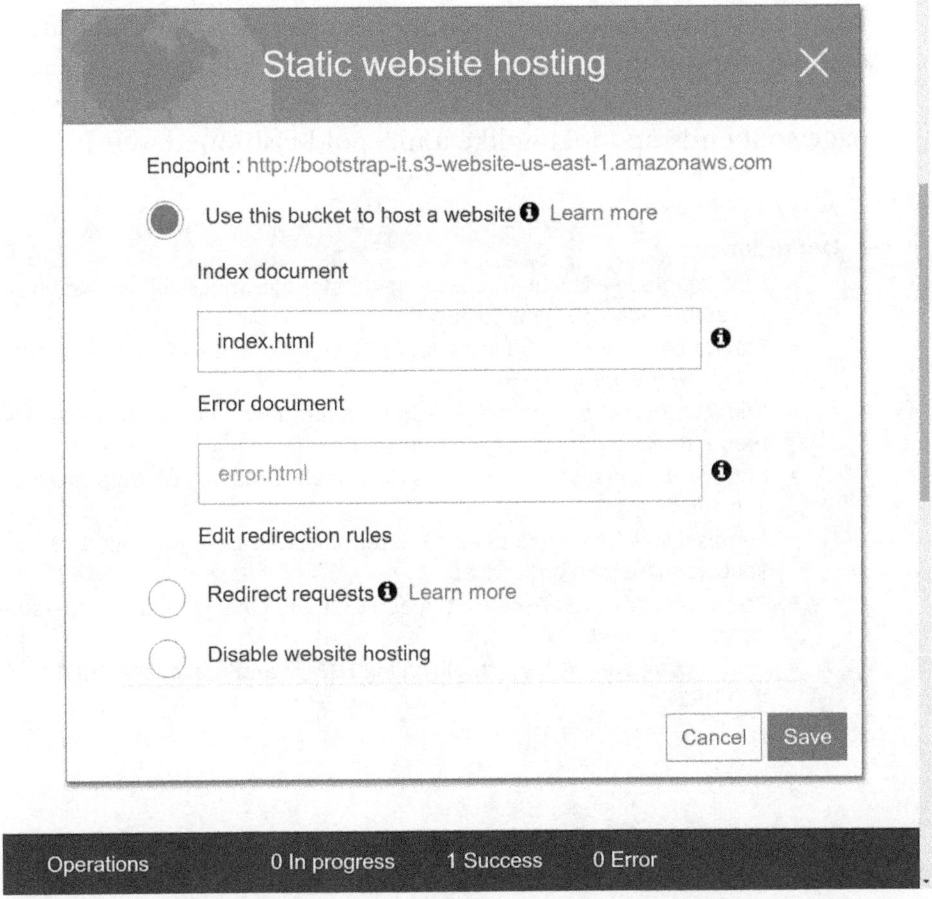

Figure 6.9 In the Static Website Hosting dialog, you can enable hosting and specify default settings, such as an index document.

Click Save. All that's left is to create a file called index.html on your computer (why not use the same HTML code you used earlier for the S3 video?) and upload all of the site's files and resources to your static website bucket. Don't forget to assign Everyone/Read permissions to all your files so they'll be publicly accessible.

Make sure you try this for yourself. Once you're finished with your own versions of the things discussed in this chapter, you're free to delete them: we won't be coming back to them later in the book.

6.4 Lab

Work through the steps for setting up your own static website. Select a default landing page (perhaps index.html), and add a few media files to a subfolder in your S3 bucket. Link to those files from your HTML page so it ends up looking like a nice, old-fashioned website.

Definitions

- *Object storage*—Nonhierarchical digital storage whose primary organization is based on individual files (objects)
- *Standard-IA storage*—S3 storage that's cheaper because it guarantees a relatively lower availability level
- *Reduced Redundancy storage*—S3 storage that's cheaper because it guarantees a relatively lower durability level
- *Server-side encryption*—The host-managed securing of data at rest on a server
- *Permissions*—The rules used to determine who gets what kind of access to specific resources or services
- *Static website*—A website that doesn't require calls to scripts or databases to serve its content
- *Index document*—A file (usually using HTML) that's accessed first by visitors to a URL

S3: cheap,
fast system backups

As you've seen, using S3 to store the application data you're actively using makes a lot of sense. But that's not the only valuable role the service can play. S3 is also a great place to host your regular backups of, say, older data you're not currently using but aren't ready to delete, or the system files currently running your server.

> **TIP** You do generate regular backups, don't you? You know what they call people who don't actively plan for significant resource failures? Unemployed.

In this chapter, we'll talk about how important it is to back up your data, and how backups relate to the needs and opportunities unique to AWS-based data. We'll also discuss how backups of AWS resources can work differently from the kinds of backup operations you may be familiar with from local deployments.

Specifically, I'll demonstrate two approaches to managing backups on AWS:

- Having AWS *take a snapshot* (make a complete copy) of an AWS Elastic Block Store (EBS) volume your EC2 instance is using and save it to S3
- Using local OS tools to compress your data into an archive file that will then be sent to an S3 bucket you specify for storage

7.1   Why back up?

When you think about how to deal with extermination-level catastrophes that might befall your local IT infrastructure, you probably primarily worry about hardware failure. That could mean the sudden, unexpected death of one or more hard drives or a destructive fire or natural disaster hitting the building where your servers live. Therefore, you should ensure that at least some of the physical media holding your backups is located in another location—the further away, the better.

When it comes to the stuff you've got running on AWS, on the other hand, hardware failure is pretty much the last thing you need to worry about. Amazon does a great job of protecting the physical servers that host your resources, by carefully guarding access to the data centers. Not many people even know where to look for an AWS building! When a data drive or server does go down, it's invisibly, instantly replaced by another one (or two or three) just like it. Even if, as has happened, an entire AWS data center suffers a massive power outage, the worst that will probably happen is a loss of service for a few minutes or hours. Once everything comes back up, AWS's layers of redundancy will ensure that your instances and volumes are just the way you left them.

Those features are part of AWS's very public *Shared Responsibility Model*. As figure 7.1 illustrates, Amazon guarantees that the cloud it provides—meaning the compute, storage, database, and networking services you purchase—will perform as promised. Your job is to secure and protect whatever you add to the cloud: software, data, applications, user-access protocols, and so on. Those cloud add-ons are where you should focus some serious attention.

7.1.1   Your AWS account: what might go wrong?

This is the first question you should ask yourself when thinking about establishing a backup protocol. The underlying hardware won't be a problem, so what should keep you up at night? The answer is, two kinds of people: hackers and administrators.

THE TROUBLE WITH HACKERS

The way I'm using the term here, *hackers* refers to criminals who wish to gain control of your data or infrastructure. Any data they get will most likely be sold and illegally reused; or, in the case of a ransomware attack, you'll be prevented from accessing your own files unless you pay

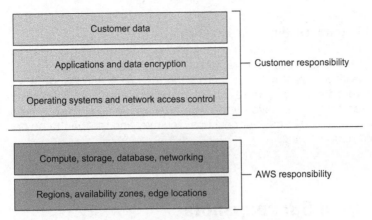

Figure 7.1 Division of responsibility between AWS and its customers for maintaining resources and services

a ransom. You'll probably never be able to regain control over stolen copies of your data as they make their way through the dark world of organized cybercrime. But having a reliable backup available from which to rebuild can definitely ease some of the pain.

Above and beyond: what about hardware hacks?
Compute, storage, and network infrastructure can be hijacked and placed in the service of sophisticated hacking activities like distributed denial of service attacks or the storage and distribution of prohibited media files. Protecting yourself from such threats requires other tools—backups aren't much use.

THE TROUBLE WITH ADMINS
Administrators like you and me may make mistakes while managing systems, irretrievably corrupting important configuration files in the process. Or people—again, like you and me—may accidentally delete EC2 instances or data volumes from their accounts. (That's far too easy to do on AWS.) All kinds of things can go badly wrong with any IT system, but the heavily virtualized bits and pieces that make up your AWS account are especially vulnerable to sudden disappearances. But with a recent, healthy backup archive just a mouse click away, a career-ending or project-killing disaster can be downgraded to a mild inconvenience.

> **Above and beyond: testing your backups**
>
> A backup archive only has value if you can, when necessary, use it to success-
> fully restore its contents to your system. Unfortunately, you'll never know if you
> can do that until you try—by which time, if the restore doesn't work, it's usually
> too late. If you don't incorporate actual tests into your backup protocol that
> attempt to restore your archives into environments identical to your production
> system, then when you need your backups, you may find that you're no better off
> than if you'd done nothing.

7.2 *Backing up to S3: snapshots*

The EBS volumes used as hard drives by your EC2 instances are where
the software that's running things is kept. By *software* I mean both the
OS kernel and directories filled with configuration files. It's sometimes
a good idea to make a quick, simple backup of an entire EBS volume.
(By default, there's at least one per instance that's known as a *root
device.*) So, for example, if you'd like to be able to quickly associate your
volume in its current state with an identical replacement EC2 instance,
having a snapshot on hand can be a great idea.

The ultimate goal, as shown in figure 7.2, is to quickly build a perfect
replica of your instance from before it failed or became corrupted and
drop it in place so that, ideally, your customers never notice the original
was gone. These three steps trace a simple way to do this:

1 Create a snapshot based on the EBS volume currently associated
   with your instance.
2 When the need arises—for example, if your old instance will no
   longer boot—/create an Amazon Machine Image (AMI) based on
   your snapshot. An AMI image, as you've seen previously in the
   book, is a template containing all the information EC2 needs to
   launch a new instance that's a perfect copy of the source instance.
3 Re-create your instance in its original state by launching the AMI
   image you created as part of a new EC2 instance (using the original security groups).

But what does all this have to do with S3? Well, where do you think
those snapshots are kept? S3, of course. But don't run to your account's
S3 dashboard and expect to see a bucket filled with snapshots; they're
stored out of sight.

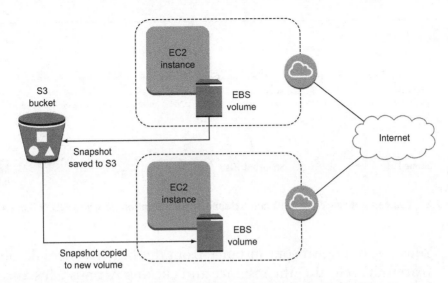

Figure 7.2 The contents of one EBS volume, saved (as a snapshot) and later reused in a second EBS volume attached to a different EC2 instance

To demonstrate how to work with snapshots, I'll assume you have an EC2 instance running (perhaps the WordPress website). Let's get started by creating a snapshot from the volume of an existing server.

7.2.1 Creating a snapshot

Click Volumes in the EC2 dashboard, and note the Volume ID of the volume attached to your running instance (see figure 7.3). If more than one volume is listed, you can confirm you're looking at the right one by clicking the corresponding instance ID in the Attachment Information column to the right. If clicking that link takes you to your WordPress instance, then that's the volume you're after.

Now you're going to create an exact copy of the storage volume used by your instance. If this volume is being used by an active instance, you'll normally want to shut down the instance before making the copy, because system files can be inconsistently copied if key processes are running during the copy operation.

> **NOTE** If you haven't attached an Elastic IP to this instance, it may have a new IP address—which, as I mentioned in chapter 4, may cause trouble with any MySQL databases you're running. Because you're playing around with proof-of-concept resources, you may be better off taking a chance and creating the copy from the instance while it's still running, rather than stopping it.

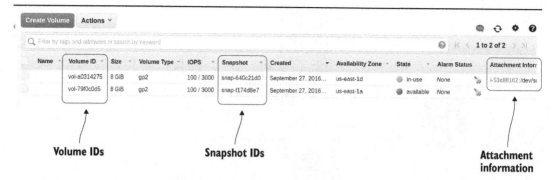

Figure 7.3   You can get the Volume ID and Attachment Information from the EC2 Volumes Console.

You can shut down your instance from the EC2 Instances dashboard by (carefully) selecting the instance and clicking Actions > Instance State > Stop (see figure 7.4.) Do *not* click Terminate: if you do, that will be the last you see of that instance or its EBS volume.

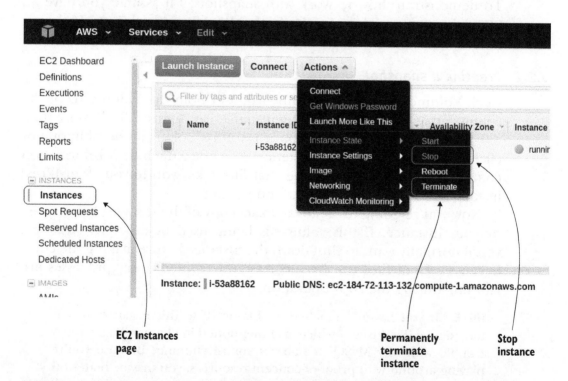

Figure 7.4   The EC2 Instance State menu where you control the lifecycle of the selected EC2 instance

You're ready to create your first snapshot. Click Snapshots in the panel at left, and then click Create Snapshot. Click once in the box next to the Volume label, and you'll be shown a list of all the volumes currently available on your account. Select the volume that matches the one associated with your instance, and give it a name to later help you identify your snapshot in the dashboard. It's always better to choose a name that's meaningful (like *WordPressInstanceBackup001*) rather than something like *snapshot* or *001*. Don't forget to restart your instance from the EC2 Instances page.

7.2.2 Creating an image

Let's turn the snapshot into an image that, in the event your worst nightmares come true, you can use to launch a replacement instance. From the Snapshots page, follow these steps:

1 Select your snapshot, and then click Actions.
2 Click Create Image (see figure 7.5).
3 Enter a name for the image in the dialog box that opens.

The other default values should all be fine, with one serious exception. Assuming your original instance was created using a mainstream AMI (if you followed along in previous chapters, it was), it used a virtualization

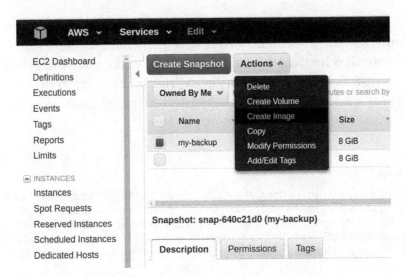

Figure 7.5 The Snapshots Actions menu, including the command to create an image from an existing snapshot

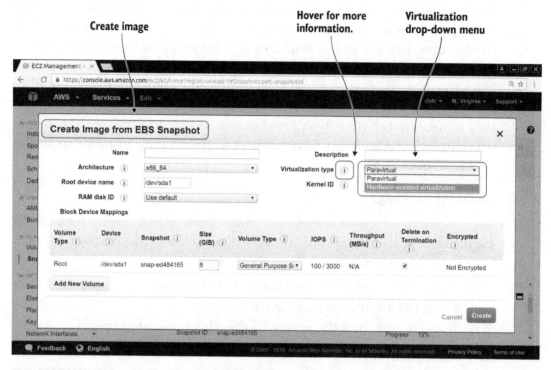

Figure 7.6   The Virtualization Type drop-down menu. Hovering your mouse over the "I" icon next to a label displays context-sensitive information.

technology known as *hardware virtual machine* (HVM). For some reason, the default virtualization type often shown by AWS is *paravirtual* (PV). The odds are that leaving this unchanged will make your image unbootable as an instance. So, click the Virtualization Type drop-down shown in figure 7.6, and select Hardware-Assisted Virtualization. When you're finished, click Create.

> **Try it now**
>
> You shouldn't trust me as much as you do. After all, how do you know that AWS will *really* push a PV virtualization type? In fact, Amazon is constantly updating its UI, so even if I'm right, the facts on the ground may have changed. So, click Create Image from EBS Snapshot, and see for yourself. If you're feeling adventurous, try booting an instance using the Paravirtual option, and see what happens.

> **Above and beyond: HVM? PV?**
> Just in case you're keen to understand the differences between HVM and PV, and when and why one or the other is preferred, feel free to read the chapter "Virtualization Concepts and Theory" in my book *Teach Yourself Linux Virtualization and High Availability* (Bootstrap IT, 2017).

Your image now exists and is ready to be launched as part of a new EC2 instance.

7.2.3 Using an image to re-create an instance

This is the easy part. Click the AMIs link in the navigation panel at left on the EC2 dashboard, select the image you previously created (and, I hope, identified with a useful name), and click Actions and Launch. That's it. From here, you're taken directly to the second step of the normal instance-launch process, where you can set networking, security, and storage options.

Confirm that everything is working by trying to log in to your new instance using SSH. You can also browse to its public website using the new IP address it's been assigned. If your original instance crashed, you'd reassign its Elastic IP address to this new instance. Hopefully, everything will work just as it did before.

7.3 Backing up to S3: manual process

AWS didn't invent the backup. No matter where it's hosted and no matter what OS you're using, it's always been possible to use a server's own tools to create copies of its data and move them to a safe place. Whether you prefer tape drives or hard drive–based network storage, it's only a matter of finding a reliable medium and moving the data to it.

So why shouldn't S3 be your backup medium? Gigabyte for gigabyte, the cost of S3 is, broadly speaking, often comparable to other formats, when you factor in their hardware and failure-replacement costs. Of course, regularly moving huge amounts of data across a network can take a long time and carries its own costs. But when the server you want to back up is already located in the AWS cloud, copying its contents to an S3 service isn't a big deal.

S3 it is, then. Here's what you'll do:

1 Use the Linux `tar` program to generate a compressed archive of the files you'd like to copy. There's no point in needlessly copying larger files back and forth when you can compress/decompress them at either end.

2 Install and configure the AWS command-line interface, which will make it easy to copy your archive to an S3 bucket that you'll create.

3 Perform the copy operation, and confirm that the file has reached its destination.

7.3.1 Choosing what to back up

Before you start, I'll devote a few moments to the problem of *what* to back up. If your Linux web server suddenly crashed, which files could be easily replaced, and which would be sorely missed?

A lot depends on how you're using your server and whether it's being accessed by other users. For instance, if you've given user accounts to a few developers, then you should probably assume they have some of their own data in their home directories (in the /home/ directory hierarchy). They may also have installed their own tools beneath the /usr/ directory. And, of course, you'll need to account for the website files that probably live in /var/, and the configuration files in /etc/.

> **Try it now**
> SSH into an EC2 Linux instance, and take a look around the filesystem. Drill down a few layers into the /etc, /var, and /usr directory trees. Note that the /sys and /proc directories are *pseudo* or *temporary* directories and will probably contain nothing worth saving.

You'll work with those locations for this example. For this to work, by the way, you'll need to create a new S3 bucket, just the way you did in chapter 6.

7.3.2 Generating a compressed archive

You're ready for `tar` (which, once upon a time, stood for Tape ARchive). To move to the directory where you'd like to save the new file, use `cd` followed by a tilde character (~) to change your working location to your account's home directory, and then run `tar`:

```
$ cd ~
$ tar czf mybackup.tar.gz /etc /var /home
```

Here's how the command breaks down. `c` stands for *create*, `z` for *zip* (which means you'd like the archive to be compressed), and `f` for *filename*. The next element must be the name you'd like to give the file you're creating: mybackup.tar.gz, in this case. The .tar.gz filename extensions aren't necessary, but they're a convenient way to remind yourself that the file will be a `tar` archive that's compressed using the gzip algorithm. Finally, you need to tell `tar` which directories or files to copy, compress, and include in the archive.

Type `ls` and then press Enter to list your directory's contents. You'll see that you're now the proud owner of a genuine file archive. If you're paranoid (and, when it comes to file management, who isn't?), you can display a full list of the file contents using `tar` with the `ztf` flags:

```
$ tar ztf mybackup.tar.gz
```

7.3.3 Installing the AWS CLI

The AWS command-line interface (CLI) is a powerful program that effectively lets you remotely control all of your AWS resources from the command line of any internet-connected computer. We'll spend a lot more time on the CLI in chapter 12. For now, though, you'll do just enough to get it running for this example.

Why install the CLI now? Because that's the tool you'll use to upload your backup archive to the S3 bucket you're about to create. Technically, you could also upload files to buckets from the S3 browser dashboard, but that's not an effective or efficient way to manage an ongoing backup operation.

You can download and install the CLI onto just about any Windows, macOS, or Linux computer running an up-to-date version of Python. You're probably fine in the Python department, but just to make sure, check the version you're running by typing `python --version` in your terminal:

```
$ python --version
Python 2.7.12
```

If it's not yet on your computer, you can find out how to download and install it on your local OS at www.python.org/downloads. Python 2 should be version 2.6.5 or higher, and 3.3 and up for Python 3 is also fine.

With that, you have everything you need except unzip—a program for decompressing files that have been compressed using the ZIP format (which is the format the AWS CLI file will use). Here's how to get it:

```
$ sudo apt update
$ sudo apt install unzip
```

> **Above and beyond: Amazon Linux and the AWS CLI**
> If you select an AMI with Amazon Linux rather than Ubuntu when you launch your instance, then the AWS CLI is preinstalled. Nice perk.

You'll use curl—a program that downloads the contents of any web address you feed it—to grab the awscli-bundle.zip file from the AWS site and then output it (-o) as a file called awscli-bundle.zip. Then, unzip the file using—you guessed it—unzip:

```
$ curl "https://s3.amazonaws.com/aws-cli/awscli-bundle.zip" -o
➥"awscli-bundle.zip"
  % Total    % Received % Xferd  Average Speed   Time    Time     Time
➥Current
                                 Dload  Upload   Total   Spent    Left
      Speed
100 8428k  100 8428k    0     0   796k      0  0:00:10  0:00:10 --:--
  :--   768k
$ unzip awscli-bundle.zip
Archive:  awscli-bundle.zip
  inflating: awscli-bundle/install
  inflating: awscli-bundle/packages/botocore-1.5.27.tar.gz
  inflating: awscli-bundle/packages/argparse-1.2.1.tar.gz
  [...]
```

unzip creates a new directory called awscli-bundle in your current directory. Type ls again to take a look. All the key tools for making the CLI work are somewhere in that directory.

Now that all the CLI program files are where they belong, it's time to install the program so Linux is made aware of your expectations. Here's how it's done:

```
$ sudo ./awscli-bundle/install -i /usr/local/aws -b /usr/local/bin/aws
Running cmd: /usr/bin/python virtualenv.py --python /usr/bin/python
➥/usr/local/aws
Running cmd: /usr/local/aws/bin/pip install --no-index --find-links
➥/>file:///home/ubuntu/awscli-bundle/packages awscli-1.11.64.tar.gz
You can now run: /usr/local/bin/aws --version
```

The install file is a short Python program that installs the AWS CLI file in the /usr/local/ directory and adds a symbolic link in the /usr/local/bin/ directory. The symbolic link is a file that, when it's run, tells the system to run the real command file in /usr/local/. The advantage of adding such a symbolic file in this case is that users can successfully run AWS CLI commands from any location on the computer. In other words, it's convenient. Lazy? Linux and AWS are here to help.

Hang in there; you're almost finished. You just need to give the CLI some information about your account so it knows whose AWS resources it should try to manage. Specifically, you need the access key ID and secret access key, both of which are available from the main AWS Console. Head over to the Console, and click your account name at upper right on the screen (see figure 7.7); then select Security Credentials. From the menu you're shown, select Access Keys and then Create New Access Key. Although you can always create a new set of keys, this will be the only time you're shown this particular secret access key; so, download the key file to a safe place or copy and paste the information you're shown.

Back in your terminal, you'll set up the AWS CLI. Run aws configure:

```
$ aws configure
```

You're prompted to type in the values of your two keys. You can paste the information by right-clicking the terminal with your mouse; you don't want to manually type in that mess, do you? Specify the region where your bucket lives as your default region; mine is us-east-1 (you can change it later if you need to). For now, don't worry about the fourth question you're asked; we'll come back to it in chapter 12.

One more step:

```
$ aws s3 cp mybackup.tar.gz s3://YourS3BucketName
```

aws tells Linux that the command that follows is intended for the AWS CLI; s3 tells the CLI that this command specifically concerns the S3 service; cp says to copy the following file; and s3:// followed by the name

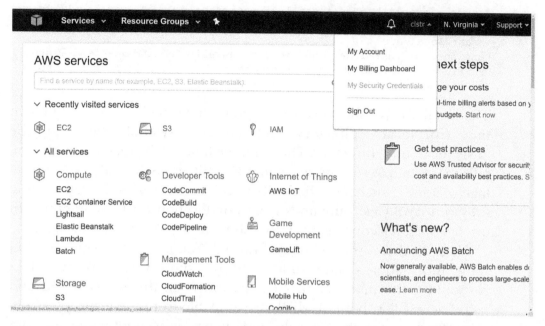

Figure 7.7   Links to basic AWS account-management tools, including Security Credentials

of your S3 bucket tells AWS where to copy the file. That's it! Go back to the AWS Console, click S3, click your bucket, and confirm that your archive is there.

The truth is, any backup strategy is far more effective if it's automated. Expecting busy administrators to do something like this regularly is optimistic. Nevertheless, having shown you how the backup process can work, I'll leave automation in your capable hands.

7.4   Lab

Practice creating a snapshot of an actual EBS volume and then launching it on a new EC2 instance. Don't assume it will work properly. Test the new instance to confirm that everything works the way it should.

> **Definitions**
> - *Snapshot*—A copy of an AWS EBS volume captured in its exact state at the moment the copy was made.
> - *EBS*—AWS's Elastic Block Store service.
> - *Volume*—A virtual hard drive managed by and made available through EBS.

- *Archive*—Any organized collection of multiple files. Archives are often (although not always) compressed.
- *Compression*—A technique for reducing the size of data files to allow more-efficient transfer and storage.
- *Root device*—Sometimes referred to as *root volume*. The primary storage device on an EC2 instance, used to host core OS files.
- *AMI*—An Amazon Machine Image, which is a template containing a core software profile that can be used to launch an EC2 instance.
- *CLI*—Command-line interface. A program that interprets keyboard commands for the underlying OS.
- *Python*—A common programming and scripting environment.

AWS security: working with IAM users, groups, and roles

The last couple of chapters showed you that Amazon S3 is a great place to store your data backups to protect you when things decide to go really wrong. But how about an early intervention? Rather than just learning how to ensure that you've got the data to successfully rebuild *after* bad stuff happens, wouldn't it be nice if you could prevent disasters in the first place?

The trick—or most of it, at any rate—is learning how to closely control exactly who and what can access your resources. Or, in other words, how to secure your AWS account.

If your entire infrastructure consisted of a single WordPress web server managed by a single administrator (you), then all this wouldn't necessarily interest you: you could open website access to the whole world and restrict admin access to yourself. But as your project grows, you may need to hire a few developers or some marketing and content professionals. Each team will need to reach the resources they're working on; but at the same time, to limit your exposure to risk, security best practices recommend permitting each user access to no more than they absolutely require. So you'll have to find a way to finely tune how people get through your front door.

The AWS security groups you've already seen can be configured to block (or allow) network traffic based on point of origin (a particular range of IP addresses, for instance) or traffic type (TCP or HTTP; port 80 or 22). But a security group can sometimes feel like a bit of a blunt instrument: either blocking everyone from everywhere other than specific IP addresses, or allowing the whole world in.

But what if you need to give access to particular users no matter where they happen to be and no matter what protocol they're using? Giving users unique account identities and letting them log in when and how they need to can let all that happen. How does that work? On Amazon, controlling access for individual users based on their authentication credentials is the job of the AWS IAM service.

8.1 Defining the pieces of the IAM picture

Controlling access through account authentication works best when it's precisely configured. And configuration works best when the admin doing it is deeply familiar with all the tools in the closet. So let's spend a little time understanding how each of IAM's many moving parts works.

8.1.1 Policies

The core of everything is the IAM policy, which defines exactly who may perform which actions on what resources. The best way to explain that is through a practical example. The policy code shown in figure 8.1 permits the user Steve—represented here as `Principal` by his unique Amazon Resource Name (ARN) identifier—to put objects into an existing S3 bucket called `designteam`. The `put` permission is set as part of the `Action` section, and the specific S3 bucket is identified by its ARN on the `Resource` line. The actual permission is enabled through the value given to `Effect`. In this case, that's `Allow`. You'll see how such a policy is applied a bit later. All this assumes, of course, that both a user account for Steve and a `designteam` bucket have already been created (stuff you'll get around to doing soon).

8.1.2 Users

An AWS user is effectively an account within an account. You, as the top-level owner of your AWS account, have the ability to create new accounts that provide access to any AWS resources you like, such as EC2 instances or S3 buckets. You can assign access policies to the account

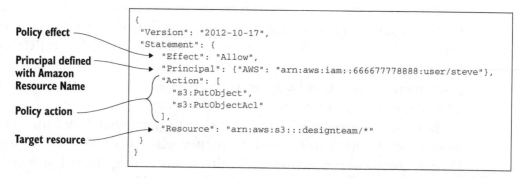

Figure 8.1   A breakdown of a typical IAM policy—this one focused on a particular S3 bucket

and generate passwords and security credentials. Once you've forwarded login details to your team members, they will have everything necessary to start work.

PROTECTING YOUR ROOT USER ACCOUNT

Although it may seem a bit strange, it's strongly recommended that you lock down your root AWS account and use a regular user account for your day-to-day activities. By *lock down* I mean do the following:

- Create a really strong password and store it in a safe place.
- Create a surrogate administrator user with somewhat limited power.
- Delete your root access keys (to prevent anyone from accessing and hijacking your root account).
- Avoid logging in to the console using your root account.

The idea is that, by definition, the root user has full power over absolutely everything. If, say, someone with hostile intentions gets hold of the root user's password, the entire infrastructure is as good as finished. An IAM user, on the other hand, starts with no powers of any sort. You can assign whatever permissions it will need to get its job done, but its reach is limited, which means an attack against it won't necessarily be as catastrophic.

I'll demonstrate how to create an administrator user and delete root access keys a bit later. But I'm afraid you're on your own when it comes to restraining your powerful urge to log in as root and finding a safe place for your password.

8.1.3 Groups

A group is similar to a user in that you can assign it specific access policies that define what's available to its members. But groups don't have their own access credentials. Instead, any users who've been added to a group will use their own credentials to gain access to the resources permitted by group policies.

The idea is that, rather than defining and frequently updating complicated policies for each user, you can update the group policies, and all of its members will automatically inherit the changes. This way, for instance, adding a new developer to the system will only require that you create a single new user account and then add it to your preexisting developers group (see figure 8.2).

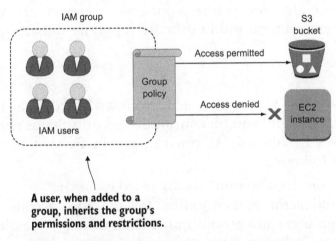

A user, when added to a group, inherits the group's permissions and restrictions.

Figure 8.2   IAM users associated with an IAM group are subject to the group policies.

8.1.4 Roles

Individual team-member access can be defined by managing users and groups. But permissions and rights can also be assigned to objects like EC2 instances and applications through *roles*.

A role is a creature of a nature somewhere between a user and a policy. Like a user, a role is an identity that has specified restrictions and permissions. But a role isn't the property of any particular user, and its privileges can't be reached through normal login methods. Instead, an object, once properly authenticated, can temporarily switch to a role whose access policies are then applied to the user, replacing any rights or restrictions that may have previously applied.

A typical use case might involve an application running on an EC2 instance that needs to access some media files in an S3 bucket. A role—and accompanying credentials—can be created and associated with the EC2 instance so that its application's request to S3 will be honored.

I'm not going to talk a lot about roles in this book because, frankly, they aren't a good match for the specific things you're trying to do right now. But as the scope and complexity of your AWS projects expand—and especially as you incorporate programmatic access into your applications—you'll probably find the role paradigm making more and more sense. I'll note, however, that it's not possible for the root user to switch to a role—because the root has access to everything, it would hardly make sense. In case you're wondering, *programmatic* means access that's automated from within software programs rather than initiated manually.

8.1.5 *Best practices*

Figuring out how to use IAM tools to make your AWS account as secure as possible is fairly straightforward: consult the Security Status checklist on the main AWS Dashboard. As you can see in figure 8.3, you're advised to do the following:

- Lock down your root account (as discussed earlier).
- Activate multi-factor authentication for the root account, and work through users and groups rather than through a single root account (as we'll discuss shortly).
- Create an IAM password policy to enforce at least minimal password quality standards.

MULTI-FACTOR AUTHENTICATION (MFA)

Considering how ineffective passwords can be at securing sensitive assets, you'd like your AWS account to be protected by something a bit stronger. AWS, like many other online providers, has added the option of applying multi-factor authentication to your account logins.

MFA requires users to log in using *both* a password and an authentication code that's been sent to a preapproved device, such as a smartphone. This extra layer of security makes it harder for a non-authorized user to gain account access even if the password has been compromised—or even if the device has been stolen. It's a good idea to require MFA for all your users.

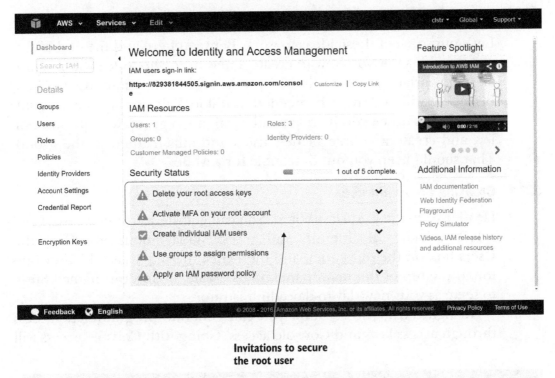

Figure 8.3 **IAM's quick Security Status checklist to remind you of the status of individual security best practice actions**

ACCESS KEYS

If all you need to do is log in and work with your AWS resources from the console, then a password (and MFA) will do just fine. But the deeper you dive into the Amazon (if you'll excuse the expression), the more likely it is that you'll need to make things happen from a command-line session on your local computer or from within an application. Trying to use passwords through such channels represents both security and usability problems.

Instead, adding the two identifying codes that make up your access keys (one access key ID and one secret access key) to a local configuration or to your application code can simplify access. I'll talk a lot more about how and when to use access keys later in the book. I'll also discuss when and how they should *not* be used. In any case, you'll need to keep tight control over your keys, because allowing them to fall into the wrong hands can quickly become unpleasant.

8.2   IAM-ifying an AWS account

Let's put some of these ideas to work. Between here and the end of this chapter, I'll show you how to create a new user who, once you assign it an appropriate policy, will become your active admin user. Then, because it will no longer be needed, you'll lock down the root account. When that's done, you'll create and configure a group with its own policy, and create a couple of new users and attach them to the group. That should keep you out of trouble for a while.

8.2.1   Creating an admin user

Head over to the IAM Dashboard. You can get there from the AWS Console by clicking the Identity and Access Management link. Click the Users link on the left panel, and then click the big blue Add User button at the top of the main panel. Let's create an account named Steve to serve as your new day-to-day administrator.

In figure 8.4, you see how you can generate programmatic access through access keys and Console access. Going with Console access will

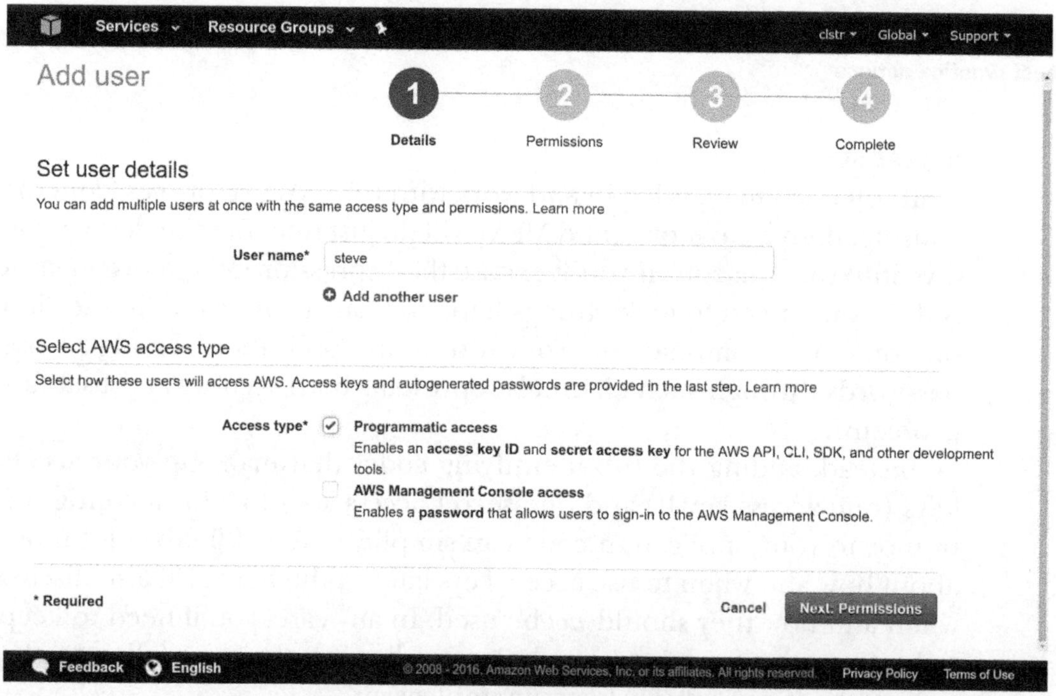

Figure 8.4   The IAM New User page with instructions for creating access keys and passwords

enable a password-creation dialog a bit further down this page (including an option that forces the user to create a new password at their first sign-in). Choosing Programmatic Access will cause access keys to be displayed in the next screen. Make sure you save them: they won't be shown to you again. Having said that, don't get anxious, because you can always generate a replacement set from the Console later.

Once all that's finished, you're taken to the Permissions page (figure 8.5), where you can assign an access profile for your new user. Because you don't yet have any groups for Steve to join, click through to review and then create the user. The final page gives you the opportunity to have an email sent directly to Steve, containing login instructions. If you're concerned about sending a password via email—and that's a reasonable concern to have—you can always communicate the new login information to Steve through a simple (and incrementally less insecure) telephone conversation.

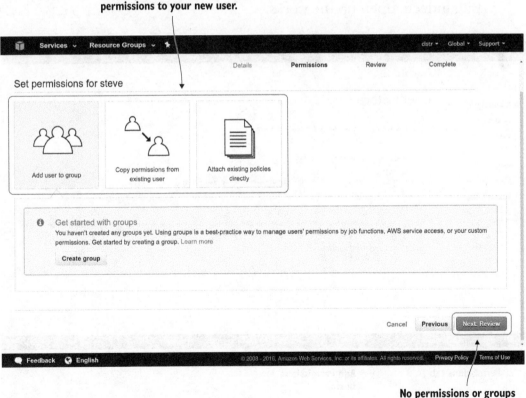

Figure 8.5 Create a unique access profile for your user.

Now you need to give Steve some permissions so he can do his job managing the account. Remember, this user is supposed to be a stand-in for the root user, so he'll need power over every area you plan to work with. You're going to attach a policy to his profile, which you can do from the user configuration page.

You get to the configuration page from the main Users dashboard by clicking the user name itself (Steve, in your case). Once there, you can manage Steve's password and access keys through the Security Credentials tab, or manage his access policies through the Permissions tab; that's what you'll do now. Make sure the Permissions tab is selected (as in figure 8.6), and click Add Permissions to return to the Grant Permissions page you skipped through while creating your user (earlier, in figure 8.5). This time, click the Attach Existing Policies Directly box.

AWS provides a long list of prebuilt policies to fit a wide range of use cases. For simplicity, you'll search for a policy that will effectively give Steve the keys to the entire shop. Type the word `admin` into the filter bar: the first option listed is AdministratorAccess (see figure 8.7) which will, indeed, open up the works.

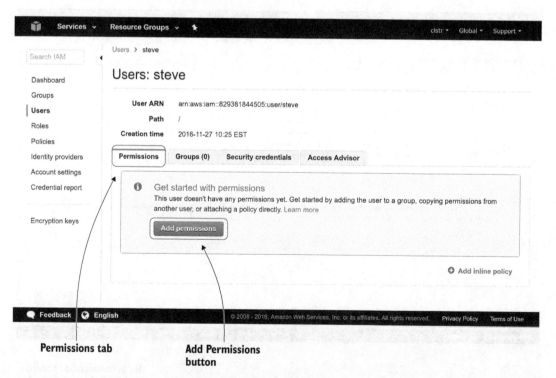

Figure 8.6   A user's Permissions tab, where you can manage resource access policies

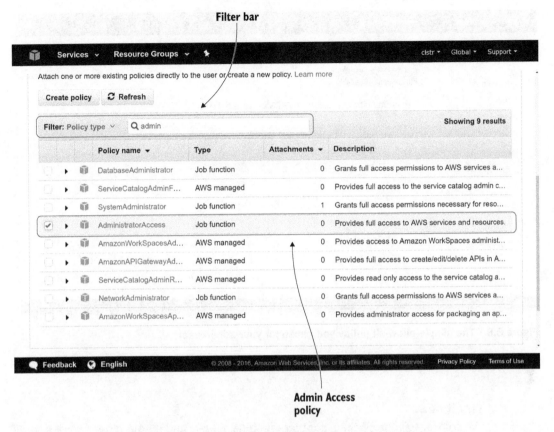

Figure 8.7 **The available prebuilt policies displayed for the filter string `admin`**

Wait a minute. Steve's account profile will now be pretty much the same as the root account it's meant to replace. This exercise doesn't seem to make much sense. But there are still some things beyond Steve's control, so once in a while you'll need to bring the root account out of retirement. I'll talk about one of those when you learn about AWS Budgets in chapter 11.

How do you know the AdministratorAccess policy is the one you want? I'll show you. Back in Steve's profile page, click the Permissions tab again, and then click the Show Policy link next to the Administrator-Access item in the policy list (AdministratorAccess is probably the only item). You're shown the policy's actual contents (see figure 8.8). Note the `Allow` value next to `Effect` and the asterisks next to the `Action` and `Resource` lines. That means any action will be allowed against any resource in the entire account.

Figure 8.8   The simple allow-all policy you chose for your admin user

> **Try it now**
> Head over to your AWS account, create a new user, and create a password. And, of course, consider using it to replace the role your root user normally uses.

8.2.2   Signing in as an IAM user

Great—you've got a brand-new IAM user who's all set to take over the farm from your tired old root user. Just one problem: how is Steve supposed to log in to the Console so he can start work? There's no email address associated with his account, so the normal login page won't work. Do you suppose there's a special account-level login page somewhere? Why, yes, there is! Go back to the main IAM page. An account-specific sign-in URL is displayed toward the top of the page, as shown in figure 8.9. All Steve will need to do is paste that URL into his browser and then enter his username ("steve") and the password you generated previously.

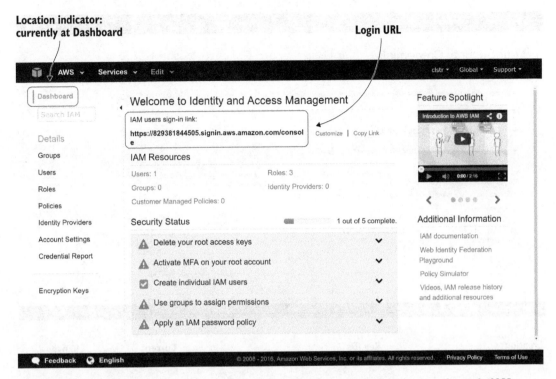

Figure 8.9   The URL where a user can log in to the AWS Console is displayed on the main IAM Dashboard.

8.2.3 Locking down the root

What's next? Now that Steve is set up and ready to step into the root user's shoes, it's time to lock down the root account. The simplest approach is to do that from the root account login. If you've already logged out of root so you could try Steve's sign-on, log back in as root, using the email address you used to create the account and your original password.

Now click the account name displayed at upper right on the page. A drop-down menu will appear that includes a Security Credentials item. Click it, and then, on the Security Credentials page, click the + character next to the Access Keys item. As you can see in figure 8.10, all of your keys are displayed with their creation dates and access key IDs. You aren't going to actively work with this user anymore, so there's no reason to keep its idle keys on the payroll, right? It's your choice: you can

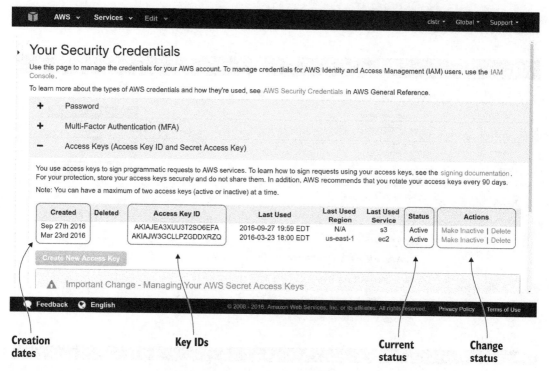

Figure 8.10   The root user's access-keys management interface

click either Make Inactive or Delete. If you're the worrying type, Make Inactive will allow you to reactivate the keys at some future time if needed.

8.2.4   Creating and configuring a group

Next, let's solve a different problem. Remember how you embedded an S3-hosted video in a WordPress page? Well, suppose your design team was regularly producing updated versions of that video. You certainly don't want to give them full access to the AWS account, but you also don't want to force them to email you the files so you can manually upload them into the S3 bucket. Is there a way for them to directly upload their new files?

You guessed it: you'll create a designers' group in IAM and add the design team members to it. Then you'll attach a policy to the group that permits both read and write access to S3 resources.

   Click the Groups link in the left panel of the IAM page to go to
Users. Then click Create New Group. Enter `designteam` for the Group
Name in the next window, and then click Next Step to go to the Attach
Policy page. You want to give group members access to your S3 bucket,
so type `s3` in the filter box to see what AWS suggests. Of the three possi-
bilities, AmazonS3FullAccess is the one that meets your needs.

> **NOTE**   Depending on what else you've got cooking in S3, you may pre-
> fer to create a custom policy that provides the group with full access to
> only some buckets.

Click Next Step to open a review page. Then, click Create Group to finish the job and return to the Group page. To add design users to the
group (for example, I created users Tony and Ann for this purpose),
select the (designteam) group and then click the Group Actions drop-
down button. Selecting Add Users to Group takes you to a page that
lists all of your users. Figure 8.11 shows that page with Ann and Tony
selected. From there, you only need to click Add Users, and the
selected users will have full access to all of your S3 buckets through their
logins. You can also fine-tune policies to, for instance, open only specific buckets to individual groups or users, but that's beyond your
immediate needs.

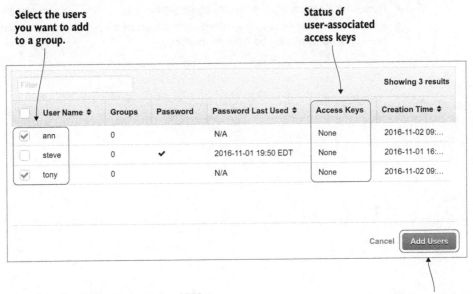

Figure 8.11   Adding users to an IAM group

> **Try it now**
>
> Create your own group, assign it a policy or two, and add some users. Then try logging in with one of those users to make sure it has the correct permissions.

8.3   *Lab*

Head over to IAM on your AWS account, where you can create your own user/group combinations and get used to searching for and applying policies to your IAM elements. Specifically, create a few new users. Add one or two of them to a *tech support* group that's been given full rights over EC2 instances, and add the other users to a separate *design* group that provides S3 access. Test it out to confirm everything works the way it should.

> **Definitions**
>
> - *Policy*—JSON-formatted rule used to define the access an element will receive
> - *User*—An IAM sub-account used to allow precise account access to team members
> - *Group*—An element with access policies to which individual users are associated
> - *Role*—An IAM identity that users can adopt to assume its access permissions
> - *Access keys*—An access key ID and secret access key pair, used to programmatically authenticate to AWS resources

Managing growth

Deciding to launch a new project without a clear idea of how much it's going to cost you is like ... well, it's dumb. Don't do it.

Sure, using a website to promote your new business rather than traditional print and media advertising does free you from paying for some expensive stuff, but that doesn't mean it's free. Yes, if you host your project in the AWS cloud, you won't have to purchase any big, bad servers and the hardware needed to support them; but that doesn't mean Amazon—out of the goodness of its heart—isn't interested in billing you. Rather, the cost burden is shifted from capex to opex.

Capex vs. opex

Capex stands for *capital expenses*: up-front stuff like new buildings and servers that may require years of revenue to cover the costs of investment. Pure cloud deployments require none of those. Opex (*operating expenses*), on the other hand, refers to ongoing costs like equipment rentals and salaries. Pure cloud deployments can have lots of those.

You may not be planning to build the next Amazon.com, but no matter how modest your vision, you need to think it through. Do you need a quick-and-dirty website with location information and a form for submitting product-support requests for a brick-and-mortar store? Or an e-commerce site with a complete database tier? Either way, ask yourself this: are the total costs you'll face justified by the value the site will deliver? Are there more-cost-effective alternatives? Are there individual elements that will add significant costs but little functionality? (You're going to put together a budget, right? Good.)

Now for some happy news: AWS provides a couple of useful tools to help you make informed and intelligent decisions *before* investing a single dollar. The Simple Monthly Calculator (https://calculator.s3 .amazonaws.com/index.html) spits out precise, detailed cost estimates based on any use scenario you throw at it. And the Total Cost of Ownership (TCO) Calculator (https://awstcocalculator.com) gives you an accurate idea of how much the operations you're currently running in your server room would cost if they were migrated to the AWS cloud. We'll take a good look at both.

9.1 *Estimating the true costs of your cloud project*

When the Simple Monthly Calculator was built, AWS fed it the entire insanely complicated cost matrix for the entire AWS system. That means the current rates for every kind of service and data transfer—including EC2 and RDS instance types, S3 buckets, and EBS storage volumes—are considered. You just tell it about all the pieces you need for your project, and the software will estimate the total costs you'll face.

As you can see in figure 9.1, links to individual AWS services run down the left side of the page. The cost of some services can vary between geographic regions, so you can select the region within which you'd like to work from the Choose Region pull-down near the top. Of course, you can also use this tool to find the cheapest regions to run your particular applications. You populate the tool by adding resources and how much of them you expect to consume in the appropriate fields.

As you add resources, the estimated total appears on the second tab along the top of the page. Clicking that tab (see figure 9.2) will give you a detailed service-by-service account of your expenses, each of which can be expanded to display more information by clicking its plus sign. Clicking the service links along the left side and adding resources

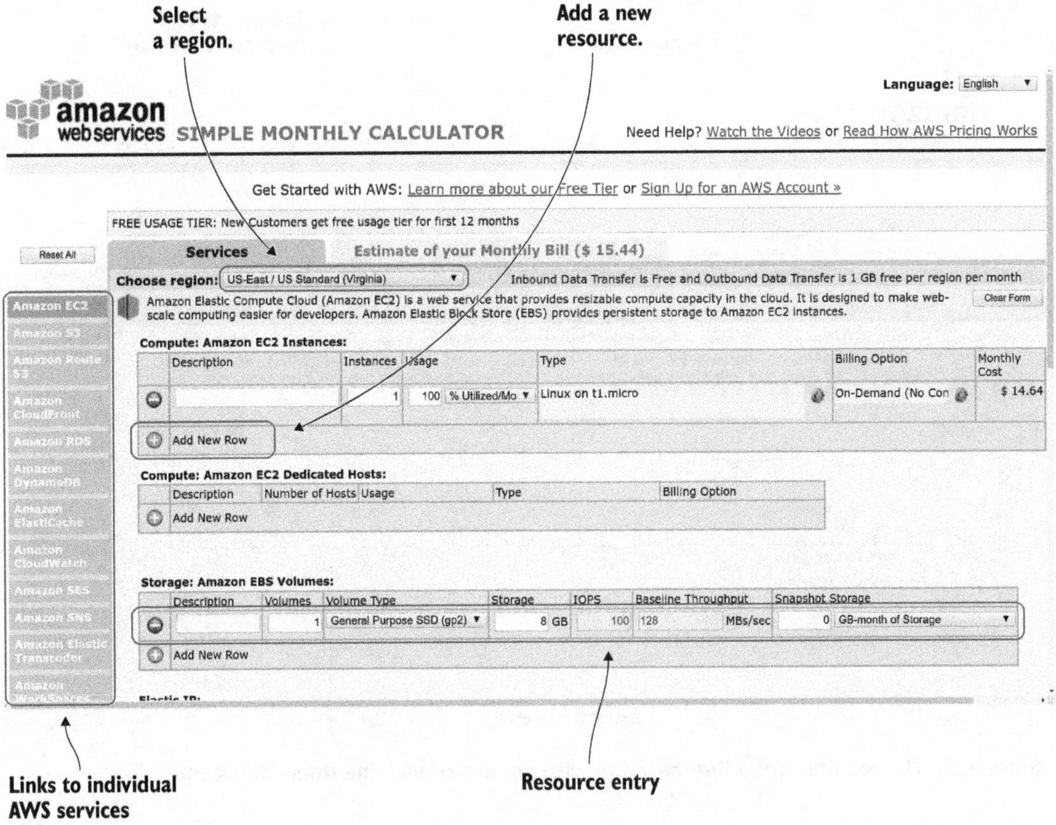

Select a region.

Add a new resource.

Links to individual AWS services

Resource entry

Figure 9.1 The EC2 page of the AWS Simple Monthly Calculator with a couple of resources entered

you're planning to use will also affect the total estimate. You can toggle the Free Usage Tier feature at the top of the screen either on or off to incorporate (or ignore) the cost discounts available for accounts in their first year.

Try it now

Don't be shy. Open the Simple Monthly Calculator page (http://calculator.s3 .amazonaws.com/index.html), and play around with the numbers. Try adding an EC2 instance by clicking Add New Row, and watch what happens on the Estimated Total tab.

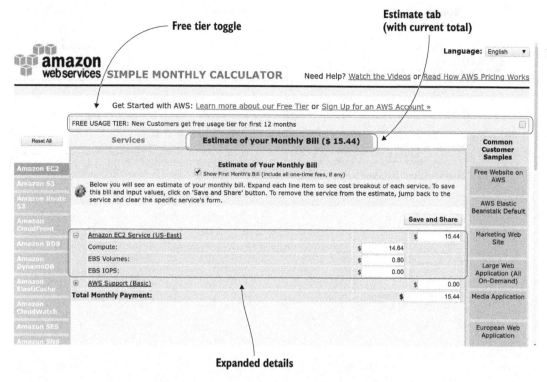

Figure 9.2   The Monthly Total Estimate tab with some detailed line items displayed

The real power of the calculator lies in how it lets you model as many alternate scenarios as you like. That means you can, for instance, accurately cost out adding a new tier of services and compare the results to the income your accounting team thinks the extra power might generate. When you've got a resource combination you think makes sense, you can—from the Estimate of Your Monthly Bill tab—click Save and Share to create a unique URL. You can then send that URL to your team members (and CEOs) for their feedback and approval (or, alternatively, scorn and ridicule). The URL will look something like this:

```
http://calculator.s3.amazonaws.com/
  index.html#key=calc-0823C17A-9085-4B6C-8EF1-AC0E68CD0FAD&r=IAD
```

To give you an idea of how it might work in the real world, AWS provides a number of example profiles used in common use cases, including Marketing Web Site and Media Application. You can access these samples via links arranged along the right side of the main page. Clicking the Large

Web Application example, for instance, first displays a schematic diagram representing the resources included in the particular profile (figure 9.3); when you click Details, you're taken to the Estimate page (figure 9.4), where you can drill down to see more detail.

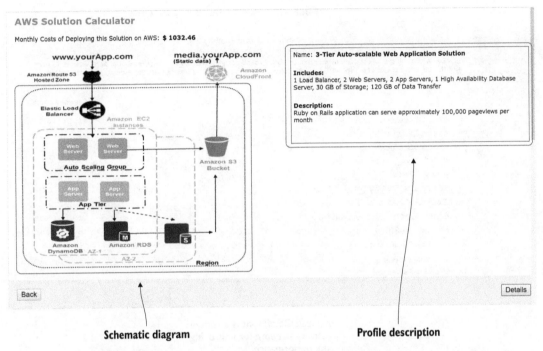

Schematic diagram   **Profile description**

Figure 9.3   Visualization and description accompanying the Large Web Application sample profile

By way of explanation, this resource profile represents the networking, compute, and database elements you'd need to run a highly available Ruby on Rails application that, as shown in figure 9.3, can handle 100,000 pageviews a month. By contrast, the Marketing Web Site example comes in at less than a quarter of the cost, largely because it serves its media directly from buckets in the S3 service rather than from an EC2 web-server instance.

9.2   Working with the TCO Calculator

Because we're talking about AWS calculators anyway, let's take a giant step backward and find out whether migrating a specific deployment to

Note the significantly higher EC2 costs compared to our previous example.

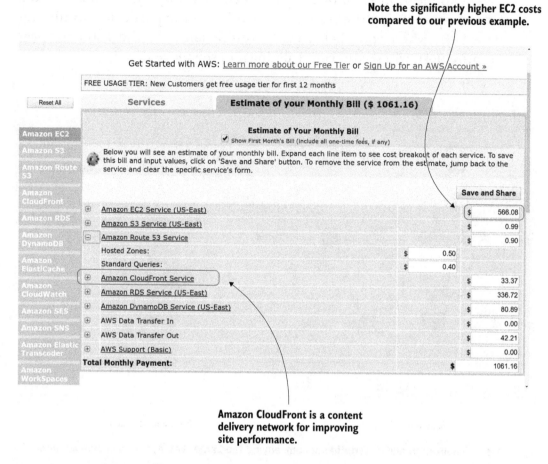

Amazon CloudFront is a content delivery network for improving site performance.

Figure 9.4   Detailed estimate of the monthly bill for the Large Web Application sample profile

the AWS cloud even makes sense. You may remember that, way back in chapter 2, I briefly mentioned how you can use the AWS Total Cost of Ownership Calculator to make detailed, accurate cost comparisons between on-premises and AWS infrastructure. Now's a great time to learn how it works.

The process is straightforward but, depending on how complicated your current setup is, may require some serious preparations to get right. As shown in figure 9.5, all the information you're asked to input—other than choosing an AWS geographic region—refers to your existing setup. So when you're asked about a workload—meaning whether you're using Microsoft's SharePoint—server type, it's in reference to the

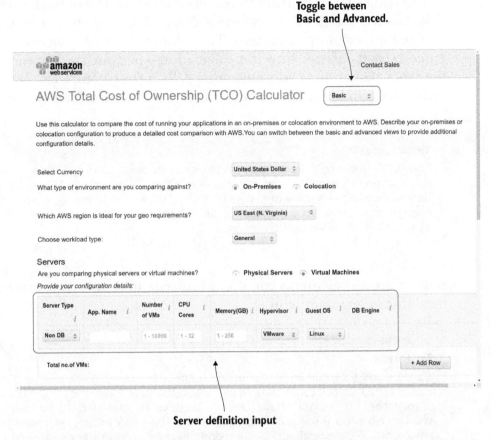

Figure 9.5 The top half of the AWS TCO input form, where you describe your current local infrastructure

ones you already have running locally. I assume that the reason Share-Point ranks a category all its own is to account for its licensing fees in the estimate.

The calculator tries to get as full a picture of your system as possible so it can determine what combination of AWS resources will be most comparable. For that reason, it's important for it to know how many and what quality of servers you're currently using, and also whether they're being run as database servers or for general-purpose use. Similarly, you'll be asked for details about things like the configuration of a particular class of server and whether you need it optimized by RAM, CPU, or storage I/O (distinctions that should remind you of the discussion in chapter 4).

Selecting Advanced from the drop-down at the top of the screen (initially labeled Basic) will reveal more-detailed data fields that let you further fine-tune your comparison. The advanced version will even let you enter IT staff salaries into the calculation—because, server for server, the labor demands of administrating AWS infrastructure can be significantly lower than for comparable work in a traditional server room.

> **Think about it**
> One detail that nicely illustrates the difference in labor costs is AWS's assumption that one IT administrator can manage 400 EC2 instances. As anyone who has ever worked at a traditional data center will tell you, purchasing, provisioning, deploying, and maintaining a fleet of just 40 physical servers would be unthinkable for a single admin. 400? Insane.

If there are any elements you don't understand, hover your mouse over the *i* (for *information*) icon.

> **Try it now**
> Spend some time gathering the technical specs for your project, and feed them into the TCO Calculator. It may make sense to enter your specs into your own spreadsheet first so you'll have a reliable baseline to come back to (and because you can *never* have too many spreadsheets). Then play around with alternative values on AWS's calculator. By all means, save a copy of the report, and try it out on your management team (just don't tell them it was my idea).

When you click the Calculate TCO button at the bottom of the page, you're taken to the results page. There you're shown a chart-rich overview of the comparison. The visual representations are followed by extremely detailed explanations of how the tool arrived at its calculations and which methodologies and assumptions were employed. For example, I calculated the costs for a multitiered e-commerce web-server project and the TCO Calculator produced a report stretching to more than 4,000 words, as illustrated in figure 9.6.

You'll be given the chance to download a full copy of the report, but not before entering your contact information and job role. You can opt to not receive communication from AWS partners; but they probably all

Note the three-year span of the projection.

Executive summary

Click to download the full report.

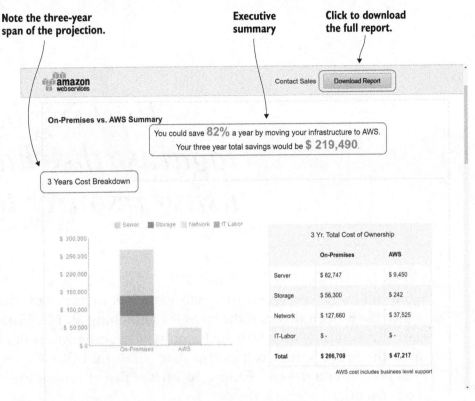

Figure 9.6   Part of the summary view of the TCO Calculator results

have loads of relevant experience, so I suspect that the partners we're talking about might prove quite useful.

That's it! You now have a great deal of valuable information on which to base an informed decision. The rest is up to you.

Definitions
- *Capex*—Capital expenses
- *Opex*—Operating expenses
- *TCO (total cost of ownership)*—An assessment of the full range of a project's costs

10
Pushing back against the chaos: using resource tags

While following along with the lab exercises in previous chapters, you've likely been through the steps for launching an EC2 instance at least a few times. With a little luck, you've also gotten yourself tangled up in the process once or twice so that "a few times" really means "I lost count after a dozen." Failure, as I never tire of reminding myself, is our friend.

Having been through the drill so often, you may be wondering about that Add Tags page I keep skipping over, mumbling excuses like "We'll get back to that a bit later." Well, "a bit later" just called: it's for you.

10.1 What are resource tags?

As you probably already figured out on your own, *tags* are key/value pairs that can be associated with individual pieces of AWS infrastructure. A *key/value* pair, by the way, is a couple of text strings used to help identify an object's purpose and context. A key called `name` might, when associated with a new EC2 instance you're launching, be given the value `MyNewEC2Instance`—to set it apart from your *old* EC2 instance, whose value for `name` might have been something like `MyFirstEC2Instance`. This label is used only for identification purposes and has no impact on the way the instance will operate. Unlike other key/value pair systems, AWS keys don't need to be unique.

I haven't used tags up to this point because I've assumed that your AWS account is fairly new and probably running only one or two examples of any particular object (one EC2 instance, one VPC, one EBS volume, and so on). When your list has only one item, there isn't much point in differentiating it from … well, from what, exactly? But my long-term goal is to turn you into a hard-core, seasoned Amazonian with all kinds of projects running on all kinds of resources. Once you've reached the "all kinds" plateau, things may get complicated if left unmanaged. So now's the time to start thinking carefully about some structural and design considerations that, over time, can make a difference.

Take your growing collection of EC2 security groups as an example. You can, of course, reuse security groups for as many instances as you like. But for me, at least, the first impulse when creating a new instance from the console is to define a new one. The downside of that approach when you're still experimenting is that the groups you create for short-lived instances are, unless you manually delete them, added to your collection. You'll probably see what I mean if you head over to the EC2 dashboard and click the Security Groups link on the left. Figure 10.1 shows how security groups are currently displayed on my account.

The Group Name column can be helpful—it identifies groups created for AWS's Relational Database Service (RDS), for instance—but look at all those Launch-wizard-x items. Without wasting significant time digging yourself deep into a dark pit of nested menus, do you have any idea which of these may require editing or are safe to remove? Tags can help.

10.2 Working with resource tags

Let's see how all this stuff works on actual AWS account resources.

10.2.1 Creating and applying a tag

Let's create a new tag for a security group. Select a security group, and click the Tags tab in the bottom panel. Then, click the Add/Edit Tags button. Click Create Tag, and choose a name for the key by typing in the Key box. You can choose an existing key name by typing the first letters of its name. Typing N in the example displays the key name Name in

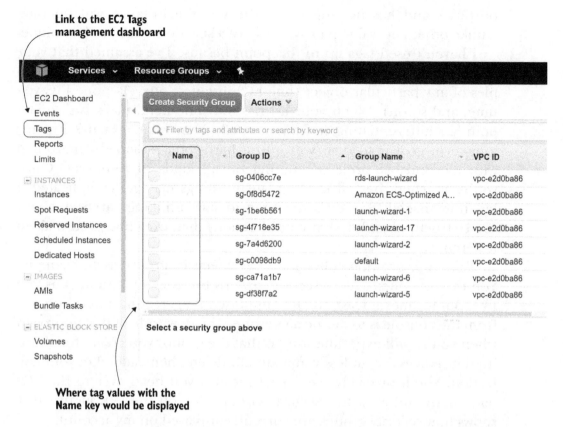

Link to the EC2 Tags management dashboard

Where tag values with the Name key would be displayed

Figure 10.1   The EC2 Security Group dashboard displaying empty tag values. Note the link to the EC2 Tags management dashboard, where you can create and administer your EC2 tags. Many AWS services have similar tools.

a large box (see figure 10.2; this example already has an existing key/value pair). Click Name to select it, and then enter a value for Value—which, in other words, will be the text displayed for this security group in the Name column.

Note that you can delete an existing value by clicking the white X (in the black circle) to the right. You can also hide or show a key column like Context or Name on the security groups page by clicking the Hide Column (or Show Column) link.

TIP   Regardless of the naming conventions you choose, be sure you don't start your names with the prefix aws: in your tags: it's reserved for internal use. Also, tags (both keys and values) may be constructed from any standard (UTF-8) characters, in addition to these special characters: + - = . _ : / @.

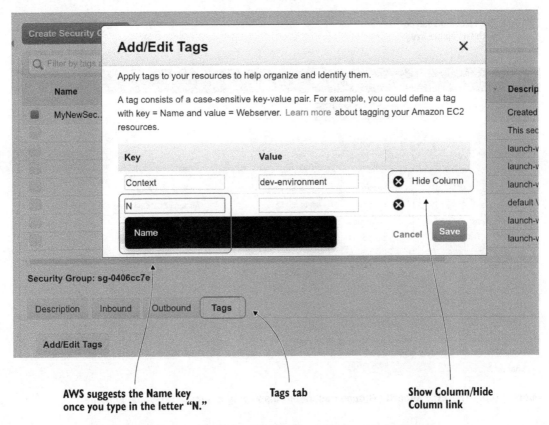

Figure 10.2   The Add/Edit Tags dialog from the EC2 Security Groups dashboard

Try it now
Don't just sit there staring. Go add a tag to a resource in your own account—perhaps one of your security groups. Then go through at least the initial steps of launching an EC2 instance, and see how much easier it is to select a security group that's been tagged from among a long list.

Figure 10.3 shows how things looked after I added values to the Name key of the first five of my security groups. The names I chose may be dumb and aren't nearly as helpful as they could be, but they're a lot better than leaving things the way they were.

Tag values displayed
with the Name key

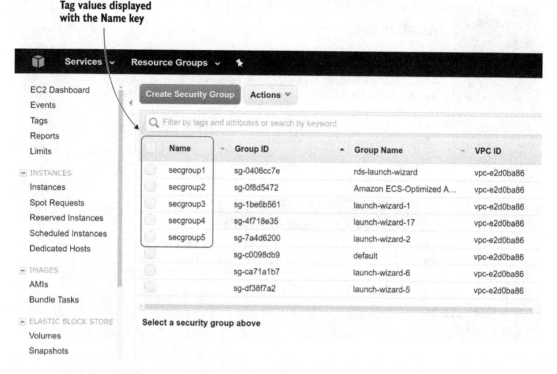

Figure 10.3   The EC2 Security Groups dashboard displaying a simple tag-value scheme

10.2.2 Designing a naming scheme

Of course, you can come up with much better naming schemes. Let's say your company has grown from a single WordPress server to include backup WordPress instances, servers handling online product sales transactions (including an RDS database instance), and a staging site where your developers can safely play with experimental code. Creating three sets of key tags, each using the key domain and values that include wordpress, transactions, and staging, could give you a naming scheme like that shown in table 10.1.

Table 10.1   How a well-organized key/value naming scheme might work

Key	Value	Explanation
domain	wordpress-instance-AZ1	WordPress instance running in availability zone 1
domain	wordpress-instance-AZ2	WordPress instance running in availability zone 2

Table 10.1 How a well-organized key/value naming scheme might work (*continued*)

Key	Value	Explanation
domain	transactions-primary	Primary transactions server
domain	transactions-backup	Backup transactions server
domain	transactions-rds	Transactions RDS server
domain	staging-instance-primary	Primary staging server
domain	staging-s3-snapshots	S3 bucket where snapshots of the staging server are stored

The idea is that you can apply these names to every piece of infrastructure in your account. Thus, you could give variations of the domain/transactions-primary key/value pair to an EC2 instance, a security group, and an S3 bucket that are associated with the primary transactions server. This would make them easy to find when searching through your resources by filtering for those keywords.

Try it now

Forget about the AWS Console for a minute, and take out a piece of paper or open a fresh document in your favorite text editor. Use it to map out how you'd organize the resources for your project. The more time you spend thinking it through now, the better your naming scheme will be when you start applying it. Believe it or not, there's an RFC guide (http://www.faqs.org/rfcs/rfc1178.html) that officially defines the best practices for naming conventions.

10.2.3 Searching your tagged resources

One place to see a naming scheme in action is on the Tag Editor page. "But how do I reach the Tag Editor page?" I hear you asking. I'll be honest: until I began to work on this chapter, I couldn't have answered that question, other than with a lame "Try searching Google." Imagine my surprise when I discovered that, as shown in figure 10.4, the Tag Editor option resides on the AWS Console main page; you can reach it via the Resource Groups drop-down.

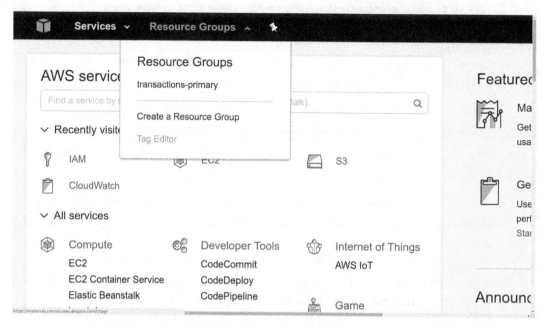

Figure 10.4　Drop-down menu leading to the Create a Resource Group and Tag Editor pages

The purpose of the Tag Editor is to make it easy for you to find resources by tag and then, if desired, create and apply new tags to all or some of the results. But I'm going to use the Tag Editor to illustrate how you can also use tags to filter for specific resources. Figure 10.5 shows how I entered the AWS region I wanted to search, along with specific resource types (I went with All Resource Types in this case), and the key *domain*. I then entered the transactions-primary value for the key and clicked Find Resources. The instance, security group, and S3 bucket were returned, but nothing else—which was exactly what I wanted.

Individual resources can have more than one tag. In fact, the upper limit is 50. Using multiple tags allows you to organize your resources in multiple ways. To illustrate, perhaps some—but not all—of your transactions-primary resources are meant to be used as models for other infrastructure purposes. You could create a new key called *template* and apply it (along with values like `primary-server`) to just the transactions-primary resources that fit this additional qualification.

Tag key field   **Tag value field**

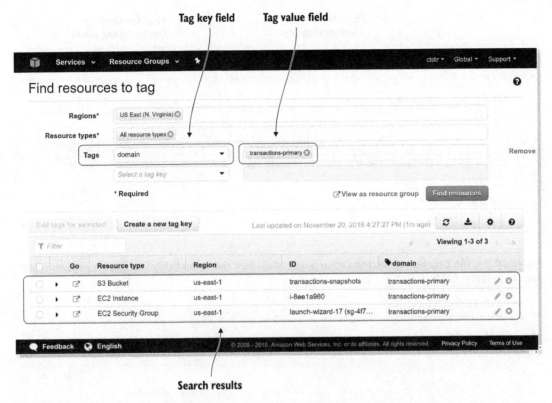

Search results

Figure 10.5 The Tag Editor page, where you can create and manage tags and also search for specific tag ranges

10.3 Working with resource groups

Tags are just the beginning. You can also create resource groups that use tags to associate resources from across your account. To do so, click the Resource Groups drop-down (the same one you use to reach the Tag Editor), and then click Create a Resource Group.

As you can see in figure 10.6, you start by giving the group a descriptive name, and then you select an existing tag. You can either click the Tags box, and the names of all your existing tags will appear, or start typing the name of the tag, and the smart people at AWS will try to guess what you're after. You can do the same for the value box to the right (my `transactions-primary` value appeared when I clicked the box). You can further narrow your selections by specifying individual regions and/or resource types.

**Fields for entering
(multiple) tag keys**

**Field for entering
(multiple) tag values**

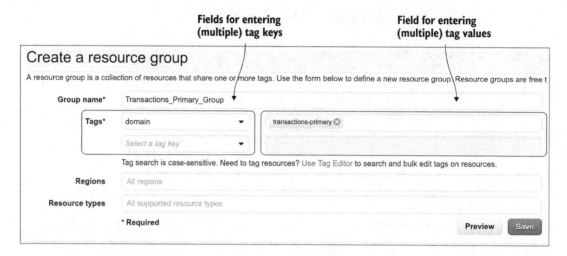

Figure 10.6   **The Create a Resource Group page. More key and value fields will appear once you add
data to existing fields.**

**Available EC2 resources
within the group**

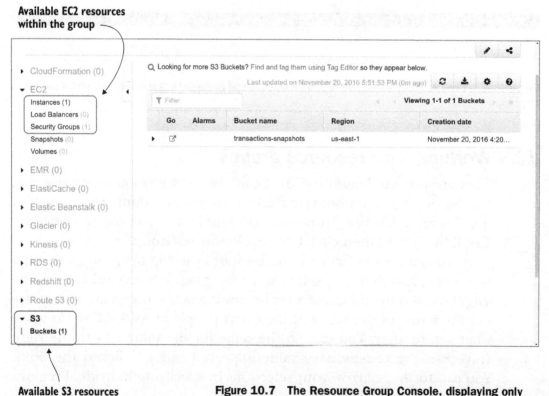

**Available S3 resources
within the group**

Figure 10.7   **The Resource Group Console, displaying only
resources that match the resource group parameters**

Now for the fun bit. Click Save, and not only will your resource group be saved, but you'll also be immediately taken to a customized console displaying only the tagged resources that are part of the group you just defined (see figure 10.7). This is a convenient place to both see and manage everything that's part of this group. From now on, you can access this custom console by clicking the Resource Groups drop-down that appears at the top of your screen and, as shown in figure 10.8, selecting your group.

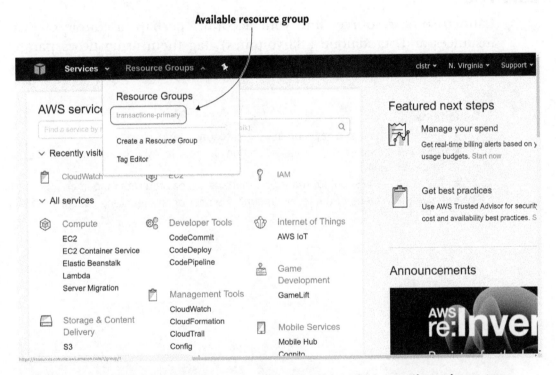

Figure 10.8   The Resource Groups pull-down menu with a link to the transactions-primary group

Try it now

Build a resource group out of tagged elements currently available in your account. Then see if you can figure out how to delete the group (without damaging the resources). If you get stuck, feel free to ask for help on the *Learn Amazon Web Services in a Month of Lunches* online forum.

10.3.1 Using tags to track costs

One of the most common uses for tags and resource groups is cost tracking. The ability to slice and dice many resources is such a great way to productively visualize what you've got running, so it stands to reason that you'll probably want to link those visualizations with the way you monitor—and control—spending. All of this, conveniently enough, is the subject of the next chapter. Don't miss it.

10.4 Lab

Launch some resources into your account (perhaps a couple of EC2 instances and standalone EBS volumes), tag them using two separate keys, and then group them together into a resource group.

> **Definitions**
> - *Key*—The name of a tag's organizing category
> - *Resource group*—A tag-based collection of links to AWS resources within a single account
> - *Tag Editor*—AWS tool for managing the tags associated with resources
> - *Value*—The name of the individual unit member of an organizing category

CloudWatch: monitoring AWS resources for fun and profit

Partly because AWS resources can be so widely scattered across dozens of service categories and geographic regions, it's easy to imagine yourself accidentally leaving things running and then forgetting about them. That thought turns a lot darker when you consider how many of those things are billed by the hour. And—in case you've forgotten—there are many hundreds of hours in a month.

You should also spend some quality time worrying about how much fun hackers could have if they gained access to your account without your knowledge. They could easily run up many thousands of dollars' worth of usage costs before you noticed anything unusual.

Failing to keep track of your active resources can get expensive. What's a poor admin to do? Fortunately, AWS provides effective tools to keep you in the loop. You just have to enable them.

11.1 AWS Budgets

Perhaps the quickest way to apply some kind of control to your account costs is through AWS Budgets. Clicking your account name at upper-right on any AWS page opens a drop-down menu that includes a My Billing Dashboard link. Click it, and then click the Budgets link on the left side of the Billing dashboard page.

Who can create a budget?

Remember how, back in chapter 8, I told you that AWS best practices encourage you to lock down your root user and use an administrator user that you created in Identity and Access Management (IAM)? Well, that may have been just a wee bit misleading: there are still cases where you'll need to dust off the root user and get it back in the saddle (although you won't have to create new access keys for this purpose). And this is one of those cases. It turns out that, even with full admin permissions, an IAM user doesn't have the power to create a budget—or do much else on the Billing dashboard.

There's powerful logic behind this: if the daily administration account could control billing limits, then successfully hacking that account would be just as catastrophic as hacking root.

11.1.1 Creating a budget

In this section, you'll create an AWS budget and set it to issue email alerts if your monthly usage charges exceed a specified limit. To start the process, follow these steps (see figure 11.1):

1 Give your budget a name.
2 Select Cost if, as in this case, your goal is to keep an eye on your account costs. Or select Usage if you're interested in tracking account activity by the number of service units consumed rather than cost—perhaps to see whether your current deployment profile requires a reset.
3 Set the budget period. This is the time period—monthly, quarterly, or yearly—you'd like to use to measure costs; any budget amount you select in step 5 will be applied in relation to the time period you set here.
4 Set the start and end dates between which this budget will remain active.
5 Set Budgeted Amount to the maximum you're willing to spend during each selected period before an alert is triggered.

The budget-creation process lets you specify expenses by areas. Suppose that, in addition to creating a general budget that monitors your overall costs, to protect against unauthorized account access, you also want to keep an eye on the way you're consuming EC2 instances. This might be useful if (as I'll discuss in later chapters) you set the number of EC2

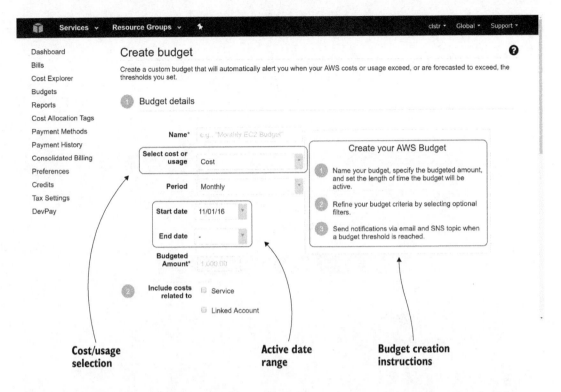

Figure 11.1 The Budget Details part of the Create Budget page, accompanied by general budget-creation instructions

instances to automatically increase (scale up) to meet higher demand. Keeping your users happy is a great thing, but every extra instance deployed for the cause will cost you more money. If you have limits on how much you can spend (and who doesn't?), you'll want a budget to watch things.

To get there, move down the page to the filter section, which is called Include Costs Related To. When you select a box next to a category, a text-entry field appears. In figure 11.2, I clicked Service and began typing ec2. Three AWS services appeared: their names included those characters *and* my account had active running resources from those services. If I'd clicked EC2-Instances, only costs associated with active EC2 instances would have been included in this budget. Of course, you aren't limited to a single active service; you can add as many as you like by entering them after EC2.

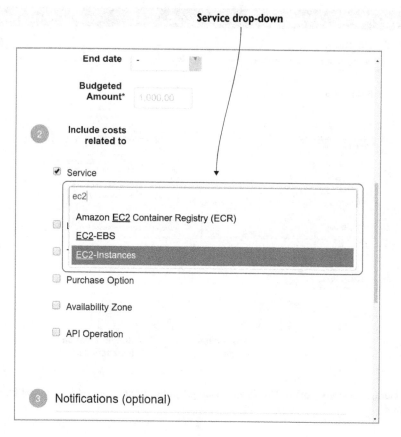

Figure 11.2   Select categories to create filters for your budget. In this image, the Service category is visible.

11.1.2 *Using tags with your budgets*

Figure 11.3 shows the Tag category. You can type a tag name into the Filters field (or select a tag that's displayed automatically), and you should be shown all the available associated values.

As I mentioned earlier, you can also use tags to create a budget that's focused on a specific subset of your AWS resources. This can be useful if you have different projects—each with its own business goals and limits—that you'd like to track individually. In this section, you can enter any tags you'd like to use as filters.

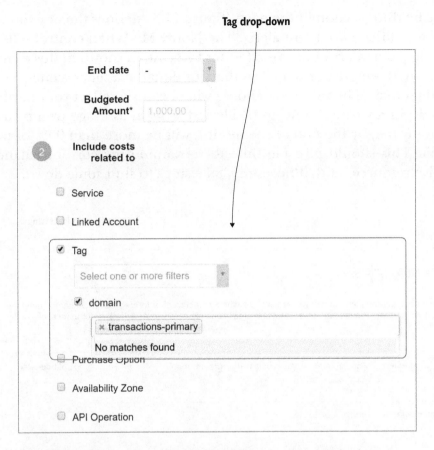

Figure 11.3   Select tags, and you'll be shown any associated values (`transactions-primary`, in this case).

Suppose you want to limit what your budget tracks to one class of resources. Perhaps you're not worried about instances running in your staging and development environments, but you do want to monitor everything that's part of the production environment. Similar to what you saw in the previous chapter, if you've already organized your resources by environment, you can easily set the budget to track resources with the `production` tag.

The third section of the page (figure 11.4) defines the way you'd like to be notified about cost alerts. The Notify Me When control tells AWS to trigger an alert when costs (either forecast, as shown in this example, or actual) are greater than, less than, or equal to a set percentage of the budget total. The value you choose will obviously reflect your particular needs; in my case, I want to be alerted as soon as usage trends suggest that my bill, by the end of the month, will be more than 90% of my set limit. This should give me time to reexamine my current balance of active resources and, if necessary, take steps to shut some down.

Trigger threshold settings

3 Notifications (optional)

You can create a billing alarm to receive e-mail alerts when your current or forecasted AWS charges meet the threshold you choose. Please provide at least one email contact or SNS topic ARN in order to receive notification.

Notify me when   Forecasted   ▾   costs are   greater than   ▾   90   % of budgeted amount

Email contacts   info@bootstrap-it.com

SNS topic ARN   Please fill in a valid SNS topic ARN   ❷   Verify
SNS topic policy statement

➕ **Add new notification**

* Required   Cancel   **Create**

Email entry field

Figure 11.4   The notifications section of a budget setup, where you can set the budget's trigger threshold and notification recipients

In order to be notified when a limit is reached, you need to enter at least one email address; you can add as many as you like, as long as they're separated by commas. Alternatively, if you find consuming alerts as text messages to be more convenient, you can send budget notifications to a preexisting SNS topic, which you identify by its Amazon Resource Name (ARN) ID.

Amazon SNS

Amazon's Simple Notification Service (SNS) allows you to automate coordination between individuals, processes, and mobile devices (using, for instance, the SMS texting protocol). An SNS topic is defined by its recipients, to whom messages are sent whenever the topic is invoked. We'll dig a bit deeper into SNS in chapter 20.

When you're finished, click Create, and your budget will go live. From now on, clicking the Budgets link will take you to the Budgets dashboard where you can edit or delete existing budgets or create new ones. Bear in mind that only the first two active budgets are free.

Try it now

Because the first two budgets are free (and assuming you don't already have two running), try creating a simple budget on your own account that sets a maximum monthly total account cost and issues an alert when it hits 75%.

11.2 CloudWatch

I can't blame you if you're wondering why I put CloudWatch in this chapter's title, given that I've utterly ignored it until this point. Ah, but I haven't been utterly ignoring it. You see, Amazon CloudWatch is the engine that drives AWS Budgets. The connection will become clear once I show you some of CloudWatch's native functionality. In addition to making billing alerts possible, CloudWatch can track the minute-by-minute health and effectiveness of your resources. I'll show you how.

CloudWatch vs. AWS Budgets

I should mention that the practical differences between CloudWatch and its younger cousin, AWS Budgets, will probably determine whether you choose one over the other. But when you get past the obvious differences in the design paradigms governing their setup interfaces, it's difficult to figure out what one can do that the other can't.

Here's one thing, at least: whereas AWS Budgets is best suited for quickly creating alerts that you can configure and forget about, CloudWatch can generate usage and cost-trend graphs that, in addition to generating alerts, can easily be incorporated into ongoing monitoring activities. We won't be spending any time on this in the book, but it's worth keeping in mind.

11.2.1 CloudWatch billing alerts

So that you can better understand their similarities, let's see how to set up the same kind of alert with CloudWatch as you did with Budgets. From the main AWS Console, click CloudWatch in the Management Tools section and then click the Billing link on the left side of the page. You'll see another charming blue button, this time labeled Create Alarm; click it.

Your alarm will need a metric. In the IT world, a *metric* is a predefined way of measuring something. It could be the estimated monthly charges that a particular AWS service (for instance, S3) is generating, or the network bandwidth being consumed by an EC2 web server.

The drop-down near the top in figure 11.5 is currently set to Billing, but you can also choose All Metrics or any individual service. Selecting Billing and then EstimatedCharges—as I did in the example—will trigger the alarm to go off on events relating to the total costs of all resources running on the account.

> **NOTE** Only metrics in the currently selected AWS region are displayed. CloudWatch alerts are region-specific.

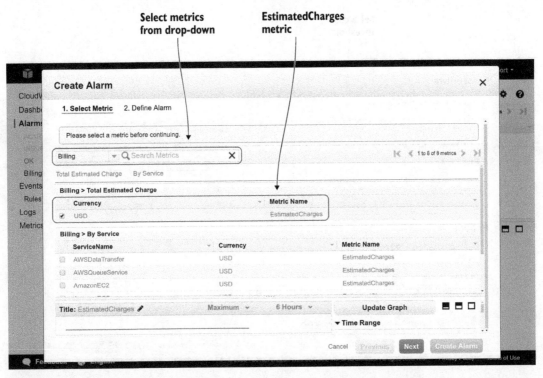

Select metrics from drop-down

EstimatedCharges metric

Figure 11.5 The Select Metric step for creating a CloudWatch alarm. Note that the Total Estimated Charge metric (in US dollars) is selected.

On the Define Alarm tab (figure 11.6), you give your alarm a name, set a cost threshold (I chose anything greater than or equal to $100), and tell CloudWatch where to send alarms. If necessary, you can click the New List link to create … wait for it … a new list, which you can populate with one or more email addresses. Click Create Alarm, and you're finished.

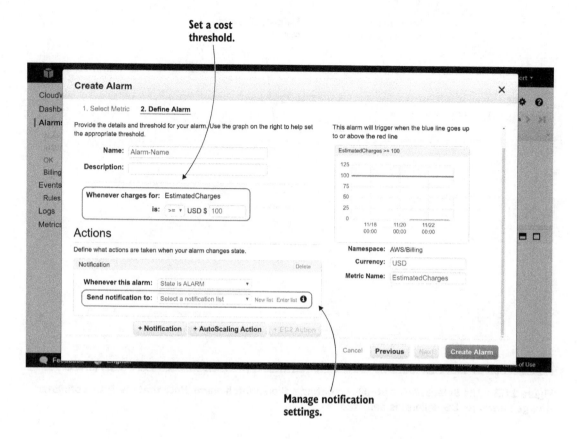

Set a cost threshold.

Manage notification settings.

Figure 11.6   Define your billing alarm. Note the chart on the right: the horizontal line at the 100 mark is your maximum limit, and the shorter line at 0 is the current estimated charge.

You can see some more differences between CloudWatch and AWS Budgets by clicking the Billing drop-down back on the Select Metric screen (figure 11.5) and then, assuming you have, say, an EC2 instance running, clicking All Metrics. Scroll down the list in the main panel, as shown in figure 11.7. AWS Budgets has nothing comparable to the depth of the selection you'll find here.

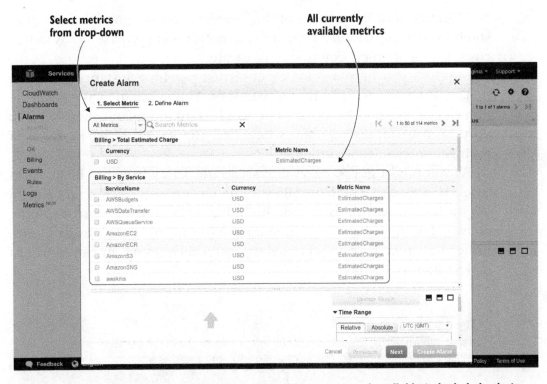

Figure 11.7 The CloudWatch metrics currently on this account and available to include in alerts

> **Cost-allocation tags**
>
> There's one more way to play this game: using cost-allocation tags. You can acti-vate either an AWS-generated tag or user-defined tags (or both) from the Cost Allocation Tags tab on the Billing dashboard. After you assign tag(s) to running resources, AWS will generate cost-allocation reports as CSV files you can down-load. These reports are an excellent way to visualize your costs from an account-wide perspective.

11.2.2 CloudWatch usage alerts

Of course you need to pay attention to how much money your AWS toys will cost you (or your boss). But you wouldn't want to ignore the toys themselves. After all, they're why we're here, right? CloudWatch offers some robust ways to keep an eye on things.

Although it isn't the focus of this chapter, now is a good time to show you how to apply CloudWatch alerts to monitoring *performance* as well as costs. I'll use a quick example to illustrate.

Suppose you have a number of virtual machine instances running that access various EBS storage volumes. You want to make sure the number of volumes is appropriate to the actual demand they face. To do that, you can create alarms based on the `VolumeIdleTime` value of each volume you're watching.

As you might guess, `VolumeIdleTime` measures stretches of time (in seconds) through which an EBS volume has no requested read or write operations. If the number is too high, it may be time to retire a volume or two. Too low? Perhaps you should add one or more new volumes. Either way, receiving an alert telling you what's going on can help you make timely decisions.

Try it now

Using CloudWatch, create an alarm that's set to go off if the CPU utilization of an EC2 instance (launch one if you need to) goes above 95%.

I'm not sure this is the simplest or most efficient way to get this particular job done, but it does illustrate the kind of deep insights into your account that CloudWatch can provide.

11.3 *Lab*

Create a budget (with appropriate alerts) that's focused on only a subset of your total running resources—say, all active EBS volumes.

Definitions
- *Filter*—A parameter used to narrow a search to a subset of a larger group
- *Metric*—A unit of measurement
- *Simple Notification Service (SNS)*—Amazon's way of communicating between participants (both human and machine) to coordinate actions

Another way to play: the command-line interface

If you only knew the kinds of contortions I had to put myself through to avoid mentioning the AWS command-line interface (CLI) until this point in the book (other than my brief lapse back in chapter 7). Pretty much everything you've done from the browser-based console could have been done more quickly and efficiently through the CLI, but I held back for two reasons:

- I believe the AWS browser-based console has a sophisticated visual design that better lends itself to quickly grasping the cloud platform's larger workflow and function. In other words, it makes it easier to learn how to use AWS.
- Although, in the long run, the CLI will probably become your best friend, getting to know it can be complicated at first. So I thought it would be best to leave it until you're comfortable with the basics.

But now, the hour of reckoning has arrived. It's CLI time.

12.1 What is the AWS CLI?

The AWS CLI is a set of commands that can run in a command-line terminal. When the CLI is invoked by the prefix aws, the subsequent characters are subjected to special rules of interpretation. Any commands that don't include the special combinations are ignored and left for the default—or parent—shell.

As figure 12.1 illustrates, when a command beginning with the letters aws is entered, it's parsed locally to ensure that the syntax is properly formed and then forwarded to the AWS account matching the local authentication configuration. If a command doesn't begin with aws, it's left for the parent shell.

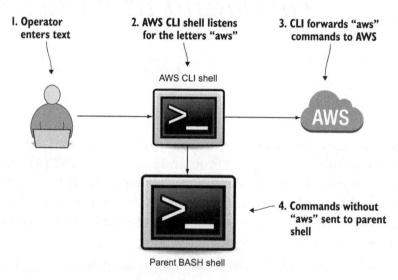

Figure 12.1   If a command starts with the letters aws, it's read by the AWS CLI and forwarded to the AWS cloud.

12.2 Why use a CLI?

By this point in the book, even those of you who were total newcomers to AWS back in chapter 1 are fairly comfortable configuring, launching, and stopping resources from the browser AWS Console. It may be starting to feel like second nature—perhaps even fun. But you've probably also wondered how it must feel to load the half dozen or so pages necessary to launch, for instance, a single EC2 instance—and then turn around and do it again a few more times to get your entire cluster running.

We live in a cloud world, and it's rare to find a reasonably sized company with only one instance, one S3 bucket, one database, and one Route 53 domain. Not only are you likely to need to fire up multiple versions of each element, but, at some point, you'll probably do so multiple times a week.

Once you're there, forget about the browser interface: it can easily become an instrument of madness. Instead, say hello to the beauty of carefully constructed commands, often woven into comprehensive scripts. Need to run a complex infrastructure combination next Thursday evening, but only for three hours and only in Ireland? You can script it and get a good night's sleep at the same time.

Of course, there are also sophisticated third-party configuration-management packages like Puppet, Vagrant, and Chef that can be integrated directly into your AWS account and provide similar functionality. But at their core, they're also scripts, relying on structures and logic that are similar to what you'll find in the AWS CLI. Exploring complex scripting is beyond the scope of this book, but I'll show you the basics that should get you most of the way there.

12.3 Installing the AWS CLI

Happily, there are all kinds of ways to install the AWS CLI on any computer running in your home or office (or your Caribbean vacation resort, if that's the way you'd like it). I'll walk you through the largely straightforward steps to get the package running on Windows, Linux, and macOS, using both native installation techniques and the pip software-management system used for Python packages.

> **NOTE** If your machine is an Amazon Linux AMI (Amazon's own cloud-ready Linux machine image) running on AWS EC2, I've got great news for you: the CLI comes preinstalled.

12.3.1 Installing with a Windows MSI file

For any Windows version back to and including XP (although you know you shouldn't be using XP anymore, right?), you can download the MSI installer file for 64-bit machines (https://s3.amazonaws.com/ aws-cli/AWSCLI64.msi) and 32-bit machines (https://s3.amazonaws .com/aws-cli/AWSCLI32.msi). If you're not sure whether you're running 32- or 64-bit, but your computer was built after 2005 or so, you can pretty much assume you're a fully credentialed member of the 64-bit club.

Once you've downloaded the file, all that's left is to run it and follow along with the subsequent installation process.

12.3.2 *Installing on Linux*

Most Linux package managers offer a quick installation option for the AWS CLI, cleverly called `awscli`. For Ubuntu or Debian-based systems, use `apt`:

```
$ sudo apt install awscli
```

The same applies to distributions that use `yum`, like CentOS and Fedora:

```
$ sudo yum install awscli
```

(Keep in mind that `yum` is eventually going to be replaced by `dnf`.)

If that doesn't work, try one of the approaches that follow.

12.3.3 *Using a bundled installer (Linux and macOS)*

For the rest of us, here's how it goes: because the CLI runs on top of Python, you'll need to make sure you have a modern-enough version of the Python environment installed on your machine. From a command line, type `python --version`:

```
$ python --version
Python 2.7.12
```

If you have Python 2, you'll need version 2.6.5 or higher. Python 3 systems require at least version 3.3.

If you don't have Python, getting it is dead easy. Because you'll probably need a couple more tools, I've included the packages for `curl`, `unzip`, and (for Ubuntu) `ca-certificates` in the commands in table 12.1.

Table 12.1 Bundled Installation—Linux and macOS

OS	Command
Linux: Ubuntu/Debian	`sudo apt update && sudo apt install python unzip curl ca-certificates`
Linux: CentOS/RHEL	`sudo yum install python unzip curl`
macOS	`brew install python`

With Python all lined up, it's time to use `curl` to download the package from Amazon. From the URL, you can see that, like all good files, it's stored on S3. You can run this command from any directory where you have permission to save files—because that's exactly what `curl` will do.

The home directory into which you were probably dropped when you logged in is fine:

```
$ curl "https://s3.amazonaws.com/aws-cli/awscli-bundle.zip" -o
➥ "awscli-bundle.zip"
```

Next, use `unzip` to decompress the archive and save its contents to a child directory automatically named awscli-bundle in the current directory. You can run `ls` after `unzip` has finished its work, to see the new directory it's created:

```
$ unzip awscli-bundle.zip
$ ls
```

Finally, run the `install` script that was among the files unpacked by `unzip`:

```
$ sudo ./awscli-bundle/install -i /usr/local/aws -
    b /usr/local/bin/aws
```

The `-i` argument installs the `aws` binary to the /usr/local/ directory, and `-b` creates a symbolic link to the binary in the /usr/local/bin/ directory. The symbolic link lets you run the binary from anywhere on the system.

12.3.4 *Installing using Python pip (all OSs)*

Honestly, I'm not aware of any advantages over the other installation approaches; but if you find it more convenient, you can also use the `pip` method as shown in table 12.2. If you don't yet have it, you'll need to install the pip package manager (whose package is named `python-pip`). `pip install` will finish the job on all platforms. You only need to add the `--ignore-installed six` argument on macOS if you run into trouble installing on El Capitan.

Table 12.2 Installing with pip

OS	Install AWS CLI	Upgrade AWS CLI
Windows	`pip install awscli`	`pip install --upgrade awscli`
Linux	`sudo pip install awscli`	`sudo pip install --upgrade awscli`
macOS	`sudo pip install awscli --ignore-installed six`	`sudo pip install --upgrade awscli`

12.4 *Configuring the AWS CLI*

Before you can add your security credentials to the CLI configuration, you need to head back to the AWS Console to create a set of credentials to add. From any page in the Console, click the drop-down menu header at upper right with your account name on it, and then click the My Security Credentials link. If you didn't lock down your root account and replace it with an IAM user back in chapter 8 (or lock it down again after its brief budget-driven rehabilitation in chapter 11), then you may be shown a pop-up box begging you to really, seriously consider doing so now. If you're still using your account for small-scale Free Tier experiments, feel free to ignore the warning and click Continue to Security Credentials. But please make a note to get to it eventually.

Once you're on the Your Security Credentials page, click the Access Keys (Access Key ID and Secret Access Key) link and then click Create New Access Key. You'll be shown your new access key ID and its accompanying secret access key: the former serves the same function as a login name, and the latter acts like its password. You can either download the access key and save it to a secure location on your computer (as though such a place existed outside of IT security professionals' daydreams) or select, copy, and paste it somewhere. Note the warning that you'll never again be shown the secret access key. (If you do lose it, you can always create a new one to replace it.)

To set things up, open a terminal on your local machine and run `aws configure` from the command line. You'll be asked for your access key ID, your secret access key, the AWS region you'd like to make the default, and the format you'd like to use for output. This example (using fake credentials) comes from the AWS documentation. You should never publicly display a real key set:

```
$ aws configure
AWS Access Key ID [None]: AKIAIOSFODNN7EXAMPLE
AWS Secret Access Key [None]: wJalrXUtnFEMI/K7MDENG/bPxRfiCYEXAMPLEKEY
Default region name [None]: us-east-1
Default output format [None]:
```

12.4.1 *Choosing a region*

The region name I used in the previous example (us-east-1) represents northern Virginia in the United States. Table 12.3 shows a more complete list of the current region choices.

Table 12.3   AWS publicly available regions and their designations

Region	Designation
US East (N. Virginia)	us-east-1
US East (Ohio)	us-east-2
US West (N. California)	us-west-1
US West (Oregon)	us-west-2
Asia Pacific (Mumbai)	ap-south-1
Asia Pacific (Seoul)	ap-northeast-2
Asia Pacific (Singapore)	ap-southeast-1
Asia Pacific (Sydney)	ap-southeast-2
Asia Pacific (Tokyo)	ap-northeast-1
Canada (Central)	ca-central-1
China (Beijing)	cn-north-1
EU (Frankfurt)	eu-central-1
EU (Ireland)	eu-west-1
EU (London)	eu-west-2
South America (São Paulo)	sa-east-1
AWS GovCloud (US)	us-gov-west-1

12.4.2 Choosing an output format

The output format you choose will largely depend on the kind of data you're likely to be generating and viewing and the size of the terminal window you'll be using to view it. Your three choices are JSON (enter `json`), table (`table`), or plain text (`text`). All you need to do to modify your settings is run `aws configure` again and enter new values only for those elements you want to change. This way, you can easily switch back and forth between formats.

> **Try it now**
>
> Edit your AWS CLI configuration to use each of the three format options. For each one, run a command that involves lots of output: for instance, `aws ec2 describe-security-groups`.

12.4.3 *Working with multiple AWS profiles*

You may find yourself with separate AWS accounts for work and personal use. This can complicate things when you're trying to access accounts from the command line. Fortunately, the CLI allows you to configure multiple accounts and specify the one you're targeting along with each subsequent command.

Run `aws configure` followed by the `--profile` argument and the name you'd like to use for the new profile. I gave the name `test-account` in this example:

```
$ aws configure --profile test-account
```

This will take you through the usual setup questions and then save a new profile in the /.aws/config file under a section entitled [profile test-account]. The default account has a [default] header. Once that's done, you can run a command against your new account by appending the profile name. The following example copies a local file called myfile to the mystuff bucket:

```
$ aws s3 cp myfile s3://mystuff1019 --profile test-account
```

12.5 *Using the help system*

Command line–based systems can often be intimidating to newcomers. There's no link to click, directing you to documentation pages; and pressing F1 won't do you any good. All you have is a blinking cursor and a largely blank screen. But you're not alone. Type `aws help` to open an overview of the AWS CLI environment that includes command-line options and a helpful list of all the AWS services that the CLI can manage:

```
$ aws help
```

There are currently more than 75 of those services, so I won't list them all here. But knowing the name of the service you're after can get you more-specific help. For instance, running `aws iam help` shows a document that explains what IAM is and how it works, and then lists all the available commands that can be used against it:

```
$ aws iam help
```

When you run that yourself, you'll see that one of those commands is add-user-to-group. This tells you that, if you want to add an existing IAM user to an existing IAM group, you type aws iam add-user-to-group. But how do you tell AWS which user and which group you're thinking about? If you're not sure of the exact syntax, add the command name to the string before the help command, like this:

```
$ aws iam add-user-to-group help
```

The help file you're shown includes this example command line, which adds the user Bob to the Admins group (assuming you have a user named Bob and a group named Admins):

```
$ aws iam add-user-to-group --user-name Bob --group-name Admins
```

Spending a little time with the AWS help system can quickly familiarize you with the basic AWS syntax conventions and make your administration work a lot more productive—and fun. I freely admit that I still get a thrill when a single command typed into the terminal fires up (or shuts down) a powerful server sitting thousands of miles away.

12.6 Using the CLI to administer your AWS account resources

Let's try performing a few real tasks through the CLI. aws s3 ls lists all the S3 buckets in your account (S3 is a global service, so buckets aren't limited to a single region):

```
$ aws s3 ls
2016-01-21 10:20:17 bootstrap-it
2016-03-21 18:50:35 elasticbeanstalk-us-east-1-829381844505
2016-11-20 16:20:45 transactions-snapshots
```

In this case, the result lists the creation dates and names of each of my three buckets.

12.6.1 Launching a new EC2 instance using the CLI

Suppose you need to double your EC2 capacity. You'd like to make a perfect copy of your existing instance so you can launch a second one. You can replicate a running instance and use it to create an Amazon Machine Image (AMI) that you can then select for new instances.

How does that work? Here's the short version. Select the running EC2 instance you want to copy in the EC2 Instances dashboard. Then click Actions, and select Image and then Create Image. After a few minutes, a new image should appear on the AMIs page of the EC2 dashboard. The next time you launch a new instance from the EC2 dashboard and arrive at the Choose an Amazon Machine Image page, click the My AMIs tab: your new AMI should be there, waiting to be selected.

I created the AMI shown based on the Apache/WordPress instance used in previous chapters. Of course, you can use any AMI to follow this demo—even a generic default AMI like the standard Ubuntu Server 16.04 (shown in figure 12.2). If you follow along and create your own AMI, it will be helpful (although not required) to leave it as is, because that will simplify some of the demos you'll encounter in the next few chapters.

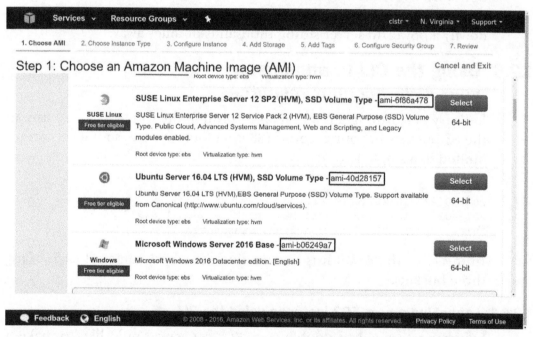

Figure 12.2   Examples of freely available AMIs, with their AMI identity numbers highlighted

The following command includes the AMI ID of my Apache/WordPress web server image. It will launch a brand-new instance that's an exact replica of the original instance I used to create the image:

```
$ aws ec2 run-instances --image-id ami-5cf5c74b \
--count 1 --instance-type t2.micro \
--key-name plural --security-group-ids sg-7a4d6200
```

Let's go through that one step at a time:

- `aws ec2 run-instances` runs a new instance whose details will follow.
- `--image-id ami-5cf5c74b` identifies the AMI's ID. You can get this information from the AMI page of the EC2 dashboard, or from the CLI using `aws ec2 describe-images --owners self`.
- `--count 1` says to launch only one instance of this image.
- `--instance-type t2.micro` is the instance type.
- `--key-name plural` is the name of the key pair you'll use to access the instance once it's running. This example uses `plural`—a key-name example from a previous chapter.
- `--security-groups sg-7a4d6200` is the name of the existing security group you'll use; you can find it using `aws ec2 describe-security-groups`. The ID displayed here is unique to the group in my account's VPC. You'll need to use a group ID from your own account.

Head back to the Console. You'll see your new instance initializing, and eventually you'll see a copy of your Apache server running.

12.7 Lab

From your own AWS CLI-equipped computer, see if you can figure out how to identify an available security group, a key pair, and any AMI, and launch your own instance entirely from the command line. Don't forget to shut it down afterward if you don't need it running.

Definitions

- *Amazon Machine Image (AMI)*—An image (or template) of a complete EC2 instance that can be launched on demand
- `ca-certificates`—A program that installs encryption certificates to allow secure remote connections and file transfers
- *CLI*—Command-line interface
- `curl`—A command-line tool for downloading files from internet sites
- *Shell*—A program used to interpret terminal commands for processing
- *JSON*—The JavaScript Object Notation text format
- *pip*—The Python package manager program
- *Shell*—A program used to interpret terminal commands for processing
- `unzip`—A Linux tool for decompressing archives compressed using compatible compression algorithms

Part 2

The AWS power user: optimizing your infrastructure

Chapters 13–17 introduce you to the concepts of elasticity, scalability, and high availability. If your cloud project isn't meant to be consumed by a large public audience (perhaps it's more of a private resource), then I suppose you can be excused if you skip this part. If only you knew what you're missing …

Keeping ahead of user demand

This is a bit of a transition chapter. Chapter 12 completed our survey of AWS's core deployment services. That means you're now familiar with the following:

- EC2 instances, Amazon Machine Images (AMIs), and the peripheral tools that support their deployment, such as security groups and EBS volumes
- Incorporating databases into applications, both on-instance and through the managed RDS service
- Using S3 buckets to deliver media files through your EC2 applications and for server backup storage
- Controlling access to your AWS resources with Identity and Access Management (IAM)
- Managing growing resource sets by intelligently applying tags
- Accessing resources using either the browser interface or the AWS command-line interface (CLI)

All of these things are represented in the schematic shown in figure 13.1. That alone would easily justify the time and energy you've invested in this book. Now we're going to shift our focus and explore some best practices for application optimization.

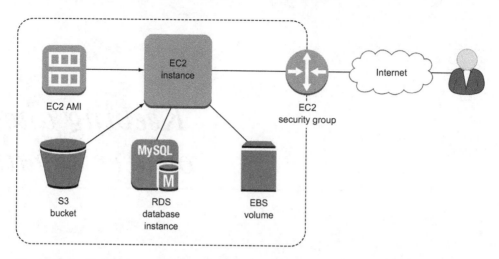

Figure 13.1 This is the kind of application infrastructure you should be able to build on your own, having read the first dozen chapters of this book.

But things are running nicely—who needs optimization? Well, as customer demand on your WordPress site continues to grow, you'll care, and in a big way. You see, for some reason—perhaps related to the fact that you discount the price of your product by 75% for half an hour each evening—most customers arrive in the early evening, local time. The single server you've been running is largely unused most of the day, but it melts under the pressure of thousands of visits squeezed into such a short stretch of time.

And then there's a question one of the guys in the office asked the other day: "Our entire business is running on a single web server. What happens if it goes down?" What indeed.

You could provision four or five extra servers and run them full time. That way, you'd be covered for the high-volume periods and for the failure of any one server. But that approach would involve colossal waste, because for much of each day you'd be paying for most of the instances to sit idle. Nor would it necessarily be much help in the event of a *network* failure, which would likely cut connectivity to *all* the servers at the same time.

You could address the customer demand issue by arranging for someone to be at the office every evening to manually fire up as many extra servers as needed; but you asked around, and no one volunteered. And besides, the best way to ensure that a daily job won't get done is to assume that an admin will remember to do it.

13.1 Automating high availability

Alternatively, you could spend some time incorporating high availability capability into your setup and let software quietly and efficiently manage things. This will be the subject of the next few chapters. You'll learn to use AWS's geographically remote availability zones to make total application failure much less likely; load balancing to coordinate between parallel servers and monitor their health; and auto scaling to let AWS automatically respond to the peaks and valleys of changing demand by launching and shutting down instances according to need.

> **NOTE** *High availability* is any server resource configuration that allows a system to remain functioning and accessible for as close to 100% of the time as possible. The basic goal can be achieved through combinations that can include redundancy, replication, failover protocols, monitoring, and load balancing.

Figure 13.2 will help you visualize how all that infrastructure can be made highly available through the magic of network segmenting, auto scaling, and load balancing. Although you probably aren't familiar with many of the tools and relationships represented in the diagram, you should make a mental note of at least a few key points:

1 A virtual private cloud (VPC) encompasses all the AWS resources in your application deployment.
2 There are two kinds of subnets—private and public—that can be located in separate availability zones and are used to manage and, where needed, isolate resources.
3 Security-group rules control the movement of data between resources.
4 The EC2 AMI acts as a template for replicating precise OS environments.
5 The S3 bucket can store and deliver data, both for backup and for delivery to users.
6 The EBS volumes act as data volumes (like hard drives) for an instance.

7 The auto scaler permits automatic provisioning of more (or fewer) instances to meet changing demands on an application.

8 The load balancer routes traffic among multiple servers to ensure the smoothest and most efficient user experience.

As you've probably noticed, the *E* in many AWS service names (EC2, ECS, EFS, EMR, and so on) doesn't stand for *electronic* the way it does in the names of some older technologies, like *email;* rather, it stands for *elastic.* You can be excused for wondering just what about the AWS vision of cloud computing is so elastic.

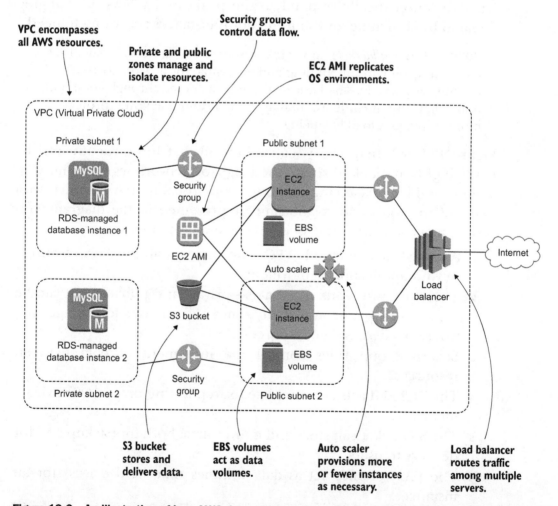

Figure 13.2   An illustration of how AWS data and security services work together to allow an EC2 instance to deliver its application

But before I answer that question, it may be useful to talk about cloud computing in general. Understanding what makes the cloud unique is essential for taking full advantage of all that it has to offer.

13.2 *Cloud computing*

The U.S. National Institute of Standards and Technology (NIST) defines *cloud computing* as services that offer users all of these five qualities:

- *On-demand self-service*—Customers can access public cloud resources whenever needed and without having to order them through a human representative.
- *Broad network access*—Cloud resources are accessible from any network-connected (that is, internet) location.
- *Resource pooling*—Cloud providers offer a multitenant model, whereby individual customers can safely share resources with each other; and dynamic resource assignment, through which resources can be allocated and deallocated according to customer demand.
- *Rapid elasticity*—Resource availability and performance can be automatically increased or decreased to meet changing customer demand.
- *Measured service*—Customers can consume services at varying levels through a single billing period and are charged only for those resources they actually use.

These five qualities describe a deeply flexible, highly automated system whose elements can be freely mixed and matched to provide the efficient, cost-effective service. But a great deal of what makes this possible is the existence of integrated systems that can dynamically adjust themselves based on what's going on around them. These adjustments are examples of elastic behavior.

13.3 *Elasticity vs. scalability*

Elasticity is a system's ability to monitor user demand and automatically increase and decrease deployed resources accordingly. *Scalability*, by contrast, is a system's ability to monitor user demand and automatically increase and decrease ... wait, didn't I just say that about elasticity?

It's complicated. The two terms are sometimes used interchangeably, but I think it's worthwhile distinguishing between them. Bear in mind that the way I explain the relationship between these two ideas is by no means the last word on the subject—look around, and you'll find some other approaches. But in the context of understanding how AWS works, my spin should be useful.

What makes an elastic band *elastic* is partly its ability to stretch under pressure, but also the way it quickly returns to its original size when the pressure is released. In AWS terms, that would mean the way, for instance, EC2 makes instances available to you when needed but lets you drop them when they're not, and charges you only for uptime (see figure 13.3).

Scalability describes the way a system is *designed* to meet changing demand. That might include the fact that you have 24-hour access to any resources you might need (which, of course, is an elastic feature), but it also means the *underlying design* supports rapid, unpredictable changes. As an example, software that's scalable can be easily picked up and dropped onto a new server—possibly in a new network environment—and run without any manual configuration. Similarly, as shown in figure 13.4, the composition of a scalable infrastructure can be quickly changed in a way that all the old bits and pieces immediately know how to work together with the new ones.

With that in mind, we can say that Amazon's EC2 is not only elastic but, because its elements—instances, storage volumes, security groups, and

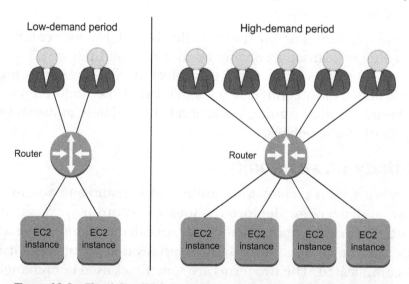

Figure 13.3   Elasticity allows for systems to dynamically add or remove resources to meet changing demand.

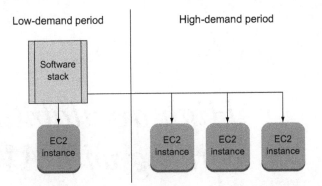

Figure 13.4   Scalable software can be easily copied for use in multiple servers deployed in multiple network environments.

so on—can be smoothly dropped into and out of running infrastructures, also very scalable. Ah, but what *kind* of scalable? There are two:

- *Horizontal scaling* is *scaling out*: you add more lightweight server nodes (or *instances*) to meet growing demand.
- *Vertical scaling* is *scaling up*: you move your application from a single lightweight server to one with greater compute capacity.

It's certainly possible to transfer AWS-based applications from lighter to heavier servers, and for some payloads—like many high-load transaction databases—it's preferred. But in an AWS context, if you hear a conjugation of the word *scale*, the odds are that it's referring to horizontal scaling.

If you want a more reliable, responsive, public-facing application (and who doesn't?), you should definitely stay tuned as we work through the book's second part, which focuses on optimizing your existing infrastructure.

Definitions
- *Cloud computing*—Networked services offering self-service, resource pooling, elasticity, and metered billing
- *Elasticity*—The ability to increase and decrease available compute resources to meet changing demands
- *Scalability*—The ability of software or infrastructure to adapt to changes in service volume
- *Scaling out*—The addition of new server nodes to handle increased demand (horizontal scaling)
- *Scaling up*—The adoption of a more powerful server node to handle increased demand (vertical scaling)

High availability: working with AWS networking tools

Back in chapter 12, you doubled the ability of your application to meet growing demand by replicating the instance, running it as an AMI, and then launching it as a new instance. But there's a far more important reason to replicate your resources: to protect against failure. All hardware (and most software) will eventually stop working; it's just a matter of time. This means the storage drive containing your OS will one day drop dead, the network connection will fail, and the application software will bug out. That's life.

But why let disaster become catastrophe? Consider high availability—the sysadmin way to provide backup resources that can be automatically deployed to replace or supplement public-facing servers showing distress. In this chapter, you'll learn about the structure and benefits of AWS VPCs and how the subnets in VPCs use sound networking principles to significantly improve the reliability of resources.

Because I'm pretty sure you want your share of all those reliability improvements, you'll finish the chapter by learning how you can deploy identical (read: redundant) application instances into two separate availability zones. That way, even if an entire complete zone fails (and don't think it's never happened), you'll be covered by the instance you have running in the other one.

14.1 Organizing AWS resources in VPCs

The secret to bulletproof infrastructure design is clever organization; and in the world of AWS, the most important organizing tool you have is the VPC. A VPC is a framework that ties together a bunch of highly configurable routing, access-control, and networking tools. When you launch resources—such as EC2 instances—in a VPC, they automatically inherit the VPC's security and connectivity settings.

Let's take a quick look at how that works. You won't make any changes right now; you're just browsing. Click the VPC link in the main AWS Console, in the Networking and Content Delivery section. If you haven't used your account for a lot of experiments, then the odds are that there's only one VPC in this region (see figure 14.1): the default VPC that comes with each region in a new account.

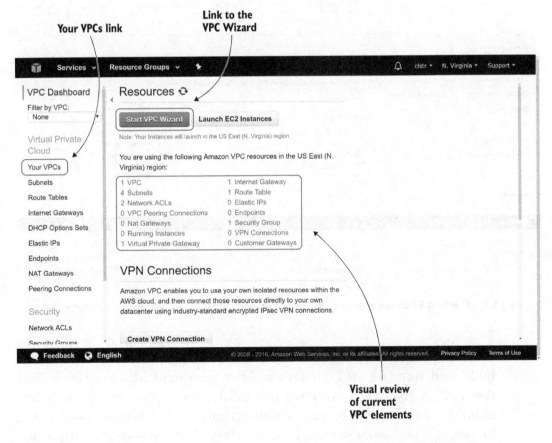

Figure 14.1 The VPC dashboard with links to VPC resource pages and the VPC Wizard

Clicking the Your VPCs link in the left panel will take you to a page that lists all of your VPCs. Here, you can also learn a lot about the elements that make up your VPCs, such as their IP address ranges and details about their connectivity to external networks (see figure 14.2). When you launch instances or other resources in a VPC, these elements define just how they will communicate with each other and with the world beyond.

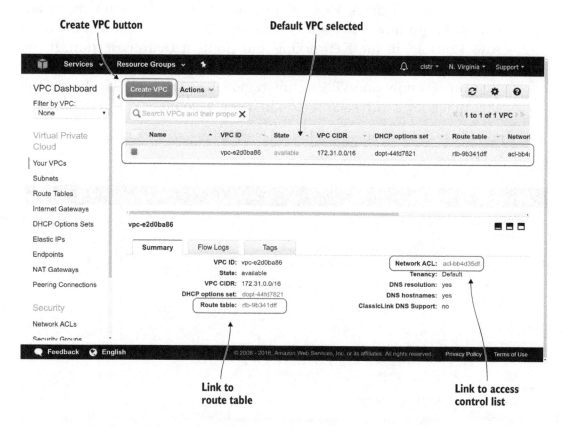

Figure 14.2   The Your VPCs page with a VPC selected, showing links to all key related elements

With a particular VPC's line selected, you're shown links to the route table and network ACL that have been automatically associated with the VPC. A *route table* contains the information that devices in a VPC need to know so they can communicate with resources—like EC2 instances and databases and even external clients—both within and outside of the VPC.

You can see what role a route table plays in, for instance, helping your EC2 application server connect with the outside world, by clicking its link. In figure 14.3, one of the active targets has an ID starting with igw. igw stands for *internet gateway*, and an internet gateway allows traffic from connected network objects to reach the internet.

Link to internet gateway

Routes tab

Figure 14.3   The Route Tables page. Note the link to an internet gateway.

A network access control list (ACL) contains rules that control what kinds of network traffic is allowed both into and out of the VPC. You can click the ACL link back on the details page for your default VPC (note that the object's ID starts with acl), and you'll be taken to the details page for the ACL.

In figure 14.4, the Inbound Rules tab is selected; by default, there are two rules. Rule 100 permits traffic using all protocols, through all ports, from any origin (source). The second rule is a standard DENY that's meant to catch and stop any traffic not explicitly allowed by previous

Inbound Rules tab

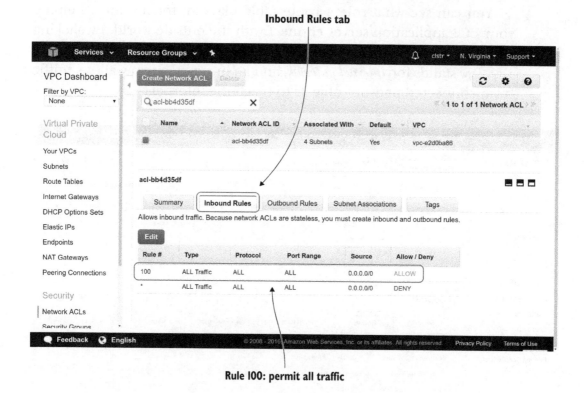

Rule 100: permit all traffic

Figure 14.4 The Network ACLs page. By default, all inbound traffic is permitted.

rules. In this case, because you've already allowed everything, nothing will make it to the second rule. Of course, your needs may require much tighter rules.

You may wonder why the default settings for an ACL are so permissive. Do you want to let just *anyone* in? Of course you don't; and even if you leave things as they are, there's no way for just *anyone* to get in. In AWS-land, the ACL is a *secondary* line of defense—the security group associated with your instances does most of the heavy lifting. Security groups, by default, are restrictive. A well-structured ACL allows you to add a relatively refined set of rules to more closely control access.

Try it now

Assuming you don't have anything critical running that might not like what comes next, add a new rule to the ACL associated with your VPC that limits inbound access to only traffic using the SSH protocol. Then, if nothing is running yet, launch a simple web server into the VPC, and confirm that its security group permits HTTP traffic. If your ACL rule works as intended, you should *not* be able to access web pages. Is there more than one way to do this with ACL rules?

14.1.1 Creating a new VPC

One of the great benefits of VPCs is the way you can use them to neatly organize your resources. Not only can you protect and enhance the stuff that lives in a VPC, but you can also define that stuff by the fact that it *doesn't* live in the VPC next door. In other words, you can segment your resources, perhaps placing all production resources in one VPC, marketing resources in another, and instances used for testing and staging in a third.

To do that, naturally, you'll need to create additional VPCs. There are two ways to do this; as I'll show you, the second method makes it much simpler to get a fully functional network environment up and running, so that's the one you'll probably prefer. But before you can fully appreciate how much simpler the second method is, I'll need to introduce the first one.

CREATING A VPC: THE MANUAL METHOD

Head back to the Your VPCs page, and then click the big blue Create VPC button. As you can see in figure 14.5, this dialog requires very little input. I chose to call my new VPC *experiment*, and I gave it a CIDR block of 192.168.1.0/24. This choice will make more sense later in the chapter; for now, savor your final fleeting moments of blissful ignorance. Click Yes, Create, and you'll be sent automatically to the Your VPCs page.

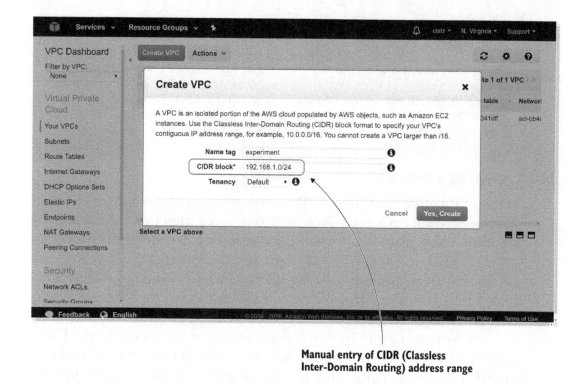

Manual entry of CIDR (Classless
Inter-Domain Routing) address range

Figure 14.5   Create VPC requires only that you enter a CIDR block—but you'll need to manually create a number of additional elements later.

You'll now see your new route table. But there's one important difference: if you click the Route Table link in the new VPC and then click the Routes tab (see figure 14.6), there's no `igw` object as there was in figure 14.3. This means the VPC isn't connected to an internet gateway. Unless you create your own and connect it, you'll be locked in.

Manually creating your own VPC works, but it doesn't automatically populate it with all the bits and pieces (like an internet gateway) that you might like to have. Nevertheless, the manual approach is useful for building nonstandard designs from the ground up, and you should keep this tool in mind.

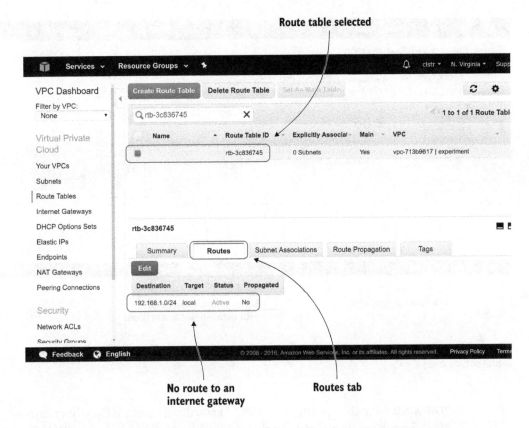

Figure 14.6 The manually created VPC: note the absence of an internet gateway.

CREATING A VPC: THE WIZARD

For most purposes, fresh new VPCs come into this world by way of the Start VPC Wizard button on the main VPC dashboard page. Head over there, and start the wizard. You can choose to create a new VPC from any one of four scenario-based templates. If, for example, you wanted to run a WordPress site with a separate RDS database instance, you might go with the VPC with Public and Private Subnets option (figure 14.7). This gives you a public subnet for the WordPress instance and a private subnet for RDS, allowing you to strictly limit database access to traffic coming from the WordPress server—not from the public internet.

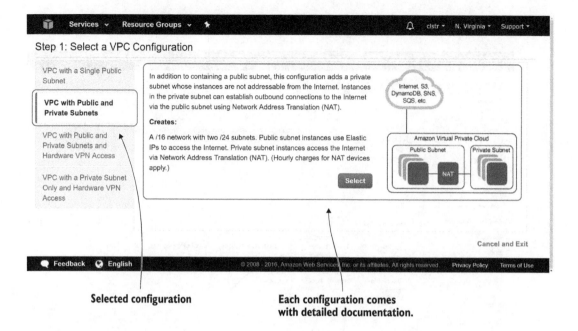

Selected configuration   **Each configuration comes
with detailed documentation.**

Figure 14.7   The VPC Wizard page, whose useful documentation can make selecting a VPC architecture easy

> **WARNING**   At this point, the VPC Wizard will automatically create a NAT instance along with each new public/private subnet VPC. The goal is to enable secure communication with resources on the private subnet. But you should be aware that the NAT instance isn't covered by the Free Tier and will incur costs for each hour it's running.

You'll encounter another common use case for dividing resources by subnet in a moment. The point is that a VPC can be structured in a way that effectively and securely organizes complex resource bundles. And using the wizard to get it done takes a lot of the guesswork and risk out of the process and ensures that you're not starting with any gaping security holes. Smart folks, those AWS people.

Try it now

Use the wizard to create your own VPC using any one of the configuration options. Once it's created, make sure you click through to each of its elements so you can explore their settings. Note that you may need to provide the allocation ID for an elastic IP address: you can get one from the EC2 dashboard.

Look through the subnets you've been given, and check to see that your route table and network ACL are functional. Because it's never good to leave unused resources lying around, once you're finished, delete the VPC—just make sure you don't accidentally delete the default VPC instead.

14.2 Availability zones and network subnets

The entire internet is built on a collection of often-ingenious network protocols, many of which are now nearly half a century old. Network protocol conventions are primarily concerned with connecting devices to each other so they can easily communicate and exchange data. But they can also be used in the service of data security and data reliability. To achieve those goals, you need to learn to properly manage your AWS resources in VPCs.

14.2.1 Network design

Why might you want to do this? Why not keep all your devices in a single network so you don't have to worry about defining individual subnets? Here's where we come to the two considerations I just mentioned: data security and data reliability.

DATA SECURITY

Your company may want to keep the resources used by various operations separate from each other. You definitely don't want to provide general, company-wide access to the HR department's database, with all of its personal information. And those fragile staging servers where your developers are doing their work—you need to make sure no clumsy-fisted Luddites from marketing accidentally find their way in. Well-planned subnets can effectively control access by resource class, ensuring that only the right traffic gets in and out.

DATA RELIABILITY

Remember the web app from the previous chapter—the one about which they asked, "Our entire business is running on a single web server; what happens if it goes down?" That was a great question. But, "What if the server happens to go down?" is just one problem. "What if the office or data center burns down?" is also a consideration.

It turns out that subnets on a single parent network can be located in availability zones many miles from each other—not only in different buildings, but in separate data centers. You can use subnetting to replicate your infrastructure across widely distant physical locations, ensuring that even if a disaster strikes one area, you'll still have the other one to fall back on.

This is the power of AWS availability zones. To fully appreciate how they work, though, we'll have to take a detour.

14.2.2 *TCP/IP addressing*

A network's most basic unit is the humble Internet Protocol (IP) address, at least one of which must be assigned to every connected device. Each address must be unique throughout the entire network; otherwise, message routing would descend into chaos.

For decades, the standard address format followed the IPv4 protocol: each address is made up of four 8-bit octets, for a total of 32 bits (don't worry if that makes no sense to you). Each octet must be a number between 0 and 255. Here's a typical example, which happens to be the public IP address for the AWS console in the northern Virginia (us-east-1) region:

```
54.239.30.25
```

The maximum theoretical number of addresses that can be drawn from the IPv4 pool is just over 4 billion (256^4). Once upon a time, that seemed like a lot. But as the internet grew far beyond anyone's expectations, there clearly weren't going to be enough unique addresses in the IPv4 pool for all the countless devices seeking to connect.

> **NOTE** Four billion possible addresses sounds like a big number until you consider that there are currently more than *1 billion* Android smart phones in use—that's in addition to all the millions of servers, routers, PCs, and laptops, not to mention Apple phones. There's a good chance your car, refrigerator, and home-security cameras also have their own network-accessible addresses, so something obviously had to give.

Two solutions to the impending collapse of the internet addressing system were proposed: IPv6, which is an entirely new addressing protocol; and Network Address Translation (NAT). IPv6 provides a *much* larger pool of addresses; but it doesn't interest us right now, because, by default, AWS VPC networks don't use it (although it's available). Instead, we'll focus on NAT.

14.2.3 NAT addressing

The organizing principle behind NAT is brilliant: rather than assign a unique, network-readable address to every one of your devices, why not have all of them share the single public address that's used by your router? But how will traffic flow to and from your local devices? Through the use of *private* addresses. And if you want to divide network resources into multiple subgroups, how can everything be effectively managed? Through network segmentation.

Here's how it works. When a browser on one of the laptops connected to your home Wi-Fi visits a site, it does so using the public IP address that's been assigned to the DSL modem/router by your ISP. Any other devices connecting through the same Wi-Fi network use that same address for all their browsing activity (see figure 14.8). In most

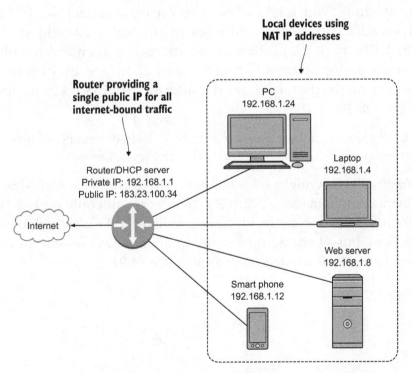

Figure 14.8   A typical NAT configuration, showing how multiple local devices—each with its own private address—can all be represented by a single public IP address

cases, the router uses Dynamic Host Configuration Protocol (DHCP) to assign unique private (NAT) addresses to each local device—but they're unique *only* in the local environment. That way, all local devices can enjoy full, reliable communication with their local peers. This works just as well for large enterprises, many of which use tens of thousands of NAT IP addresses, all behind a single public IP.

The NAT protocol sets aside three IPv4 address ranges that may only be used for private addressing:

- 10.0.0.0–10.255.255.255
- 72.16.0.0–172.31.255.255
- 92.168.0.0–192.168.255.255

Local network managers are free to use any and all of those addresses (there are more than 17 million of them) any way they like. But addresses are usually organized into smaller network (or *subnet*) blocks whose host network is identified by the octets to the left of the address, leaving octets to the right available for assigning to individual devices.

For example, you might choose to create a subnet on 192.168.1, which would mean all the addresses in this subnet would start with 192.168.1 (the network portion of the address) and end with a unique, single-octet device address between 2 and 254. One PC or laptop on that subnet might therefore get the address 192.168.1.4, and another could get 192.168.1.48.

> **NOTE** Following networking conventions, DHCP servers generally don't assign the numbers 0, 1, and 255 to network clients.

In the example, you might subsequently want to add a parallel—but separate—network subnet using 192.168.2. In this case, not only are 192.168.1.4 and 192.168.2.4 two separate addresses, available to be assigned to two distinct devices, but—because they're on separate networks—the two might not even have access to each other (see figure 14.9).

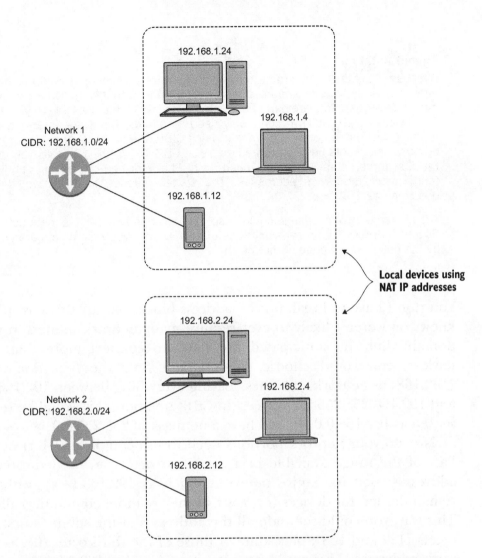

Figure 14.9   Devices attached to two separate NAT subnets in the 192.168.x network range

Subnet notation

Because it's critically important to make sure systems know what kind of subnet a network address is on, we need a standard notation that can accurately communicate which octets are part of the network and which are available to be used for devices. There are *two* commonly used standards: Classless Inter-Domain Routing (CIDR) notation and netmask. Using CIDR, the first network in the previous example would be represented as 192.168.1.0/24: the /24 tells you that the first three octets (8*3=24) make up the network portion, leaving only the fourth octet for device addresses. The second subnet, in CIDR, would be described as 192.168.2.0/24.

These same two networks could also be described through a netmask of 255.255.255.0. That means all 8 bits of each of the first three octets are used by the network, but none of the fourth.

You don't have to break up the address blocks exactly this way. If you knew you weren't likely to ever require many network subnets in your domain, but you anticipated the need to connect more than 255 devices, you could choose to designate only the first *two* octets (192.168) as network addresses, leaving everything between 192.168.0.0 and 192.168.255.255 for devices. In CIDR notation, this would be represented as 192.168.0.0/16 and have a netmask of 255.255.0.0.

Nor do your network portions need to use complete (8-bit) octets. Part of the range available in a particular octet can be dedicated to addresses used for entire networks (such as 192.168.14.x), with the remainder left for devices (or, *hosts*, as they're more commonly called). This way, you could set aside all the addresses of the subnet's first two octets (192 and 168), plus some of those of the third octet (0), as network addresses. This could be represented as 192.168.0.0/20 or with the netmask 255.255.240.0.

Where did I get these notation numbers? Most experienced admins use their binary counting skills to work it out for themselves. But for a chapter on AWS VPCs, that's a bit out of scope—and unnecessary for the normal AWS work you're likely to encounter. Nevertheless, I'll draw your attention to one of the many online subnet calculators that will do the calculation for you. Figure 14.10 shows the results of a calculation provided by the http://jodies.de/ipcalc website.

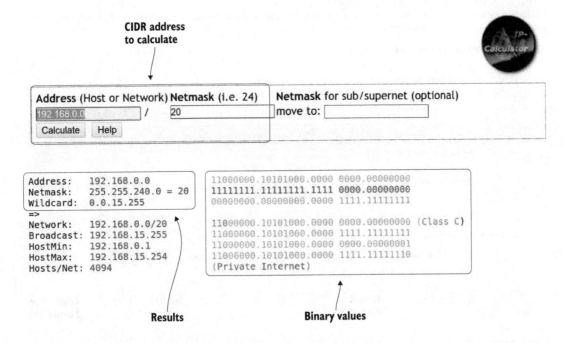

CIDR address
to calculate

Address (Host or Network) Netmask (i.e. 24) Netmask for sub/supernet (optional)
192.168.0.0   /   20   move to:
Calculate   Help

Address: 192.168.0.0   11000000.10101000.0000 0000.00000000
Netmask: 255.255.240.0 = 20   11111111.11111111.1111 0000.00000000
Wildcard: 0.0.15.255   00000000.00000000.0000 1111.11111111
=>
Network: 192.168.0.0/20   11000000.10101000.0000 0000.00000000 (Class C)
Broadcast: 192.168.15.255   11000000.10101000.0000 1111.11111111
HostMin: 192.168.0.1   11000000.10101000.0000 0000.00000001
HostMax: 192.168.15.254   11000000.10101000.0000 1111.11111110
Hosts/Net: 4094   (Private Internet)

Results   Binary values

Figure 14.10   Online subnet calculator. Enter an IP address with a netmask, and it calculates the network ranges and binary values.

14.3 Deploying a website across two availability zones

The best way to explain how all this networking goodness is applied through availability zones is to show you. Head over to the EC2 dashboard, click Launch Instance, and then select any old AMI (if you can't find an AMI called "any old," you can settle for our familiar friend, Ubuntu Server 16.04). Go with your favorite instance type (I'll bet it's t2.micro).

This time, so you can learn how deployments with multiple availability zones work, pause on the Configure Instance Details page: this is where all the subnetting action takes place. Click the Subnet drop-down menu (see figure 14.11), and you'll be shown a number of subnets—the exact number varies by region and account. In my case, there are four subnets, each with an ID beginning with the word *subnet* and identified by something like us-east-1d (an AWS data center somewhere in the

Step 3: Configure Instance Details

Configure the instance to suit your requirements. You can launch multiple instances from the same AMI, request Spot instances to take a pricing, assign an access management role to the instance, and more.

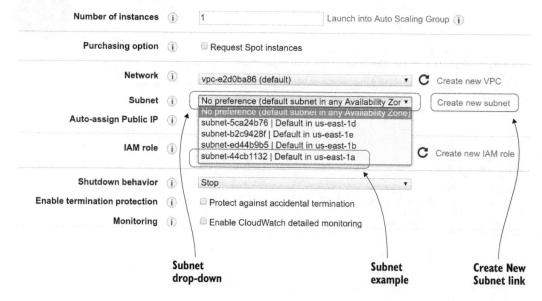

Figure 14.11   The Configure Instance Details page from EC2 setup, including subnet configuration

northern Virginia region). us-east-1a, us-east-1b, and us-east-1c are other data centers in the same region.

To learn more about a particular subnet's specific values and connection settings, click the Create New Subnet link to the right of the Subnet drop-down. You'll be taken to the main Subnets page, where you *could* create a new subnet. But you won't.

Instead, as shown in figure 14.12, explore the information that's displayed. Notice the way the subnet IDs and availability zone designations for each subnet are listed, along with which VPC the subnet belongs to and, most important, the IP address block CIDR. This gives you everything you need to know to choose a subnet for the instance you're launching.

You could, for instance, load this instance into us-east-1a and then load a second instance into us-east-1b. There: you've just doubled your capacity *and* durability. You can cancel this instance launch now, if you like—I only brought you here to show you how it's done.

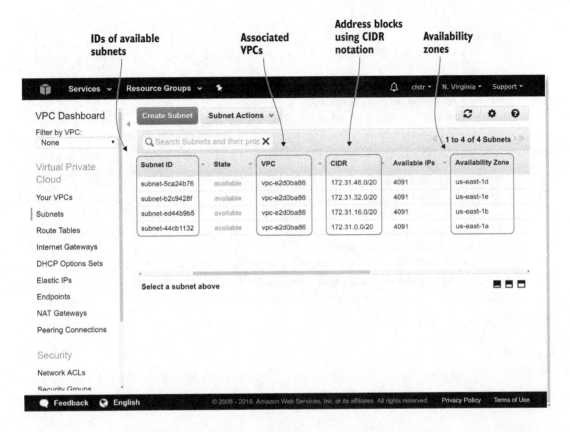

Figure 14.12 The Subnets page, showing available subnets along with their status and details

Because all the existing subnets in the selected AWS region are linked here—even those from multiple VPCs—you can also use the interface as a springboard to further fine-tune the way your resources work together. Is there data running in one VPC that needs to be accessible to instances in another? Do you need to create a tunnel between resources in two VPCs? This is where all that starts.

14.4 Lab

Using the wizard, create a new VPC with at least two subnets. Then, launch identical copies of a EC2 instance into *separate* subnets, and test to confirm that they're both available. Once everything is running, take it all down (including the new VPC), and make sure you haven't left any resources running. Don't forget to budget for any accompanying service charges.

Definitions

- *Classless Inter-Domain Routing (CIDR) notation*—A way of representing subnet blocks.
- *Internet gateway*—Network endpoint through which traffic between a VPC and the internet can be routed.
- *IPv4*—Version 4 of the IP protocol. IPv4 addresses have four 8-bit octets.
- *IPv6*—Version 6 of the IP protocol. IPv6 addresses have eight groups of four hexadecimal digits and are 128-bit (rather than 32-bit).
- *Network access control list (ACL)*—Rules that act like a firewall to filter inbound and outbound network traffic.
- *Network Address Translation (NAT)*—A system for managing privately networked devices and resources.
- *Route table*—Instructions defining a VPC's available routes for sending and receiving network packets.
- *Subnet*—Block of IP addresses carved out of a larger network.
- *Virtual private cloud (VPC)*—Organizing structure for AWS resources.

High availability: load balancing

15

So where are we? In the early chapters, we played with the basics: EC2, S3, RDS, IAM, Route 53, CloudWatch, tags, and the AWS CLI. That was great. Then I introduced you to the wonders of elasticity and scalability and touched on making instances more highly available through the use of AWS availability zones.

But to be perfectly honest, nothing discussed so far will make things more highly available—or scalable or elastic, for that matter. Why not? Because you don't have a high-level administration mechanism to coordinate between your front-line and backup instances. As it stands, even if you did have a running replica of a recently failed instance, how would your website visitors know where to go to find it? You need to add a load balancer to the mix that can monitor the health of your running instances and, if one goes dark, redirect incoming traffic toward active resources.

15.1 What is load balancing?

Like all load-balancing tools, Amazon's Elastic Load Balancing (ELB) system is designed for more than just managing failovers. *Failover*, you'll recall, is the automatic transfer of server tasks from a failed instance to an identical replacement. As the term *load balancer* suggests, ELB's overall mandate is to balance traffic loads among multiple resources to satisfy defined efficiency and performance needs.

For instance, if one of your servers has a greater capacity than the others, you'll probably want it to receive a greater proportion of user traffic. Or suppose each of your application servers is optimized for customers coming from specific geographic locations—perhaps because you're providing pages translated into multiple languages. You can configure a load balancer to direct traffic among your destinations based on where it's coming from.

But for the purposes of this chapter, we're mainly interested in how load balancing can generate high availability (figure 15.1). A well-designed balancer can do the following:

- Listen for traffic aimed at your web application
- Keep track of the health and availability of each of your application servers
- Redirect incoming traffic among only the servers that are currently able to respond

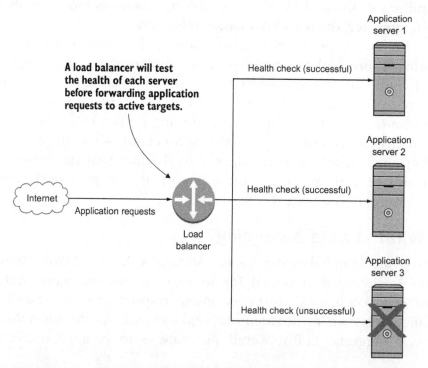

Figure 15.1   Site visitors only have direct contact with the load balancer, which confirms server health before forwarding requests.

Once a load balancer is configured with the addresses of all of your servers, organized into what AWS called *target groups,* its own network address becomes the only URL your users need to access. Visitors don't need to know the individual DNS or IP addresses of each of your servers—nor do they have to worry about which ones are best prepared to handle their needs. As long as you've set your load balancer to listen for requests against a particular address and associated your application's DNS address with the balancer's endpoint—which, for AWS balancers, is provided as part of the balancer description you'll see later—all that is taken care of automatically and invisibly.

As you saw in the previous chapter, spreading instances across multiple availability zones greatly increases their durability. Even if an entire AWS data center should go offline, resources hosted in a second zone can pick up at least some of the slack. Creating a load balancer to manage your instances in more than one zone is the puzzle piece you've been missing until now. The load balancer itself, because it effectively consists of settings rather than infrastructure, should survive any service disruption.

All this sounds attractive, given your vulnerable web-application server from chapter 14. It's high time you added some resilience to it.

15.2 Building a multizone load balancer

In this section, I'll walk you through the process of setting up a load balancer to handle the kind of application server cluster you're after. You'll first launch four EC2 instances into two separate availability zones (or subnets). For convenience, those four instances will all use the WordPress-based AMI created in chapter 12. But you can use anything you like, as long as each instance has a web server package (Apache) installed.

To make it easier to keep track of things, create an index.html file in the web root directory (/var/www/html on my Ubuntu AMI) of each instance. This file should contain a simple welcome message identifying the instance by the name you gave it and by its IP address.

NOTE Even though you're launching four concurrent instances, assuming they're Free Tier eligible, they should cost you nothing—as long as you shut them down once the demo is complete. This is because the Free Tier permits 750 hours of a t2.micro instance over the course of a single month, regardless of how many of those hours you use at a single time.

What does load balancing cost?

AWS load balancers are charged per hour of active use and for the data they transfer, which includes just about anything moving in or out through the balancer. To give you a general idea of how that works, at the time of writing you'd be billed $0.025/hour to run a balancer—which is $18 for a month—and $0.008 per GB of transferred data. 100 GB of total monthly transfers would come to $0.80. This, naturally, is over and above any charges you incur for running EC2 instances.

Once the instances are running, you'll need to jump through these five hoops to get a load balancer on the job:

1 Create a target group, and configure a health check.
2 Register your four instances with the target group.
3 Create a load balancer, and associate it with the two subnets hosting your instances.
4 Create a security group for both instances and for the load balancer.
5 Associate your target group with the load balancer.

When that's finished, you'll wait a few minutes for the balancer to provision, point your browser to the balancer DNS endpoint, and then refresh the page over and over again so you can see the balancer cycling through all of your instances. Finally, you'll disable one of the application servers and, again, cycle through using a browser to see how the balancer skips the failed instance.

I don't know about you, but I'm all set to start by launching those EC2 instances.

15.2.1 *Launching four instances*

To launch instances based on your existing AMI, click Launch Instances from the EC2 dashboard and then click the My AMIs tab at left on the page. Any AMIs stored in this region are displayed, anxiously waiting for you to click Select. Do just that for the WordPress AMI. On the Configure

**Specify the number of
instances you want to launch.**

Step 3: Configure Instance Details

Configure the instance to suit your requirements. You can launch multiple instances from the same AMI, request Spot instances to take advant:
role to the instance, and more.

| Number of instances (i) | 2 | Launch into Auto Scaling Group (i) |

You may want to consider launching these instances into an Auto Scaling Group to help
scaling in the future. Learn how Auto Scaling can help your application stay healthy and

| Purchasing option (i) | ☐ Request Spot instances |

| Network (i) | vpc-e2d0ba86 (default) ▼ | C Create new VPC |

| Subnet (i) | subnet-44cb1132 | Default in us-east-1a ▼ | Create new subnet |
4091 IP Addresses available

| Auto-assign Public IP (i) | Use subnet setting (Enable) ▼ |

| IAM role (i) | None ▼ | C Create new IAM role |

| Shutdown behavior (i) | Stop ▼ |

| Enable termination protection (i) | ☐ Protect against accidental termination |

**Specify the subnet into
which to launch the instances.**

**Figure 15.2 In the subnet drop-down menu, you can specify particular subnets into which to launch
instances.**

Instance Details page, let's diverge from what you've done until now in
two important ways: enter 2 in the Number of Instances field (see figure
15.2), and select the us-east-1a subnet in the Subnet drop-down.

The only other thing is to remember to create a security group that
opens HTTP (port 80) access to any incoming traffic. Name the group
cluster-instances, because you'll use it not only for these instances, but
also for the load balancer.

You're creating only two instances in this round because right now
you're focusing on one specific subnet: concentrating all four instances
in one subnet would defeat the purpose. With those two launched,
repeat the entire process to launch two more instances into a second
subnet. Once the second pair is also up and all the running instances

are displayed in the EC2 dashboard, give each instance an easily identifiable name, as shown in figure 15.3 (including az-1a-alpha for the first instance in availability zone us-east-1a and az-1b-beta for the second instance in AZ us-east-1b).

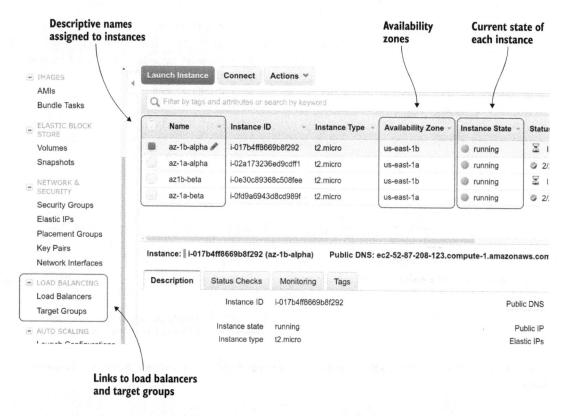

Figure 15.3   The EC2 Instances dashboard, displaying each running instance's zone and state

15.2.2 Creating a target group

You'll build a load balancer in the next step. First, you need to add all of your instances into a target group that defines how the load balancer will redirect incoming traffic to your app servers and, just as important, how it will perform health checks. As shown in figure 15.4, choose a descriptive name for the group, identifying it as part of the cluster infrastructure, and go with the HTTP protocol. The only other choice— secure HTTPS—would normally be a better option, assuming your web servers are all encrypted. But you're probably just experimenting, and adding SSL/TLS encryption is an extra complication you can safely bypass for now. The default port (80) will work fine, because that's the port you already opened in your security group. Make sure the VPC is the one into which your instances were launched.

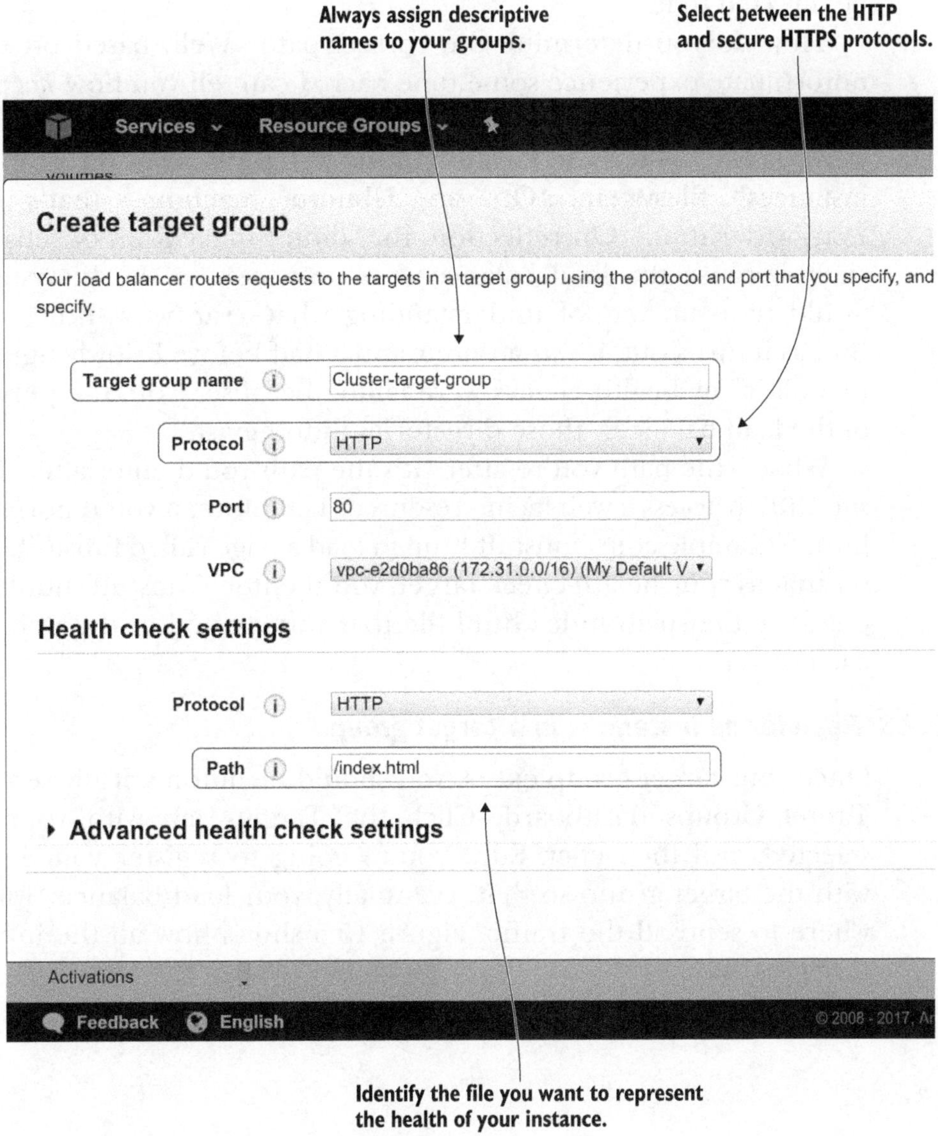

Always assign descriptive
names to your groups.

Select between the HTTP
and secure HTTPS protocols.

Services ∨   Resource Groups ∨   ✦

Create target group

Your load balancer routes requests to the targets in a target group using the protocol and port that you specify, and specify.

Target group name (i)   Cluster-target-group

Protocol (i)   HTTP   ▼

Port (i)   80

VPC (i)   vpc-e2d0ba86 (172.31.0.0/16) (My Default V ▼

Health check settings

Protocol (i)   HTTP   ▼

Path (i)   /index.html

▸ **Advanced health check settings**

Activations   ∨

🔴 Feedback   🌐 English   © 2008 - 2017, A

Identify the file you want to represent
the health of your instance.

Figure 15.4 The target group configuration includes setting the path to the file you want to use for health-check confirmation.

Entering the correct path to be used for health checks is a big deal. This path points to a file on an application server that the load balancer will regularly try to load. As long as the file loads successfully, the load balancer will assume everything's fine. But if the request fails a preset number of attempts, the server will be declared dead, and no new traffic will be directed to it.

How do you determine the correct path? Well, based on my own unfortunate experience some time back, I can tell you how *not* to do it. For some reason, I assumed that the path—which must start with a forward slash (/)—was the location of the web server root directory on my instances' filesystem. On an Ubuntu machine, that's usually /var/www/html/. On reflection, that didn't make a lot of sense, especially because the load balancer has no access to the filesystem and would have no way of understanding what /var/www/html/ means. But, as it turns out, it was an hour and a half before I slowly figured out that all of my health checks were failing because, from the perspective of the load balancer, those directories didn't exist.

What *is* the path you're after? It's the path you'd enter after the website URL to access a web-facing resource. Therefore, if you'd normally use http://example.com/funstuff.html to load a page called funstuff.html, to set that as your health-check target, you'd enter /funstuff .html. In this case, use the small index.html file that you created in the web root of each server.

15.2.3 *Registering instances in a target group*

Once your target group exists, you should be automatically sent to the Target Groups dashboard. Click the Targets tab with your group selected, and then click Edit. You're going to register your instances with the target group so that, eventually, your load balancer will know where to send all the traffic. Figure 15.5 shows how all the infrastructure looks now.

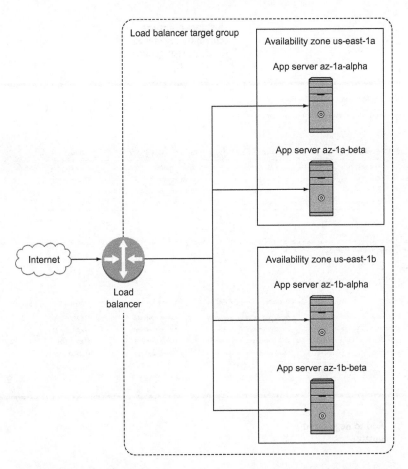

Figure 15.5 A visualization of a load balancer directing internet traffic to the inhabitants of a target made up of four servers spread over two availability zones

You want to use all four instances that are displayed, because they're all part of the application cluster. So select all four, and click Add to Registered. As shown in figure 15.6, they'll now appear in the Registered Instances list. Click Save.

Instances that are
currently registered
in the target group

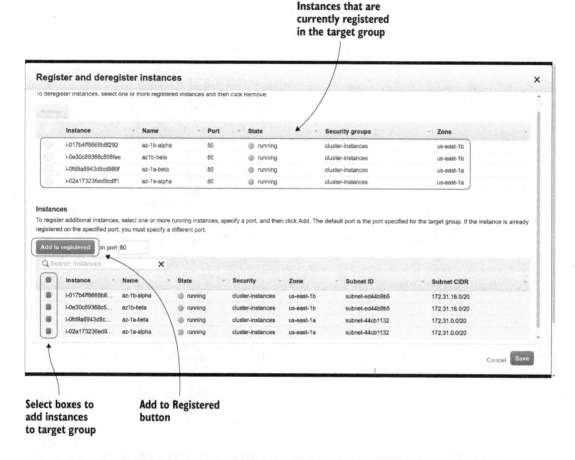

Figure 15.6   The four instances, now fully registered in the target group

Select boxes to
add instances
to target group

Add to Registered
button

15.2.4 *Creating a load balancer, and associating it with a security group*

With four running instances all tucked into their target group, it's time to create a load balancer and put it to work orchestrating the whole arrangement. The most obvious way to get to the Load Balancers page is to click its link in the left panel of any EC2 page (just above the target group link). From there, click the blue Create Load Balancer button, and you'll be presented with—a tough choice. Do you want an Application Load Balancer or a Classic? What's the difference?

It's not complicated. This is one of those cases where AWS introduced a new version of a service that's clearly an improvement for all but a very small number of scenarios. Because AWS didn't want to block access to those edge cases (which might, for instance, require support for the pre-VPC era EC2-Classic networking architecture or TCP and SSL-based listeners), it left Classic as an option. But in this case, the choice is a no-brainer: Application Load Balancer all the way.

Give the balancer a descriptive name. Assuming you're just kicking the tires, rather than launching an actual production environment, stick to the HTTP protocol for your listener (the other option is HTTPS), and use the other default values. Of course, when you're ready to apply this to a real web application, HTTPS will be the only choice.

Scroll down the page to the Availability Zones configuration (figure 15.7), and select the two zones (subnets) into which you launched your instances from the Available list. To select a zone, click its plus icon; the zone will appear in Selected Subnets. When you're finished, click Next: Configure Security Settings. Because your balancer will have access needs similar to those of your application servers, you can select the same security group you created for the four instances.

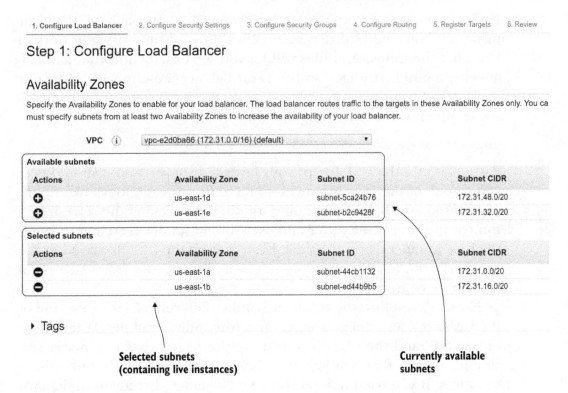

Figure 15.7 **You must add subnets from at least two availability zones to benefit from a load balancer.**

15.2.5 Associating the target with the load balancer

The last step in the Load Balancer Setup Wizard is the Configure Routing page. Here's where you connect the target group you created—with its registry of active instances and health-check settings—with the load balancer. Rather than creating a new target group, click the Target Group drop-down menu and select Existing Target Group. Assuming your target group was created properly, the Name field will become a drop-down menu from which you can choose your target group. The other fields on the page will then change to read-only, because the configuration automatically inherits the values you set in the target group.

Now pull the trigger: click Review, and create the load balancer. It may take a few minutes for all the pieces to fall into place; but when they do, the value of State on the Load Balancer dashboard will change from Provisioning to Active. At this point, you should be live. Let's test it out.

15.3 Testing the cluster

Earlier, you created unique index.html pages on each of the four instances. You could still access the WordPress account using its normal URL, but the index.html files will let you see exactly how the load balancer is handling things. On the Load Balancers dashboard, with your cluster load balancer selected, you're shown the balancer's public DNS name, which looks something like this:

```
Cluster-load-balancer-579837535.us-east-1.elb.amazonaws.com
```

Paste that into the URL bar of your favorite browser, and it should take you to one of the four instances—which, in this case, looks like figure 15.8. If the load balancer is doing its job, then clicking the refresh button (or pressing Ctrl-R) over and over should send you cycling through the four instances, one at a time. Even though the URL displayed in the browser's URL bar remains the same, you'll know your test is successful if the page contents change.

Now let's test how the balancer handles failover. SSH into any one of the instances, and delete (or rename) the index.html file. Wait a minute or two, and then begin refreshing the page in your browser. You should notice that you're now being cycled through only three instances. If you tried to load the failed instance directly using its own

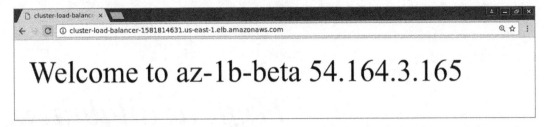

Figure 15.8   The index.html page of one of the four instances. Contrast the instance's 54.164.3.165 IP address with the URL in the browser's URL bar.

IP address, you'd see an error screen. But the load balancer skips right over it, giving you only active, useful pages, exactly as it should.

The instances themselves can be shut down, but you may want to hold off deleting this load balancer. It will be an important part of the mix as your infrastructure grows in the next two chapters.

15.4 Lab

You put together a fairly large number of pieces in this chapter. See if you can deploy multiple instances of your own AMI into an application load balancer; then, see what happens when you take down (fail) three instances, one after another. See how quickly your balancer recovers when you begin restoring the failed instances. If your balancer is working properly, the results should be predictable. Bonus: experiment with the settings in the Advanced Health Check section of your target group. Double bonus: see if you can define and launch those four EC2 instances into two availability zones using only the AWS CLI. Remember, the AWS `help` command and internet search engines are your friends.

Definitions
- *Cluster*—Group of application servers providing a unified service and managed by a high-level software system
- *Failover*—Moving compute tasks away from failed servers to active servers that have free capacity to handle the load
- *Health check*—Periodic attempt to load a resource on a remote server to confirm that the server is running
- *Target group*—AWS framework containing configuration information and health-check settings for registered instances

High availability:
auto scaling

Although load balancers are good at gracefully accommodating the sudden loss of a server, one thing they can't do is replace the lost *capacity* that the now-dead server originally provided. In other words, if one of your three servers has crashed, the two left behind will now have to manage the full workload on their own. Helping out in that area is well beyond your load balancer's pay scale.

And then there's that elasticity thing: load balancers can keep what you've got running nicely, but they're not built to manage change. If you're worried that unexpected server downtime or increased demand can leave your application unable to properly do its job, you'll need to find a way to *add* capacity. But you'll have to look beyond load balancers, to auto scaling.

It's been a rough week for your web application. Load-balanced EC2 instances have been periodically crashing for no apparent reason (note to self: have a frank discussion with the lead developer ASAP), and customers have been complaining about slow service from your site during high-demand times. Something's got to change. And here's where it's going to happen.

In this chapter, you'll learn how to use auto scaling to do two things: automate the replacement of instances when they fail, and increase or decrease the number of instances you're running to keep up with changing customer demand.

Predictably, the two main principles of auto scaling are

- *Auto*—Things made to happen without active human intervention
- *Scaling*—Where capacity is scaled up or down depending on need

You do this by creating a *launch configuration*, which defines details like which EC2 AMI, instance type, and security group you'd like the auto scaler—when required—to launch. Instructions for *how* and *when* to apply capacity changes to your infrastructure are then defined as part of an *auto scaling group*.

You're going to design your launch configuration and auto scaling group to keep the number of instances running within your operation between two and four. The configuration should work to automatically scale the instances up and down between those numbers according to demand. You'll also integrate your group with the load balancer you created in the previous chapter, so that traffic will be intelligently distributed among your instances—even instances launched automatically. Figure 16.1 illustrates how all this will work.

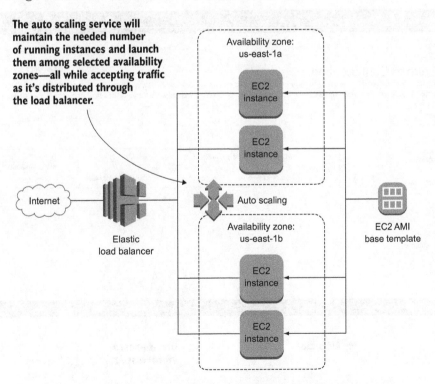

Figure 16.1 A load balancer to distribute traffic between instances, and an auto scaling service to maintain instance numbers, deployed together

16.1 *Creating a launch configuration*

As I said, the launch configuration defines exactly what gets scaled, so that's what will come first. On the EC2 dashboard, click Launch Configurations, and then click the blue Create Launch Configuration button.

The first step is to choose the AMI you want your auto scaler to launch when new instances are needed. Because you're after more instances of the WordPress server, click the My AMIs tab shown in figure 16.2 and select the wp-clone1 AMI you created earlier. Of course, everything you'll do in this chapter will work just as well with any AMI, as long as it's set up as a web server of some kind.

Next, select an instance type. Because this is just a demo, go with the light (and cheap) t2.micro. The main thing is that it should ideally match whatever type you're using for the rest of the instances in this cluster. If you can't decide, take another look at the longer discussion of instance types back in chapter 3.

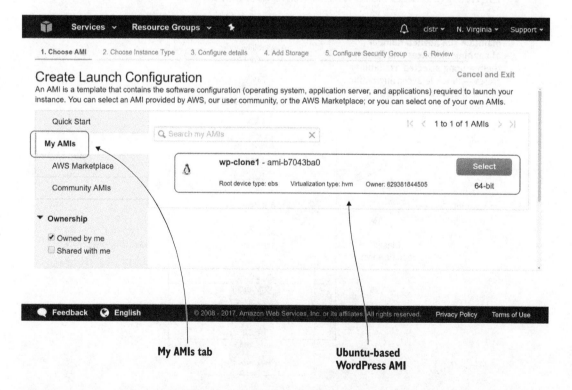

My AMIs tab

Ubuntu-based
WordPress AMI

Figure 16.2   The My AMIs tab with the WordPress clone from which a running WordPress instance can be launched

With that done, give your configuration a name. If you want to permit users or services access to the instance you're creating, you can, as you saw a few chapters back, assign it an IAM role (see figure 16.3). You can also select Enable CloudWatch Detailed Monitoring. The more complex your AWS infrastructure grows, the more important it will be to keep a watchful eye on things using AWS's resource-monitoring service the way you saw back in chapter 11.

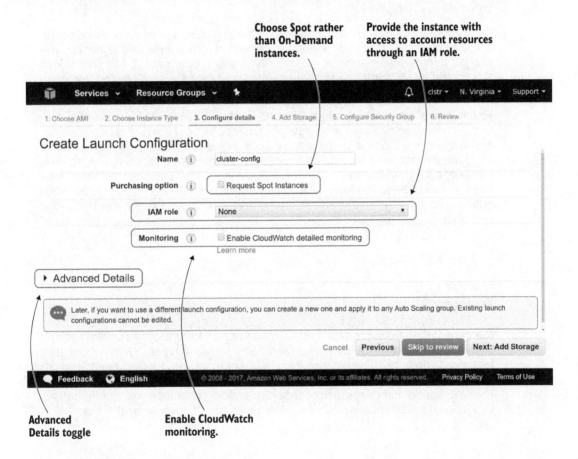

Figure 16.3 Give your launch configuration a name, choose a purchase option, and control access through an IAM role.

EC2 instance pricing

Now is a good time to take a bit of a detour and mention that there are three ways to purchase EC2 instances: on demand, spot, and reserve pricing. Throughout this book, we've gone with on-demand pricing, meaning you launch the instance and pay for every hour it's running until you shut it down again. For the kind of short-term needs you've had so far, that's fine. But it's also the most expensive option, ranging from just over half a penny per hour for the t2.nano to $5.50 an hour for the d2.8xlarge (exact costs may vary between regions). Your t2.micro instance would cost just over $8.50/month, assuming that it wasn't still eligible for the Free Tier.

You can also purchase reserve instances for long-term use of up to three years. If you're confident that your needs will remain steady over a longer period, you can get a three-year reserve instance of a t2.micro for around $150. That's less than half what an on-demand instance would cost over the same period (although that $150 doesn't include the cost of an EBS volume).

Finally, there's the spot market. If you're using your instances to, for instance, perform intense ongoing mathematical calculations or pharmaceutical research, and nothing will break if a running instance's plug is suddenly pulled, then you can save even more money by automating the purchase of spot instances. You can configure your application to buy and run instances only until the spot price rises above a limit you set. When one instance shuts down, the application keeps an eye on the market for dropping prices so it can fire up new instances and resume the calculations.

Try it now

Click the Launch Instance button on the EC2 Instance page, select an AMI, and then choose an instance type in the "m" family (m4.large, for example—at this point, you can't get spot instances for smaller instance types). On the Configure Instance Details page, select the Request Spot Instances box, and look through the configuration options that appear. This should give you a good idea of how the AWS spot market works. Note that if you decide to launch your configuration, you'll be charged, because "m"-type instances aren't covered by the Free Tier.

Now, back to our regularly scheduled demo. Clicking the Advanced Details drop-down on the configuration page displays a few more options. The Kernel ID and RAM Disk ID settings shown in figure 16.4 are ways of closely controlling the instance hardware environment— mostly to accommodate specialized virtualization needs. The simple example I added to the User Data field will start the Apache server and

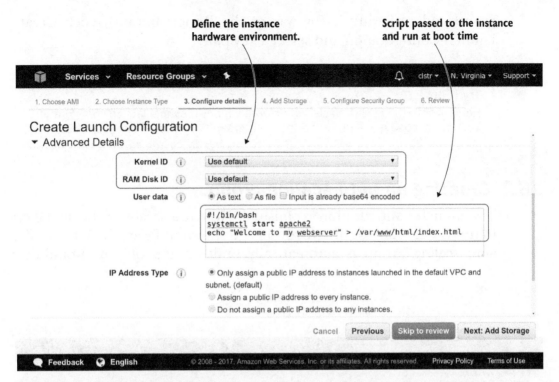

Define the instance hardware environment.

Script passed to the instance and run at boot time

Figure 16.4   The Advanced Details section of the Create Launch Configuration setup page. Use it to customize and define the launch environment.

populate an index.html file with some text. This illustrates how you can add your own scripts to customize your instance as it boots.

When you're finished with the config page, you're taken through the same storage and security-group steps with which you're already familiar. If you have an existing EBS storage volume containing data that will be needed by this instance, here's where you tell AWS to attach it. But taking cost and performance considerations into account, it usually makes sense to keep that data in an S3 bucket and preload the AMI with the information and authorizations it needs to directly access the bucket contents. If necessary, you can create an IAM role to allow access to your S3 bucket from the instance.

On the Security Group page, click the Select an Existing Security Group radio button, and use the same cluster-instances group you've been so attached to since the previous chapter. Because your access needs haven't changed, the original group's rules will work fine here. (If it ain't broke, don't fix it.) Once you're done setting up a security group and reviewing it (by way of the Review button), click Create Launch Configuration and select a key pair.

> **Try it now**
>
> Head over to the EC2 Console, and create your own simple launch configuration. You can choose any AMI for the task—it doesn't have to be one you created.

16.2 Creating an auto scaling group

The launch configuration is finished. Now you're automatically taken to the Create Auto Scaling Group page shown in figure 16.5. Here, the auto scaling group is automatically built on top of your brand-new

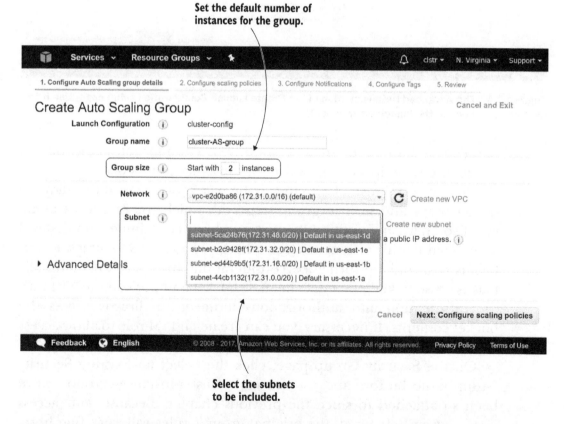

Figure 16.5 Setting the main auto scaling group configuration details to define how your scaled instances will be provisioned

cluster-config launch configuration. In the interest of high availability, let's start with at least two running instances, which you'll spread across two subnets: the same us-east-1a and us-east-1b that you've been using for your load balancer.

16.2.1 Integrating a load balancer

You'll obviously still be running your load balancer, which is an integral part of your high-availability plans. But to make it all work, you need to specify how to find your balancer—or, more specifically, the target group being used by your balancer.

Maximize the Advanced Details section of the Create Auto Scaling Group page, and select the Load Balancing check box. Clicking in the Target Groups box (see figure 16.6) shows you a list of all existing target groups. In my case, the only choice is the cluster-target group I created for use with the balancer in the previous chapter. Selecting that group means access to all instances—whether they're originals or launched later out of an auto scaling group—will be managed by the load balancer.

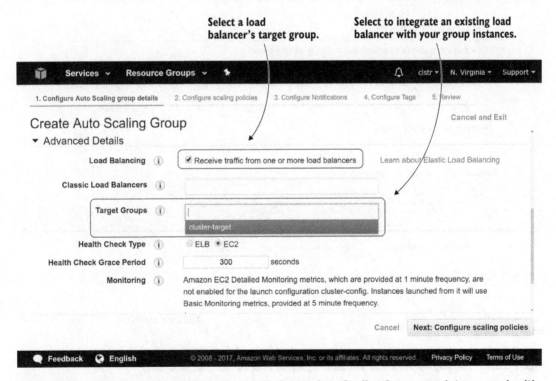

Figure 16.6 The Advanced Details section of the Create Auto Scaling Group page lets you work with a load balancer and define health-check and monitoring behavior.

16.2.2 Configuring scaling policies

You need to set a couple of policies to control the way your instances will be scaled up and down. When you're finished with the basic subnet and load-balancing settings, click Next: Configure Scaling Policies. You'll find yourself on what looks like a strange click-through page with two radio buttons: Keep This Group at Its Initial Size, and Use Scaling Policies to Adjust the Capacity of This Group. As you can see in figure 16.7, if you select the second option, the click-through page suddenly becomes a lot less empty.

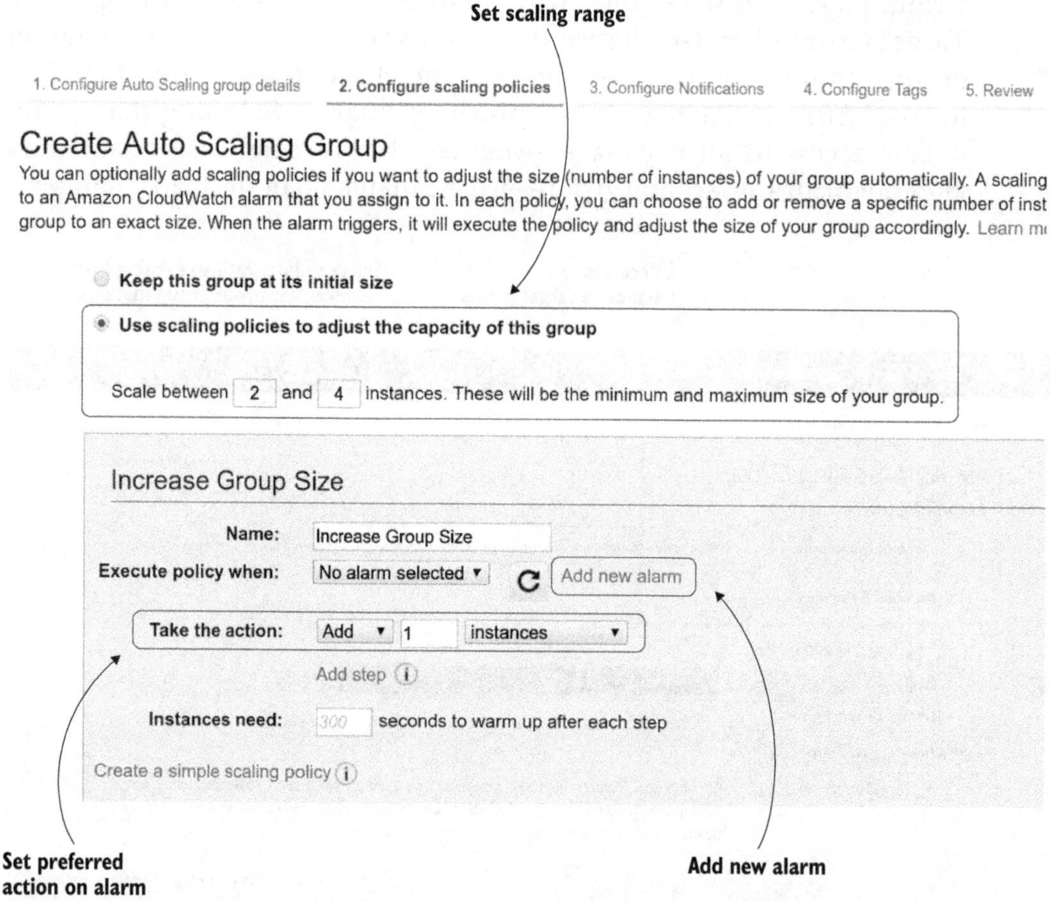

Set scaling range

1. Configure Auto Scaling group details   **2. Configure scaling policies**   3. Configure Notifications   4. Configure Tags   5. Review

Create Auto Scaling Group

You can optionally add scaling policies if you want to adjust the size (number of instances) of your group automatically. A scaling to an Amazon CloudWatch alarm that you assign to it. In each policy, you can choose to add or remove a specific number of inst group to an exact size. When the alarm triggers, it will execute the policy and adjust the size of your group accordingly. Learn m

○ **Keep this group at its initial size**

● **Use scaling policies to adjust the capacity of this group**

Scale between ⌈ 2 ⌉ and ⌈ 4 ⌉ instances. These will be the minimum and maximum size of your group.

Increase Group Size

Name:	Increase Group Size
Execute policy when:	No alarm selected ▾ ⟳ Add new alarm
Take the action:	Add ▾ 1 instances ▾
	Add step ⓘ
Instances need:	300 seconds to warm up after each step

Create a simple scaling policy ⓘ

Set preferred action on alarm

Add new alarm

Figure 16.7   The page where you set scaling limits and define trigger events

I chose to set the minimum number of running instances to two and the maximum to four. That means even if there are no live instances when the scaling group starts up, two will immediately be launched and maintained. If demand grows, the scaling group will raise that number as high as four, but no further.

Why four? Well, your numbers will probably be different, but here are the basic principles. You may want to set such an upper limit to ensure that, no matter how high demand rises, you always stay within an IT budget allocation. This can also protect you against unnecessary costs if you're ever targeted by a DDoS-type of external attack—which can simultaneously direct thousands of hijacked networked devices against a public-facing application.

Of course, there's also the risk that you may miss out on an unexpected surge of legitimate interest in your product. But business is all about making tough decisions, isn't it?

Of course, scaling won't work unless you set some kind of alarm to tell the scaling group that it's got work to do. Click the Add New Alarm link to define the environment conditions that will trigger your alarm (see figure 16.8). I chose to trip the alarm whenever the average CPU

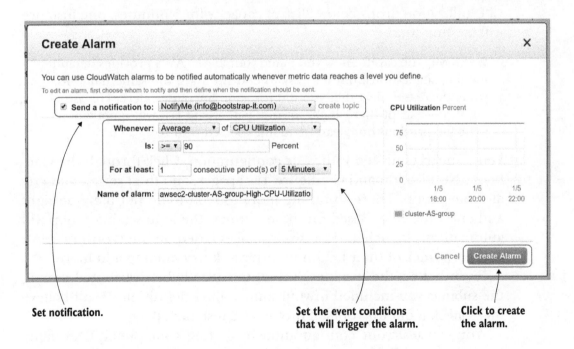

Set notification.   Set the event conditions   Click to create
                    that will trigger the alarm.   the alarm.

Figure 16.8   Create an alarm to trigger a scaling event based on changing environmental conditions.

utilization of my existing instances equals or exceeds 90% of capacity for at least 5 minutes. When that happens, the scaling group will add one instance, as defined with the Take the Action setting back in the Increase Group Size dialog.

Of course, you may pick different figures. But the overall goal is to try to spot developing trends (increasing demand, for instance) and react to them appropriately so you can invisibly and automatically maintain service levels.

You can also add a notification to a topic that defines an email or text-messaging address where alerts can be sent. You can create a new topic or, as I did, use the one created back in chapter 11. Why notify? These changes may be a sign of Amazon's services working together nicely and doing their job, but they could also indicate trouble. It's always a good idea to have a pair of human eyes take a look.

You'll also want to anticipate the need to scale down the number of instances you have running as demand drops. Scrolling down the scaling policies page takes you to the Decrease Group Size dialog (figure 16.9). Here, too, you can add a new alarm whose values will be displayed in the Execute Policy When section. In my case, when average CPU utilization drops below 20% of capacity for 5 minutes, one instance will be shut down.

> **WARNING**   Be careful how you name your alerts. AWS provides default naming suggestions, but it's easy to end up using the same name for your "decrease" alert that you did for your "increase" alert. This is no big deal—except that whichever one you create last will quietly overwrite the previous one, leading to unexpected results.

You're nearly finished with your configuration. Click through the Configure Notification and Configure Tags pages, and then review and create your group. There's nothing more for you to do but hang on tight and enjoy the ride. Based on these settings, the auto scaling group will automatically launch at least two instances based on the WordPress AMI and keep track of their health in order to know when to add more.

Even better, the instances will automatically be distributed among the subnets you included in your auto scaling definition. Don't believe me? Check it out for yourself on the EC2 instances page.

You can test your configuration by getting your public DNS name from the Load Balancer dashboard and pasting it into your browser's

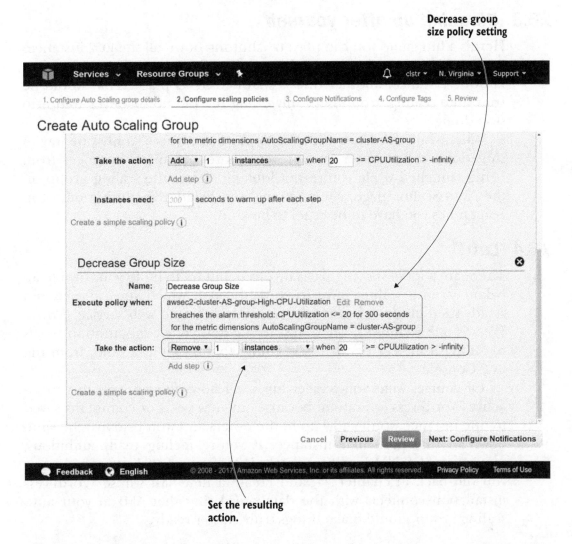

Figure 16.9 The Decrease Group Size dialog after an alarm has been created. The resulting action will be to remove one instance.

URL field. In my case, I saw the index.html page that I created with each instance through my boot-time script. Kill off (by which I mean *terminate*) one of the instances on the EC2 Instances page, and reload the balancer's DNS address in the browser. You should see an identical page. You should also see a new instance being launched on the Instances page.

16.3 Cleaning up after yourself

Here's a fun game you can play: try shutting down all the EC2 instances from the Instances dashboard. It's a futile effort, right? The minute you kill one instance, another one is spawned in its place. That would be your auto scaling group faithfully doing the job no one ever told it to stop doing.

When you're finished with the deployment, there's only one way to shut down the monster and prevent more and more instances from being launched while you're not looking. Select the scaling group on the Auto Scaling page, click Actions, and delete the stuffing out of it. Sometimes you have to be cruel to be kind.

16.4 Lab

There are a lot of moving parts involved, but try to build your own load-balancer/auto scaling infrastructure through which you can access a steady-sized cluster of instances running the same web service (Word-Press is one example). Then, test to see how your configuration reacts to failing instances by manually killing them, one at a time, from the EC2 Console.

Of course, what you've seen up until now isn't enough to run an active WordPress operation, because any new posts or comments saved to one instance won't show up in the others and won't survive the shutdown of that particular instance. If you're feeling really ambitious, move your MySQL WordPress database to its own RDS instance (the way you did back in chapter 4), and create a new AMI whose WordPress installation connects with the database. Using that AMI in your auto scaling group should make things truly cluster-ready.

Definitions

- *Launch configuration*—Settings that define which AMI will be targeted for scale-up operations.
- *On-demand pricing*—Hourly-based purchases of EC2 instances.
- *Reserve pricing*—Long-term purchases of EC2 instances. This approach is cheaper than on-demand.
- *Scaling policy*—The defined conditions and actions controlling scaling behavior.
- *Spot pricing*—Purchasing EC2instances from the short-term spot market can provide the cheapest costs of all.
- *User data*—Scripts or files that can be passed into a scaled instance on boot.

High availability: content-delivery networks

Before beginning this final high-availability chapter, let's see what you have so far. You first learned how to "robustify" your resources by spreading them among multiple availability zones (chapter 14). You then added centralized coordination of your replicated instances through load balancing (chapter 15). And finally, in chapter 16, you took control of the launch process by placing your prebuilt AMI in an auto scaling group. This let you automate the process of replacing failed instances and, when necessary, adding new ones to meet growing demand.

What's missing? Well, considering the fact that your infrastructure is now robust and self-healing, nothing—but it could still be faster. Remember, this is all about providing the best service. And "best" includes ensuring that your customers experience as few delays as possible.

What kinds of delays am I talking about? Anything that unnecessarily prolongs the time between a customer's request for data and the delivery of that data. And considering the fact that a serious percentage of users will abandon your website if a page takes longer than 2 or 3 seconds to load, this is a big deal.

All kinds of things can cause delays. Some pages are badly written or overloaded with fancy scripts and large images. But other factors can be controlled through the use of good networking practices and, in particular—as you've probably guessed from the chapter's title—by the use of a content-delivery network (CDN) like CloudFlare or Akamai.

To that end, this chapter will introduce you to Amazon's CDN: CloudFront. You'll learn what kind of configuration is required to get a CloudFront distribution going and how to integrate it into the existing elements of your application—in particular, your load balancer.

17.1 How does Amazon CloudFront work?

A CDN (sometimes also known as *edge caching*) takes snapshots of your website that it can store on a network of servers spread all around the world. If the URL used by a user on a different continent routes its request to load a page on your website through the CDN, your web server may never need to know about it. That's because, rather than transporting the original data all the way from your web server to the distant user, the cached version kept on the CDN server that's physically closest to the customer is sent. Figure 17.1 illustrates how this works; keep in mind that there are many, many more edge locations than those depicted in this image.

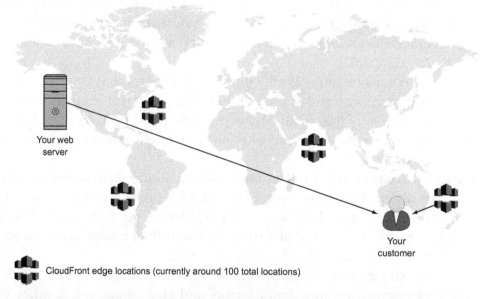

Your web server

CloudFront edge locations (currently around 100 total locations)

Your customer

Figure 17.1   The practical advantage of serving an Australian customer with data stored in Australia rather than on your North American server

Sending data 100 miles will obviously be quicker than sending it 10,000 miles. In addition to making the world a smaller place, most CDNs can also be configured to take advantage of all kinds of networking tricks, like compressing packets to further reduce in-transit latency.

Of course, that's not the end of the story. Because subsequent session actions may involve writing data to, say, your back-end database (as a commercial transaction would), just pulling down a cached image of your page won't be enough. To make that work, CloudFront can enable two-way data exchanges by acting as a proxy and invisibly relaying all server-bound requests (including cookies) back to the origin server.

When you create a distribution, you tell CloudFront what content you'd like it to distribute. This content's source is known as an *origin server*. Origin servers come in a number of flavors:

- Static content stored in an S3 bucket, like the static websites you saw back in chapter 6
- Dynamically generated content from a web server as your source, whether hosted on an AWS platform like EC2 or elsewhere

In this chapter, you'll create a CloudFront distribution that will serve the content of your WordPress application through the cluster load balancer you've been using over the past couple of chapters; see figure 17.2. You'll point CloudFront to your load balancer endpoint (URL) and work through the configuration details.

Where a CDN might not make sense

CloudFront edge locations give priority to data objects that are accessed frequently (think: Netflix videos). Because available space in any cache is always limited, this means less-popular content may be dumped from the edge-location cache after going too long without any requests. Such content will, therefore, often need to be reloaded from its origin to answer each incoming request, significantly reducing performance. For that reason, it often makes more sense to serve media and other site content that isn't as popular directly from an S3 bucket, rather than CloudFront.

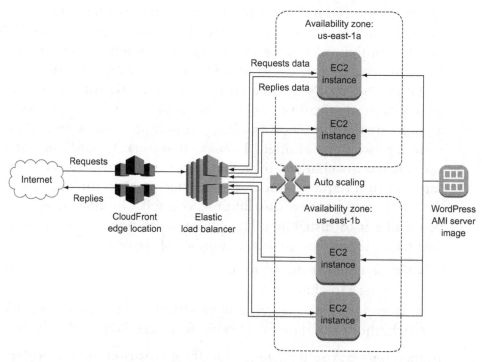

Figure 17.2   The entire AMI-based, load-balanced, auto scaled infrastructure being served to users through CloudFront

17.2 *Creating a CloudFront distribution*

Now that you know how the system functions, let's work through the process of building a distribution for the WordPress application. Because you'll encounter so many individual settings—many of whose default values will work fine for this application—I'm not going to dig into each of them. If your particular needs require something a bit different from what you see here, feel free to click any of the *i* icons or Learn More links on the Create Distribution page for helpful explanations.

You get to CloudFront from the Networking and Content Delivery section of the main AWS Console (https://console.aws.amazon.com). Click Create Distribution and then the Get Started button under the Web section to reach the Create Distribution page, where you enter the resource IDs and settings that will define your distribution. Appropriately, the first value you're expected to provide is the Origin, meaning the URL of the content CloudFront will be distributing.

Click in the Origin Domain Name field to display a list of domain names for all the compatible resources currently in your account. Figure 17.3 shows what's available in my account, including the load balancer I've been using through the last couple of chapters. By selecting it, all the high-availability goodness you've worked into your infrastructure through load balancing and auto scaling will be instantly integrated into your CloudFront distribution. That way, requests sent by CloudFront back to your servers will be properly balanced. It's that easy. Once you've chosen a Domain Name, AWS will automatically populate the Origin ID field.

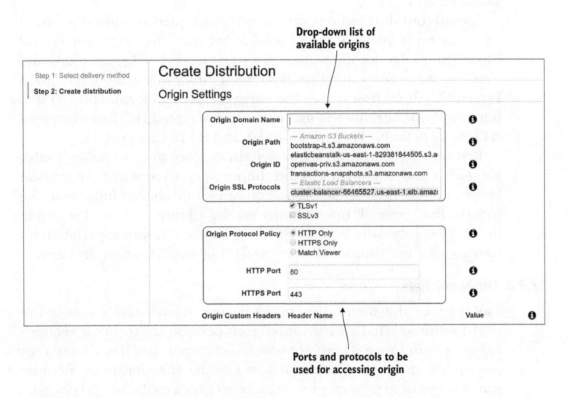

Figure 17.3   Here's where you tell CloudFront where and how to access the data on your origin server.

17.2.1   SSL/TLS encryption

You no doubt remember how—way, way back in chapter 2—we discussed encrypting SSH sessions to ensure that data being transferred between remote locations can't be read by anyone along the way. Well, a lot of data is routinely transferred between remote locations every time you open a page on a website; what's to keep prying eyes along the way from seeing things they shouldn't? The answer is website encryption—although, hopefully, using Transport Layer Security (TLS) rather than the long-deprecated Secure Sockets Layer (SSL) encryption technology. (You'll still often hear people use the SSL acronym, but they almost always mean TLS.)

CloudFront distributions can enforce encrypted communications at either or both of two stages: transfers between the origin server and CloudFront edge locations, and transfers between edge locations and your end users. You can set encryption for either one without the other. Figure 17.3 shows how you set the *origin* protocol policy and port(s) that transfers *to* CloudFront will use: either unencrypted HTTP or encrypted HTTPS. By default, HTTP uses port 80, and HTTP uses port 443.

Because edge locations are by definition more open to public access, it's much more common (and important) to enforce encryption between *CloudFront and your users.* You can set this by scrolling down the page to the Viewer Protocol Policy setting (figure 17.4) and selecting the HTTPS Only radio button. Of course, if you'd rather experiment on your own using a simpler unencrypted HTTP configuration, feel free.

17.2.2   Other settings

This part of the menu also controls your distribution's time-to-live (TTL) settings. What's TTL? CloudFront periodically forwards requests to your origin to see if your content has changed. If it has, CloudFront can update the cached copies it stores on its edge locations. Because you don't want to generate unnecessary network traffic by updating the cache too often, but you also don't want to miss important changes to the content, you'll look for an appropriately balanced TTL setting.

The Default TTL value, set initially to 86,400 seconds (24 hours), is the amount of time CloudFront will wait before looking for an update at the origin. The primary factor to consider in setting your own value will usually be how often you normally make changes to your site. If

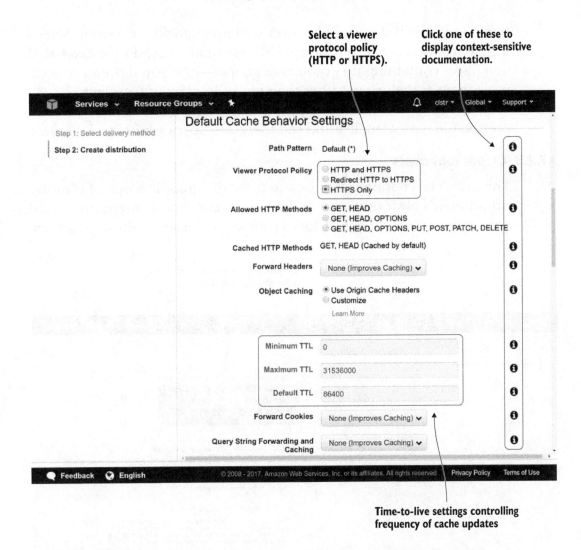

Figure 17.4   Distribution behavior settings, including selecting an access protocol and time-to-live configuration

you're pushing updates a few times each day, then you'll want to set your TTL a bit lower—perhaps to once every couple of hours. The Minimum TTL and Maximum TTL values kick in only when special instructions are passed to CloudFront from your origin by way of HTTP headers included with the objects your server sends your users.

When Yes is selected for the Compress Objects Automatically control, all objects are automatically compressed by CloudFront before being sent to end users. But CloudFront will only send a compressed version of a file if the user's browser settings explicitly request it. Selecting No makes sense if your files are all very small—say, simple text-based web pages containing no graphics or scripts—or if you'd prefer to compress them at the origin rather than have CloudFront handle it.

Why would you want to compress in the first place? Because a compressed file is a lot smaller and can therefore be transmitted a lot faster.

17.2.3 *CloudFront costs*

The price class option you choose sets the geographic scope of your distribution. It's obviously more expensive to have your content stored and served from every single CloudFront edge location throughout the

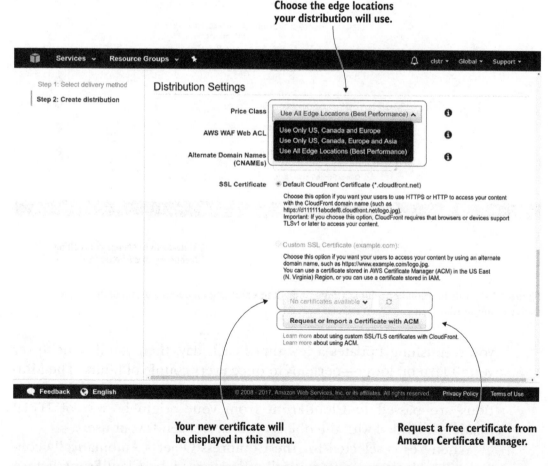

Figure 17.5   The Price Class setting, which determines which edge locations will be deployed as part of a distribution and, consequently, how much the distribution will cost

world, but that option is also more effective at delivering content to global customers. Your decision should take into account the location of the greatest numbers of your users. If they're mostly located near each other, then using fewer edge locations makes sense. Your project's budget will also play a role as you determine where limited funds should be best spent. Figure 17.5 shows how you can choose among three levels.

What does it cost to run a CloudFront distribution? Well, it's complicated. It turns out that what you pay depends on all kinds of factors. Figure 17.6 (taken from https://aws.amazon.com/cloudfront/pricing) shows how CloudFront primarily charges according to the amount of data that's transferred out to the internet. But those rates vary according to the viewers' geographic region and overall monthly volume—rates decrease as volume increases. The number of requests and use of HTTP versus HTTPS also go into the cost mix.

I used the AWS Simple Monthly Calculator (https://calculator.s3 .amazonaws.com/index.html) to put together an estimate for a relatively small distribution that transfers 10 MB videos totalling 100 GB out

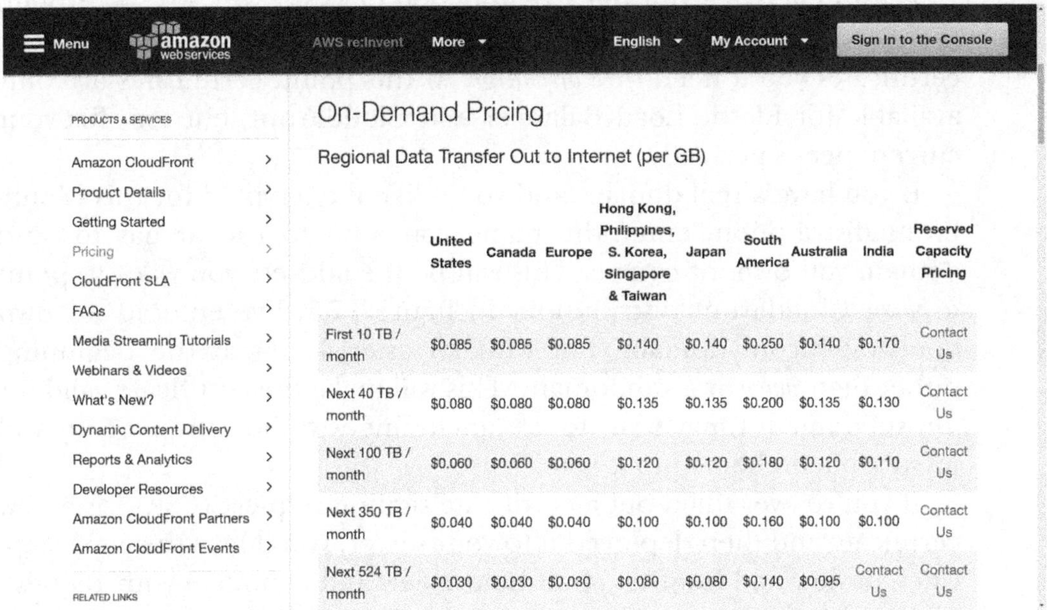

| | | | | | | | | | Reserved |
	United States	Canada	Europe	Hong Kong, Philippines, S. Korea, Singapore & Taiwan	Japan	South America	Australia	India	Capacity Pricing
First 10 TB / month	$0.085	$0.085	$0.085	$0.140	$0.140	$0.250	$0.140	$0.170	Contact Us
Next 40 TB / month	$0.080	$0.080	$0.080	$0.135	$0.135	$0.200	$0.135	$0.130	Contact Us
Next 100 TB / month	$0.060	$0.060	$0.060	$0.120	$0.120	$0.180	$0.120	$0.110	Contact Us
Next 350 TB / month	$0.040	$0.040	$0.040	$0.100	$0.100	$0.160	$0.100	$0.100	Contact Us
Next 524 TB / month	$0.030	$0.030	$0.030	$0.080	$0.080	$0.140	$0.095	Contact Us	Contact Us

Figure 17.6   CloudFront transfer costs broken down by region and volume. Notice the Reserved Capacity Pricing option in the right column, for large enterprise operations.

to a broad range of global regions. The total monthly cost was only around $5.00—but just imagine what a lucky blog post could do to that total by driving the video viral!

> **NOTE**   The Free Tier allows you 50 GB of data transfer to the internet and 2 million HTTP and HTTPS requests each month.

17.2.4 SSL/TLS certificates

Take another look at figure 17.5. The SSL Certificate option is currently set to use the default CloudFront certificate. That means as long as incoming traffic is all aimed at the CloudFront domain name you'll be given once the distribution is live, you'll be protected by AWS's own certificate. That domain name will look something like this: https://d111111abcdef8.cloudfront.net/index.html.

But the odds are that you won't want the world to associate your business with such a lovely piece of prose as https://d111111abcdef8 .cloudfront.net/index.html. I'll bet you'd prefer something catchier like—oh, I don't know—bootstrap-it.com. No problem. All you need to do is import your certificate by clicking Request or Import a Certificate with ACM.

Haven't got a certificate? I've got good news for you. AWS—through the AWS Certificate Manager—will painlessly provide you with all the certificates you'll need, *free of charge*. At this point, certificates are only available for Elastic Load Balancer and CloudFront, but that fits your current needs perfectly.

If you have a real domain and you'd like it encrypted for this Cloud-Front distribution, enter the name you want to use. It has to be a domain you own, of course. This will be the address you want to point to your CloudFront distribution. In figure 17.7, I've entered my own bootstrap-it.com domain, but with an asterisk (*) at the beginning rather than *www* or a subdomain. This will make the certificate valid for *any* subdomain I may want to use, including www.bootstrap-it.com and mysubdomain.bootstrap-it.com.

If you've ever filled out a certificate signing request (CSR) for a new certificate and then deployed it to your server, you'll love this next step. Click Review and Request, and then review and complete your request. That's it! Once your certificate has been issued, all that's left is to head back to the CloudFront Create Distribution page (figure 17.5) and pull

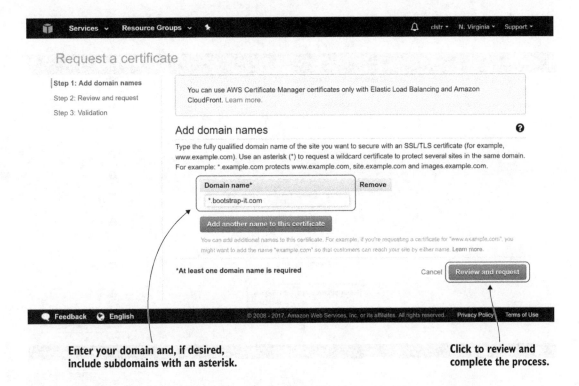

Enter your domain and, if desired,
include subdomains with an asterisk.

Click to review and
complete the process.

Figure 17.7 Request a certificate to protect a domain that you want to associate with your
CloudFront distribution.

down the now-active menu that previously read No Certificates Available. If you entered your domain name accurately, the menu should
now display your new certificate—which you should select.

17.2.5 Wrapping it all up

Fear not. Nearly done. Figure 17.8 shows the last part of the Create Distribution page. The optional Default Root Object tells CloudFront to
load a specific file on your origin server when viewers arrive at your root
URL (for example, bootstrap-ip.com). This can be useful if, for some
reason, your server's filesystem needs to follow an unorthodox design
and your root HTML file isn't where browsers normally expect it to be.

To keep track of the traffic coming through your distribution, you
can turn on logging, specify an S3 bucket where log data should be
stored, and specify a log prefix to make log data easier to pick out
among many thousands of lines of data. Clicking Create Distribution

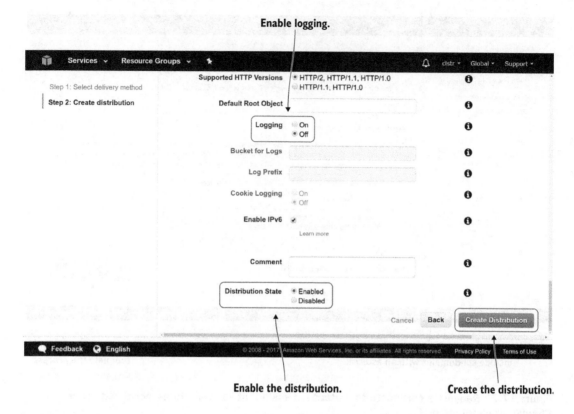

Enable logging.

Enable the distribution.

Create the distribution.

Figure 17.8   The final steps in creating a new distribution: enable logging, enable the distribution itself, and click Create Distribution.

will, as advertised, create the distribution—but won't start it running. That happens only if you've set Distribution State to Enabled (as shown in figure 17.8).

17.3 Lab

Now it's your turn. Create a working CloudFront distribution that uses any resource you may have running as its origin server. You can use an active load balancer or even a static website in an S3 bucket. To keep it simple, use the distribution end point (and default certificate) that you'll be given once the distribution is live. This should easily be within your Free Tier limits, assuming your account is still eligible for Free Tier.

You can test the distribution by directing browsers on different computers (both logged in to your AWS account and not logged in) to the

URL CloudFront gives you. You can also use the `curl` tool from a command line on a remote server if you don't have a fleet of spare physical computers lying around in various locations.

Definitions
- *Cache*—A digital memory store from which data can be quickly retrieved
- *Edge locations*—CloudFront servers positioned around the world to be as close as possible to end users
- *Origin server*—The computer or data repository (like an S3 bucket) from which a CloudFront distribution takes its data
- *Time-to-live (TTL)*—The length of time before CloudFront will check for updates to the origin server and, if necessary, update the cache at the edge locations
- *Website encryption*—Using TLS certificates to protect the data in transit between the origin server and CloudFront, or between CloudFront and the end user

Part 3

Food for thought: what else can AWS do for you?

Chapters 18–21 are my attempt to briefly explore some of the many dozens of AWS services that I couldn't cover properly in the previous chapters. We'll look at some popular and highly useful hybrid, automation, and developer-centric tools. The idea is to give you a feel for the kinds of things you can do on AWS. Your imagination can take over from there.

Building hybrid infrastructure

18

Life is a moving target. Just when you get used to the way all your stuff has been working until now, something completely unexpected lands on the front lawn. As you cross the line separating this book's practical, hands-on sections from the big-picture-overview chapters to come, expect some change. Of course, if you've already read the table of contents, this won't necessarily come as a surprise.

No single book could adequately cover *all* the many tools AWS offers and *all* the countless ways you might use them. But I can at least introduce you to the kinds of things you can accomplish using some of the less-traveled AWS resources out there scattered across the cloud. So I've assembled a collection of services that—to some degree, at least—*represent* the functionality of all the others. Again, because a single month contains only so many lunches, as you work through these secondary collections, I'm won't show you *how* to do these things; rather, I'll describe *what* you can do. You can always find the main console or official documentation pages for any of the services I'll discuss through simple web searches or by browsing the well-designed AWS site.

I'll start the ball rolling with a subject dedicated to those people who just can't fully commit: hybrid cloud solutions. We'll explore data storage, backups, network connectivity, and resource management.

18.1 Why go hybrid?

Cloud computing is definitely not a zero-sum game. There's nothing wrong with deploying your resources both locally and on AWS. In fact, there's no law preventing you from using multiple cloud providers at the same time. The trick is properly coordinating the administration of remote infrastructure. You'll learn about some pretty powerful coordination tools as you move through this chapter. But first, just why would you want to split things up? Here are some possibilities:

- *Staged migrations*—Even if you understand the value proposition of AWS, it will often be impractical to shift all the pieces of a complicated operation into the cloud at once. It sometimes makes sense to move things over in stages. You might begin by transferring a few databases to RDS or moving backup archives to S3.
- *Using existing infrastructure and skills*—If you've recently invested in a rack of high-performance servers, now is probably not the best time to send them off to a landfill. Ditto the six months of training your junior sysadmins just completed. But that doesn't mean you can't plan (and upgrade your skills) for the future while moving what can be easily moved.
- *Regulatory and compliance restrictions*—Although this happens less and less, some deployments may, due to security concerns, require specialized local care and handling.
- *Costs of data transfer*—For some businesses, migrating server workloads to the cloud is a no-brainer, but finding a way to upload a few dozen terabytes of back-end data can be complicated. Even if you're lucky enough to have a gigabyte internet connection, that doesn't mean you'll get anything like those speeds for real-world uploads. Do the math: a 10 TB archive sent at a rate of 500 Mbps will take close to 48 hours—and probably severely limit everyone else's internet use for the duration. That's assuming you're getting 500 Mbps. The more common rate of 25 Mbps would take well over a month. I'll talk about some interesting alternatives in the next section.

NOTE Although faster internet connections are becoming more common, the volumes of data many companies must deal with are, if anything, increasing even more quickly. It would take more than *3 years* to upload 10 petabytes over a 1 Gbps connection.

18.2 Hybrid storage solutions

Let's take another look at storage. In many ways, this is the easiest category to migrate. After all, why should the rest of your infrastructure care whether its data is spinning on a hard drive just up the hall or chilling out with the gang in an AWS data center? Files are files.

18.2.1 S3 and Glacier

If all you're looking for is a place to store moderate amounts of easily accessible data, then S3 is probably where you want to put it. Do your saved archives lose their relevance over time? Once your files are safely parked in S3, it's trivial to arrange for them to be automatically transitioned between S3 and the much cheaper Glacier storage service.

Just enable versioning for a particular bucket and then, on the Lifecycles tab in the S3 console, click Add Lifecycle Rule. As you can see in figure 18.1, you can arrange for S3 to automatically move data to Glacier once it's been there for more than, say, 60 days, and then delete it after 120 days. The only downside of Glacier is that it can take a few hours to recover data that's stored there.

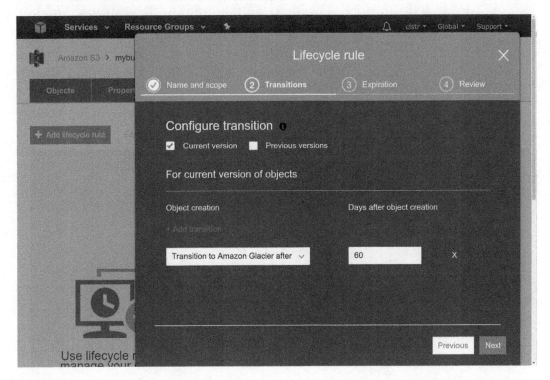

Figure 18.1 As stored S3 data ages beyond a set number of days, you can schedule its archival to the cheaper Glacier storage class.

> **Try it now**
>
> Upload a file or directory to a new S3 bucket. Then, tell S3 to automatically move the bucket's contents to Glacier after it's been there for 30 days and delete it after 90 days.

18.2.2 AWS Storage Gateway

Just because AWS S3 has earned its reputation for flexibility and reliability won't make it any easier to tell all of your applications that their precious data has moved. Updating the legacy scripts and processes running on your locally hosted servers won't be simple—especially if you've been automating backups to tape or NAS devices.

If backups are critical to your operations but making the connection with off-site storage is a problem, why not pretend that everything's in the same room? AWS Storage Gateway, which makes a living by imitating on-premises storage devices, can simplify the process. Once you've installed the Storage Gateway as a virtual machine on a local server, it can be mounted as a compatible storage device—including as an iSCSI device (iSCSI is a common standard for managing data transfers). That means it can present itself to your local infrastructure exactly the way your legacy hardware did, while, in reality, its data is stored in the AWS cloud.

For faster access times, Storage Gateway can optionally be configured to maintain a local cached copy of your volume, combining the safety of cloud storage with the immediacy of local copies. Figure 18.2 shows the Storage Gateway intro page from the AWS site.

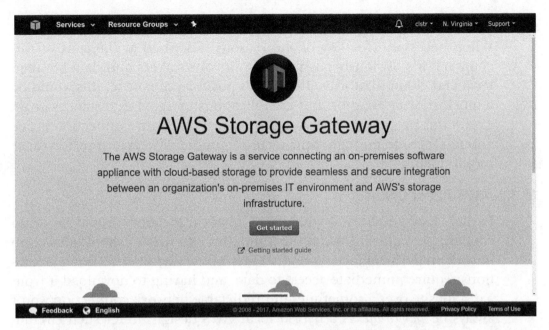

Figure 18.2   The AWS Storage Gateway introduction page with links to useful documentation

18.2.3 AWS Snowball

Don't have three years to wait, but still want to move large volumes of data to AWS? Consider having Amazon send you a petabyte-sized physical storage device: you can load your data onto it and then ship it back. This service is called Snowball, and the device comes with 256-bit encryption and multiple layers of security and tracking features to protect it through its journey back to AWS.

Assuming you're in a location where the Snowball service is available (consult AWS documentation for details), the entire process can take less than a week, and it will end up a great deal cheaper than the cost of bandwidth for an upload. Snowball can also be used in the other direction: if your local system fails, and you need to retrieve a huge data backup from S3, you can order an export.

18.3 Hybrid connectivity

When necessary (for any of the reasons described at the start of this chapter), it's obviously possible to split your servers and data between local and cloud platforms. If it wasn't possible, of course, this would be a much shorter chapter. But complications increase as distances grow. To do this properly, you'll need to ensure that your connection is fast enough, private enough, and secure enough. AWS has apps for those requirements.

18.3.1 AWS Direct Connect

Earlier, I suggested that your data's physical location should be of no concern to your infrastructure and, by extension, should have no impact on performance. Well, that may not always be true. Some operations require immediate access to data, and having to download it from a distant site over a sometimes-unpredictable network connection won't always be *immediate*. Is a hybrid local/AWS design under such circumstances workable?

Allow me to introduce you to AWS Direct Connect. Direct Connect is built on a pool of third-party providers, each of which can create and maintain a fast, dedicated network connection between your office or data center and your AWS-based resources. Companies called AWS Partner Network (APN) Technology and Consulting Partners are available to help you establish connections to Amazon's Direct Connect locations. You can hook up with an approved partner through links on AWS's site: https://aws.amazon.com/directconnect/partners.

You're billed for Direct Connect usage in two ways: hourly, according to the port speed you choose, and per gigabyte of data that you transfer (in many cases, between $0.02 and $0.03 per GB). Figure 18.3 shows hourly rates according to the various available port speeds.

18.3.2 The hardware virtual private gateway

Even if your internet connection is already fast and reliable enough for the things you're doing, you may be uncomfortable sending your private data across an unprotected public network like the internet. A common solution involves creating a tunneled connection using a special virtual private network (VPN) to connect your local servers to the resources you have running within an AWS Virtual Private Cloud (VPC).

Port Speed	Port-Hour Rate	Port-Hour Rate in Japan
50M*	$0.03/hour	$0.029/hour
100M*	$0.06/hour	$0.057/hour
200M*	$0.12/hour	$0.114/hour
300M*	$0.18/hour	$0.171/hour
400M*	$0.24/hour	$0.228/hour
500M*	$0.30/hour	$0.285/hour
1G	$0.30/hour	$0.285/hour
10G	$2.25/hour	$2.142/hour

PRODUCTS & SERVICES

AWS Direct Connect
Product Details
Pricing
Getting Started
Developer Resources
FAQs
Partners
Partner Bundles

RELATED LINKS
Documentation
Management Console
Release Notes
Discussion Forum

Manage Your Resources

Menu · amazon webservices · AWS re:Invent · Products · More · English · My Account · Sign In to the Console

* Contact an APN Partner supporting AWS Direct Connect to order these connection speeds.

Except as otherwise noted, our prices are exclusive of applicable taxes and duties, including VAT and applicable sales tax. For customers with a Japanese billing address, use of the Asia Pacific (Tokyo) Region is subject to Japanese Consumption Tax. Learn more.

Figure 18.3 Hourly port-hour rates charged for Direct Connect service. These rates are in addition to data-transfer charges that are billed by transfer volume.

Tunnels are designed to shield data while it travels through an unprotected public network like the internet. VPCs, as you'll recall from chapter 14, are the networking tools that give structure to the way your AWS resources connect to the rest of the world.

Using an AWS virtual private gateway service, you can establish a VPN connection between your local servers and your AWS VPC through some kind of internet-facing routing device (like a firewall) that you have running locally. The device (known in AWS terms as a *customer gateway device*) might be a compatible hardware router from a company like Cisco or Juniper, or even a software application. Once the VPN is up, you'll need to identify the location and configuration profile of your appliance as part of the virtual private gateway setup at the AWS end.

The process can be complicated (which carries its own costs), but a virtual private gateway can go a long way toward simplifying the close integration of local and cloud resources. VPN connections are charged at around $0.05 per VPN connection-hour (in addition to your normal use of AWS services). Figure 18.4 shows how the connection might work.

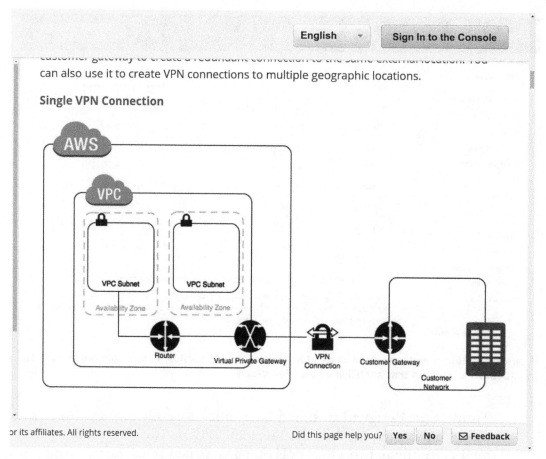

Figure 18.4   An example (from the AWS documentation web pages) of a virtual private gateway VPN connection between an AWS-based VPC and a customer's local network

18.3.3 *AWS Directory Service*

Securing your hybrid infrastructure involves more than just ensuring that the network connections are strong enough to keep bad guys on the internet from eavesdropping on your data transfers. You'll probably also want to manage the way your users authenticate themselves to gain legitimate access. After all, there's no point in securing the network and then turning around and letting everyone in through the front door. But creating a new authentication system *in addition* to whatever you're using on the rest of your company's networks can introduce some serious pain into the process. For example, just think how much fun you'd

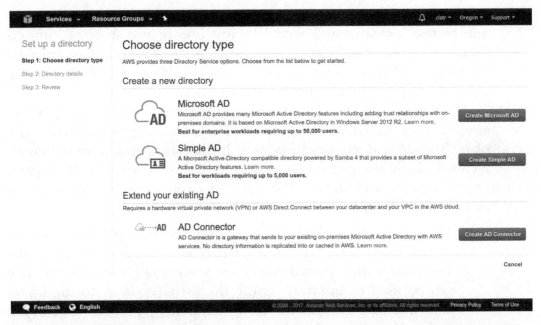

Figure 18.5 AWS Directory Service comes in more than one flavor. Note: not all of these options are available in every AWS region.

have creating login accounts for each of the 500 people who need access to the back-end services you're running.

So that you won't need to reinvent the wheel, the AWS Directory Service allows close integration between any existing local Microsoft Active Directory (or AD-compatible) system and AWS resources. This can permit system-wide deployment of features like Kerberos-based single sign-on, RADIUS-based multi-factor authentication, and LDAP. Some directory type options are illustrated in figure 18.5.

18.4 Disaster recovery

Even if you decide to keep every last byte of your live deployments off-cloud and local, there's still plenty of value to be found in using AWS as part of your disaster-recovery plan. You do have a disaster-recover plan, right? I mean the kind of plan that includes clear and realistic *recovery-time objectives* (the maximum amount of time you can tolerate a service outage) and *recovery-point objectives* (the maximum amount of transaction data loss you can tolerate). You obviously want to be able to return your application and its data to a fully functioning state as quickly as possible.

If your servers and storage media are all currently concentrated in one or two locations and served by just one or two network connections, it's not hard to imagine something physical, political, or criminal bringing it all down. How quickly you'll be able to get it all back up again will depend on the quality of your plan.

Maintaining a backup deployment on AWS that can be triggered to assemble and launch itself when needed can play a big part in an effective plan. The AWS documentation (see https://aws.amazon.com/disaster-recovery) includes a white paper that describes a number of disaster-recovery models in detail. The solutions you can read about there include the following:

- The *pilot-light model*, where you keep a synchronized, constantly updated copy of your back-end database running on AWS RDS. The goal is that, should your local servers fail, the RDS database can be used to instantly "ignite the furnace" by restoring up-to-date application data to freshly launched, prebuilt AWS-based AMIs. All you'll need to do is redirect your DNS records away from your local infrastructure to your AWS VPC so users are sent to the new servers.

- The *warm-standby model*, where you run a full-tiered copy of your actual application but, to save costs, in a scaled-down version. If the local resources fail, pointing your DNS traffic to AWS will automatically cause your auto scaler to quickly increase capacity to meet demand. This can be more expensive to maintain than a pilot-light infrastructure, but you get quicker recovery as a return on your extra investment.

The nice thing about working with an AWS disaster-recovery solution is that, in addition to providing the comfort of a solid recovery plan, it also gives you the kind of excellent, hands-on experience with AWS that will make a full migration later much easier.

18.5 The Amazon EC2 Systems Manager

EC2 Systems Manager is essentially a collection of administration tools that were recently added to the EC2 family. It's an AWS in-house answer to an entire class of third-party provisioning tools like Puppet and Chef, to Linux-based cron jobs, and to first-party tools like a keyboard and a wall full of monitors.

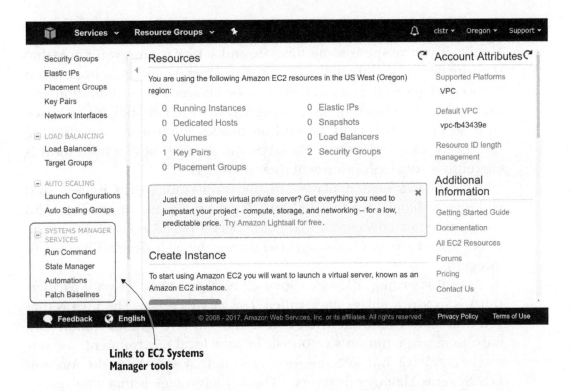

Links to EC2 Systems
Manager tools

Figure 18.6 **The EC2 dashboard, with links to the four Systems Manager services highlighted**

The EC2 Systems Manager tools provide one-stop, centralized control over all of your Linux and Windows instances, allowing you to schedule software and OS updates, run regularly scheduled or one-off scripts (both Linux and PowerShell), and apply updates to underlying AMIs. As you can see in figure 18.6, the four members of the Systems Manager services group are all accessible from the regular EC2 dashboard.

All that sounds great. But what does it have to do with hybrid designs? Well, you see, once you register on-premises servers or VMs through a managed-instance activation and install the SSM agent on each of them, you'll be able to administer the entire cluster using the Systems Manager tools. Thus, EC2 Systems Manager is a true cross-platform, hybrid-friendly administration tool for bridging the cloud/local gap.

18.6 *VMware integration*

Finally, if you've spent some time around server rooms, you know that they involve more than just racks, bare metal, and monitors. Even before you get to the cloud, there can be all kinds of virtualization and management-abstraction layers designed to either simplify or enhance your administrative tasks. Given how quickly enterprises are adopting the use of cloud platforms like AWS, integrating those admin tools is currently a very high priority of their providers.

One of the biggest players in the on-premises virtualization and cloud technologies world is VMware. For a brief moment, the Palo Alto company reportedly considered going head-to-head against AWS in the public cloud space. One long, cold shower later, it decided instead to integrate.

As of this writing, VMware Cloud on AWS (an AWS/VMware partnership) is in a prerelease stage called *Technology Preview*. The idea is that you'll be able to use the tried and tested VMware administration software to manage not only resources in your local environment, the way you always have, but AWS instances as well. In a way, this is the Amazon EC2 Systems Manager in reverse. The key advantage is that your team's hard-earned VMware skills and existing VMware infrastructure need not be abandoned as you move to the cloud.

Definitions
- *Hybrid solution*—A combination of cloud-based and on-premises infrastructure.
- *Migration*—Shifting IT infrastructure between local and cloud environments.
- *Virtual private network (VPN)*—A network tunnel through which private communications can be safely exchanged over a public network.
- *Recovery-time objective (RTO)*—The estimated maximum amount of time that a company could survive without its key data/compute service.
- *Recovery-point objective (RPO)*—The estimated maximum amount of unsaved data that a company could lose in a system crash. This value determines the maximum time between backups.

Cloud automation: working with Elastic Beanstalk, Docker, and Lambda

Automation is the running of processes with as little human intervention as possible. This has advantages: humans make dumb mistakes, expect to be paid lots of money, have trouble watching more than one thing at a time, and, if YouTube usage patterns are any indication, are fairly easy to distract. They also often have trouble understanding complex stuff (like how to operate a photocopier).

Automated systems? Not so much.

Cloud computing is all about automating user access to compute and network resources, so it makes sense that the resources themselves should be offered behind an increasingly automated interface. In this chapter, you'll learn a little about three AWS services, each operating on its own level of automation abstraction:

- *AWS Elastic Beanstalk*—The infrastructure exists but is hidden from the user.
- *Docker on AWS EC2 Container Service*—The infrastructure is virtualized.
- *AWS Lambda*—The infrastructure doesn't even pretend to exist.

19.1 AWS Elastic Beanstalk: what you don't see won't hurt you

System administrators love diving into new technologies. I hope you've enjoyed learning your way around all the AWS services covered in the book so far at least as much as I have. But the world is a large, diverse place filled with all kinds of people—developers, for instance, some of whom prefer writing code over calculating TCP/IP subnets.

Looking for the perfect gift for the overworked developers in your life? Forward them a link to Elastic Beanstalk: https://console.aws.amazon.com/ elasticbeanstalk. In the view you're shown the first time you use the service (see figure 19.1), you tell Beanstalk what kind of environment you'd like to provision—all the most up-to-date favorites are there—and click Launch Now. Amazon will immediately—and silently—get to work building the complete infrastructure your deployment will need, including EC2 instances, auto scaling, health monitoring, and a load balancer.

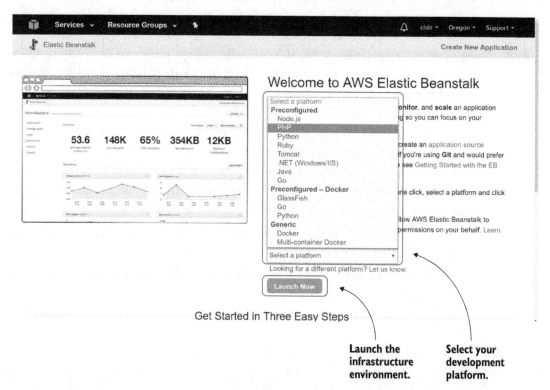

Figure 19.1   The first-visit page where you can choose a development environment and click to launch all the infrastructure your app will need

Once the underlying environment is running, there's only one thing left for you to do: click Upload and Deploy and upload your application code. Select a local file containing code in the language you selected in the previous screen, add some text describing the current version, and click Deploy, as shown in figure 19.2. That's it.

There's obviously more you can do to tweak the underlying configuration. But to a large degree, if your application is fairly straightforward and you'd prefer to avoid facing the details, Elastic Beanstalk can give you a robust, scalable, highly available, public-facing application in a couple of minutes.

By way of example, remember that two-tiered, load-balanced, auto scaled WordPress application you spent most of the book building?

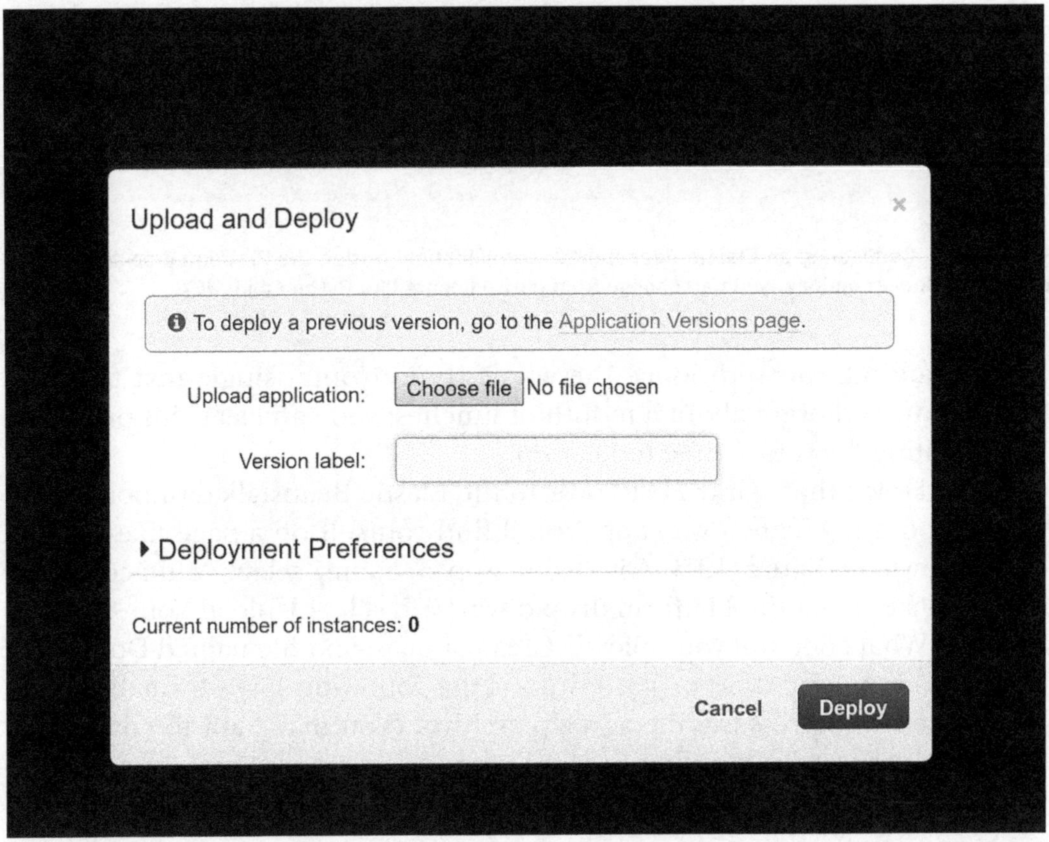

Upload and Deploy

ⓘ To deploy a previous version, go to the Application Versions page.

Upload application: [Choose file] No file chosen

Version label: [   ]

▶ Deployment Preferences

Current number of instances: **0**

Cancel   **Deploy**

Figure 19.2   The dialog where you upload initial or updated versions of your application code. Version Label should be a description of this version's origin and purpose.

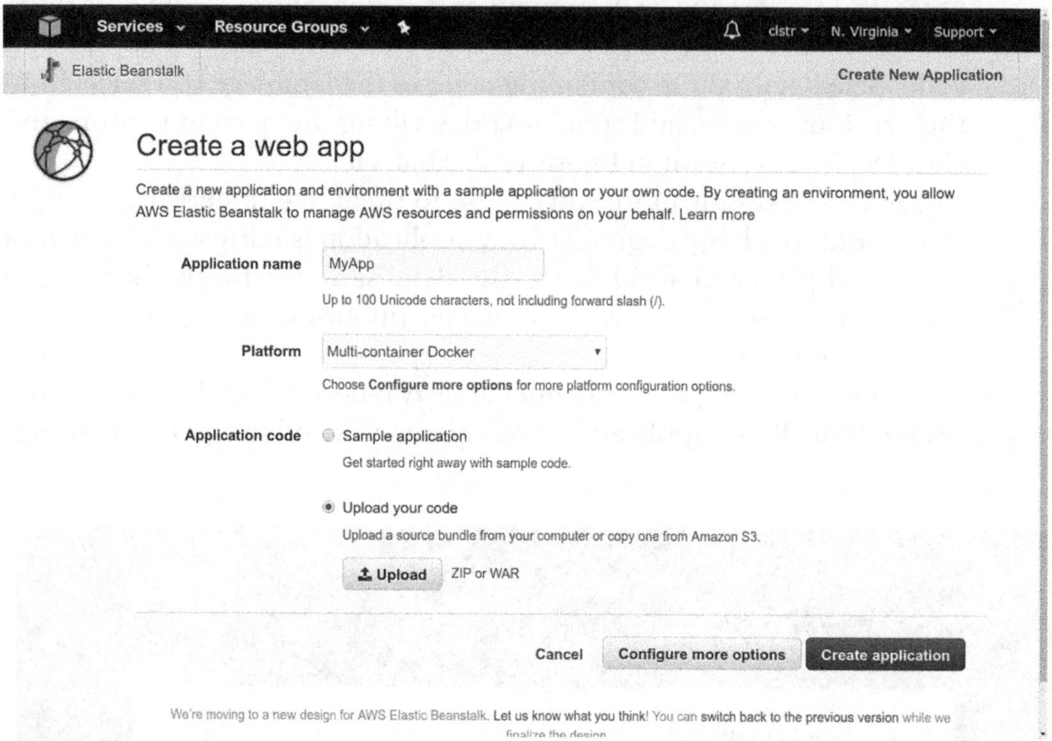

Figure 19.3   Configuring an Elastic Beanstalk web application. Notice the Platform drop-down: in addition to Docker options, you can choose from environments like Python and .NET.

Beanstalk can reproduce the whole thing from a single text file. In 5 minutes. Forget about a month of lunches; you can clear this one while waiting for your coffee to heat up.

How's that work? Head over to the Elastic Beanstalk dashboard, and choose to create a web app. You'll find yourself on a page like the one shown in figure 19.3. Give your app a name, select Multi-container Docker from the Platform drop-down, and select Upload Your Code.

What code will you upload? Create a plain-text file named Dockerrun .aws.json, and type or paste into it the following JSON-formatted text. Then, compress the file as a zip archive. (You may want to change the two password values first.)

Listing 19.1 Dockerrun.aws.json

```json
{
    "AWSEBDockerrunVersion": 2,
    "containerDefinitions": [
        {
            "name": "mariadb",
            "image": "mariadb:latest",
            "essential": true,
            "memory": 128,
            "portMappings": [
                {
                    "hostPort": 3306,
                    "containerPort": 3306
                }
            ],
            "environment": [
                {
                    "name": "MYSQL_ROOT_PASSWORD",
                    "value": "password"
                },
                {
                    "name": "MYSQL_DATABASE",
                    "value": "wordpress"
                }
            ]
        },
        {
            "name": "wordpress",
            "image": "wordpress",
            "essential": true,
            "memory": 128,
            "portMappings": [
                {
                    "hostPort": 80,
                    "containerPort": 80
                }
            ],
            "links": [
                "mariadb"
            ],
            "environment": [
                {
                    "name": "MYSQL_ROOT_PASSWORD",
                    "value": "password"
                }
            ]
        }
    ]
}
```

Once the file is uploaded, click Create Application, and wait the 5 or 10 minutes it will take for your application to load. Then, follow the URL you're shown to visit your WordPress setup page, all fully supported by some serious resource infrastructure.

Give the containers a few extra minutes to get themselves settled, and then, from the WordPress setup page, try using *root* for the username; and instead of localhost for the database host, try *mariadb* (the name you gave to the database container). Enter the password you included in the Dockerrun.aws.json file.

> **NOTE**   This code is just an illustrative example, stolen shamelessly from my Pluralsight course on Docker and Elastic Beanstalk. To get it working fully, you may need to do some manual configuration on the EC2 host, which will require associating a key pair with the instance, updating the application, and using SSH to gain access.

Don't forget to shut down the application by clicking Actions and Terminate Environment when you're finished with it.

> **Try it now**
>
> Go ahead and try launching your own Beanstalk application. By default, a sample Hello World application written in the language you select is already included, so you can direct your browser to the URL you're given in the Beanstalk dashboard to confirm it works. Don't forget to delete the application once you're finished. Confirm that things are working by monitoring the activity on the EC2 Instances dashboard.

19.2   AWS EC2 Container Service: running Docker in the cloud

A Docker instance is called a *container*. If you haven't yet run into one in person, here's what to expect: containers are extremely lightweight, software-driven virtual servers that can be configured and launched to perform highly customized tasks. The technology isn't exclusive to AWS; but the things Docker does well fit so nicely with the environments that AWS offers that the two were destined from birth to marry. The happy couple can currently be found spending time together in, among other places, the EC2 Container Service: https://console.aws.amazon.com/ecs.

Containers are built from images, which are in turn made up of layers of software. An image might have a Linux OS like Ubuntu as its base layer, with individual applications like the Apache web server and the MySQL database forming additional layers. You can pull images with prebuilt, ready-to-run applications and deploy them in clusters of containers where they're integrated with other containers running their own applications (see figure 19.4).

What makes Docker so attractive is how simple it can be to quickly create carefully defined server environments. And once a Docker image exists, it can be widely and reliably shared. Teams working remotely can launch and test perfect copies of each other's work, incorporate changes and updates into new images, and send them back for the next step in the development cycle.

The scriptability and responsiveness of Docker containers make them perfect candidates for deployment in huge cluster orchestrations. It's not uncommon to use a new container for every web page or service a user requests. Every single Google search, for example, spawns a unique container—although of the Kubernetes variety, rather than Docker. Individual containers can independently undertake tasks as part of much larger systems, sometimes involving many thousands of

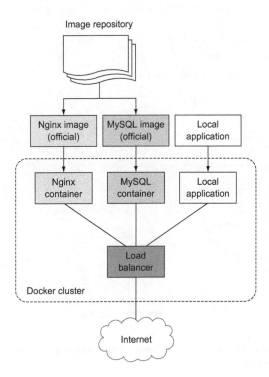

Figure 19.4 Images can be pulled from repositories, deployed into Docker clusters as interdependent containers, and connected to public networks.

containers. Global companies like PayPal and BBC use Docker extensively in their operations.

This is exactly where AWS—with its keen interest in fostering large-scale automated operations—comes in. The EC2 Container Service (ECS) makes it easy—well, perhaps makes it *possible* is a bit more accurate—to manage large clusters of Docker containers. To get started, you can deploy purpose-built, Docker-ready EC2 instances, launched using the official Amazon ECS-optimized Amazon Linux AMI; you can get this AMI during the EC2 launch process by searching the AWS Marketplace for *ecs*.

With AWS's special EC2 instance running, you're ready to configure an ECS cluster; by defining services and tasks, it allows you to launch and control containers. Figure 19.5 shows how you create a task definition

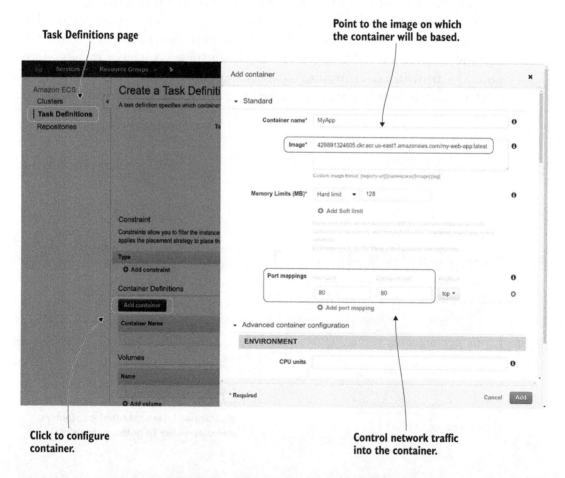

Figure 19.5   The Add Container pop-up window on the AWS ECS Task Definitions page. Here's where you define the capacity and behavior of your container.

that will determine how containers in your cluster will run. The Add Container pop-up is where you tell ECS which image you'll be using for the container, along with various environment and networking details.

ECS does a good job handling the dirty details of cluster and container management for you, along with scaling and integration with the broader AWS resources that make it all happen. AWS even has its own image repository called the Amazon EC2 Container Registry.

The kind of interdependent microservices cluster that the Elastic Beanstalk WordPress example illustrated is just as possible using ECS. But whereas Beanstalk is built around code and scripts of one sort or another—and can also be used for non-Docker applications—ECS adds a more hands-on, visual, ongoing administrative experience.

> **TIP** To be honest, fully understanding the ECS structure and workflow can be a challenge. The precise function played by clusters, services, tasks, and containers may feel arbitrary at first, which can make it tough to get started. At the risk of being accused (and convicted) of shameless self-promotion, I'll mention my "Using Docker on AWS" course at Pluralsight (https://app.pluralsight.com/library/courses/docker-aws-using/table-of-contents). The first section is a general introduction to Docker, but the rest is focused on showing you around ECS and then guiding you through actual cluster deployments.

19.3 AWS Lambda: *going serverless*

The thing about a trend is that, after a while, remembering what it was supposed to be about is sometimes complicated. Take server virtualization. For years, one ingenious technology after another has delivered software that can impersonate full-bore servers while demanding ever-lighter footprints. As long as you don't go looking for a physical box that's running it, you'd be perfectly justified in assuming that the Xen and VMware virtual machine or the LXC or Docker container you're using is the real deal. The fact that it's all an illusion doesn't make it any less wondrous.

But at least your interactions with all of those virtualization platforms were server-like—by which I mean, you could log in to the VM, and it would have the same filesystem architecture and running processes on it that you'd expect to find on any Linux or Windows machine. It looked and behaved like a physical server, even if it wasn't.

That was then. These days, you can't walk down the hall of a respectable data center without tripping over an abandoned virtualization paradigm—the virtual server, for instance. Using *serverless* architectures like AWS Lambda, cloud-based compute functions can now be launched, executed, and shut down completely independent of anything that even looks like a server. There's no logging in to a Lambda *server*, because there's no server to log in to.

The idea behind serverless is that events happening in other AWS services can be configured to trigger the quick execution of a function using only the bare minimum of cloud resources needed to spawn an action. The classic example to illustrate the way it works is the old generate-a-thumbnail-from-an-image-file trick; and really, who *doesn't* need to generate thumbnails from images every now and then?

Here's how it goes: whenever a customer of your online image-storage business saves a photograph to your S3 bucket, a Lambda function springs to life, creates a small thumbnail version of the image, saves it to a second bucket, and associates the two images so the thumbnail will appear as a proxy of the original in website displays. You don't need

Figure 19.6   The Lambda Configure Triggers page with some of the possible trigger-service choices available in the drop-down menu

to run (and pay for) an entire EC2 instance 24 hours a day, just in case a few cute kitten pictures show up. Instead, you run exactly what you need, exactly when you need it.

Of course, because it's far more efficient, all of this can be done from the AWS command-line interface or through APIs; but figure 19.6 shows how you can use the Console to select the service whose events should trigger Lambda. You just select from the drop-down menu and click Next.

With the service selected, you need to choose an event. Again, as you can see in figure 19.7, there's a drop-down menu for that. Finally, on the Configure Function page (figure 19.8), you upload or write the code you'd like Lambda to run in response to triggers.

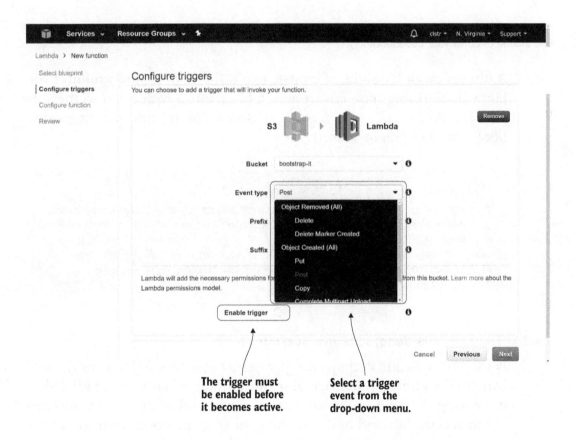

Figure 19.7   With a trigger service selected, choose a specific event from the Event Type menu, along with other configuration details.

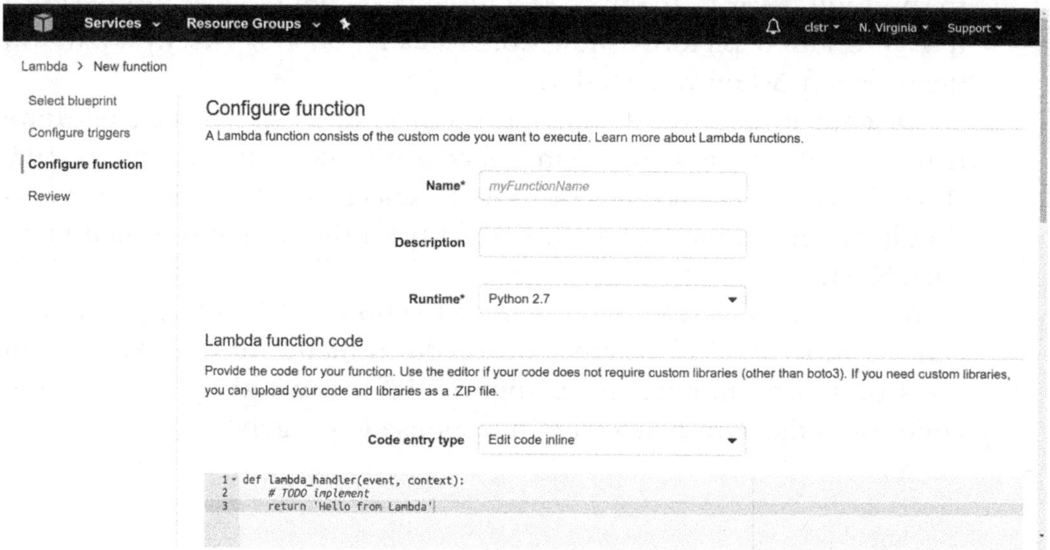

Figure 19.8   You can select a runtime environment (such as Python 2.7) for the Lambda function, and upload or enter your code manually.

A discussion of Lambda, of course, could fill a book. And wouldn't you know it, Manning happens to have a book entirely devoted to the subject: Danilo Poccia's *AWS Lambda in Action* (2016, www.manning.com/books/aws-lambda-in-action).

> **Try it now**
>
> Why not fire up some Lambda goodness by selecting one of the prebuilt blueprints available from the Get Started Now button on the Lambda home page? Try the S3-get-object-python blueprint—but first, create a new bucket in S3, go back into Lambda, select the bucket from the drop-down menu, and then choose an event type. See what happens when you trip the trigger.

19.3.1 *The server is dead; long live serverless—?*

Is the server dead? Perhaps not just yet. Despite sometimes overheated hype to the contrary, the virtual server paradigm has loads of life left in it. Leaving rhetoric and politics aside, it comes down to what you're trying to accomplish and how you and your team go about your work.

Just about everything you've done in this book (up until this chapter, at least) has focused on migrating or building traditional server-based infrastructure on AWS. So, some important process-oriented tools like OpsWorks, CloudFormation, and Simple Queue Service—alongside Lambda—have been among the many services I've ignored. But the use cases I've highlighted are among countless thousands that will work best using the server model.

When should you choose Lambda? If your task is relatively small, infrequent, and independent of other processes, then Lambda is a no-brainer. On the other hand, if it's one piece in a larger, deeply interconnected mega-process driven by a very large code base that would be hard to refactor, you should think carefully before jumping on the Lambda bandwagon. Everything that falls somewhere in between will require you to make a judgment call, weighing all the factors as you find the right balance.

Thirsty for more? Check out Manning's *AWS Lambda in Action* or AWS's own introductory documentation at http://docs.aws.amazon .com/lambda/ latest/dg/welcome.html and https://aws.amazon.com/ lambda/getting-started.

Definitions
- *Cluster*—A group of independently running virtual servers
- *Docker container*—A virtual server that's defined by a text-based template, sometimes called a Dockerfile
- *Docker image*—A packaging format for sharing container definitions
- *EC2 Container Registry*—AWS's Docker image repository
- *Lambda function*—The software code that is run in response to a trigger event
- *Lambda trigger*—An event designated as the spark to spawn a Lambda function

Everything else (nearly)

This book wasn't meant to be encyclopedic, so covering all of the many AWS services was never part of the plan. Still, deciding what to include and what to leave out was a struggle. My goal was to introduce you to the core tools and principles necessary to successfully launch robust server-based applications. There is, of course, no single "right" way to use AWS, but I think my approach should open doors to the widest possible range of scenarios.

In addition to the core services that I gave the full treatment, chapter 18 summarized categories of services useful for hybrid solutions, and chapter 19 briefly looked at three automation tools. Now it's time for the "none of the above" section.

Before I get started, I'll point out that we certainly haven't been wasting our time. The first 18 chapters of the book (skipping over chapter 19) explored more than a dozen individual services; see table 20.1.

Table 20.1 Services covered in this book, arranged by AWS service category

Category	Service	Chapter(s)
Compute	EC2	2, 3, 15, 16
Storage	S3	6, 7
	Glacier	18

Table 20.1 Services covered in this book, arranged by AWS service category *(continued)*

Category	Service	Chapter(s)
	Storage Gateway	18
Databases	Relational Database Service	4
Networking	VPC	14
	CloudFront	17
	Direct Connect	18
	Route 53	5
Migration	Snowball	18
Management tools	CloudWatch	11
Security	IAM	8
	Certificate Manager	17

In addition, the book has discussed important general-purpose tools and concepts like the AWS CLI, elasticity, load balancing, auto scaling, and hybrid designs. So I think you can now consider yourself well educated in things AWS. But there's still a great deal I haven't yet touched.

This chapter is about *many* (although not all) of the hidden treasures I've left out previously. In many cases, the services I'll discuss here should probably be fairly high on your list of "I'll have to get to that sometime." As I've said more than once, no two people share an exact set of needs, but the popularity of these services is pretty broad.

As in chapter 19, you won't learn how to use these services, but you'll learn that they exist and what they do. Let their names and descriptions roll around in your mind for a while, and see what creative ideas start to percolate.

These descriptions will, by necessity, move by quickly. If you don't understand some of the terminology or concepts discussed here, it probably means they're not part of your technology space anyway, so I wouldn't worry. If you're the worrying type, get in touch with me through the Manning book forum, and I'll be happy to help: https://forums.manning.com/forums/learn-amazon-web-services-in-a-month-of-lunches.

20.1 Databases

There's more than one way to manage data. In addition to RDS, Amazon has a whole whack of database engines, including DynamoDB, Redshift, and ElastiCache.

20.1.1 DynamoDB

Back in chapter 4, I talked about the differences between traditional relational databases (like those supported by AWS RDS) and those that use the less-structured NoSQL model. We didn't spend a lot of time exploring the inner workings of NoSQL and Amazon's managed NoSQL service, DynamoDB—and, unfortunately, I won't be able to expand any more on that now.

But I'll note that the data you add to your DynamoDB table is organized in key-value stores. A *key* is an identifying string or number used to partition data within large data tables. A primary key of `CustomerID`, for instance, allows searches for all entries whose `CustomerID` value equals a specified string (david_clinton, for instance). If you choose to add a secondary *sort* key, you can further narrow results to, say, customer transactions within a specified date range.

DynamoDB databases can be managed from the AWS Console; figure 20.1 shows how to set up a database. You can do a surprising amount of configuration, monitoring, and even data importing and exporting from the console. But the most common way to consume the service is from program code, using DynamoDB bindings that are available for all major programming languages.

20.1.2 Redshift

Just about any database tool can be poked and bullied into doing what you need. But it'll save you a boatload of time and trouble to pick the right tool for the job from the start. If you're looking to efficiently manage petabyte-scale data stores (often referred to as *data warehouses*) and dynamically mine them for their business intelligence, then forget about RDS or DynamoDB. It's Redshift you're after.

Redshift is a hosted and managed service designed for massive parallel processing, built on the PostgreSQL relational database engine. Having said that, the rather outdated 8.0.2 version of PostgreSQL was used. To avoid confusion, AWS maintains a web page with updated information on the kinds of things people familiar with more modern Postgre releases may expect to be able to do, but can't: http://mng.bz/88an.

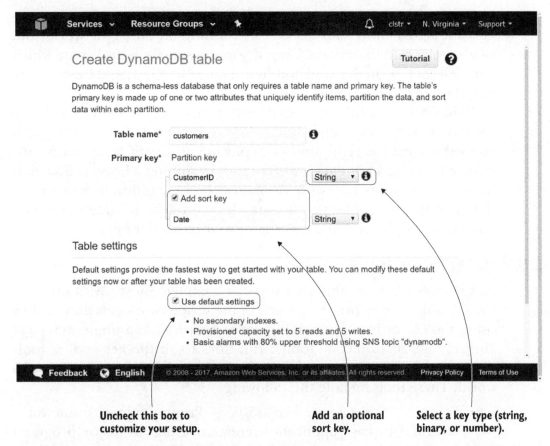

Figure 20.1 Setting up a new DynamoDB table can be as simple as entering these three values. Datasets can be imported later through pipeline templates.

Redshift can connect to data sources using either the Open Database Connectivity (ODBC) or Java Database Connectivity (JDBC) API. Once connected, you should be able to deeply analyze and transform data and generate useful business intelligence–oriented reports.

20.1.3 ElastiCache

A *cache*, in the English spoken during those simpler days before IT took over the world, is a hidden hoard of some kind of treasure. Now that IT *has* taken over the world, *cache* is selected data that's stored in a way that makes its retrieval quicker. This usually works by keeping the data in a volatile memory store (like RAM) rather than on a disk. Storing data that way is usually more expensive, but the resulting improved performance often justifies the cost.

The cache advantage can be applied not only to individual computers, but across entire clusters of VMs running on public networks. But that's easier said than done. Even if you can somehow anticipate which data will soon be in demand and figure out where it should be sent, getting it there can be complicated.

ElastiCache is a fully managed service that can use either the Memcached or Redis caching engine. When launched, fed its data, and applied against the right kind of deployments, ElastiCache can greatly reduce bottlenecks in data transfers and, by shifting a heavy transaction burden away from back-end databases, even significantly cut operational costs. It might be worth your while to research some of the creative ways people are using caching in your particular field.

20.2 Developer tools

As I've noted before, although you can complete most AWS stuff from the Console in your browser, much of the serious work gets done either using the CLI or in programming code. Amazon has a single web page (https://aws.amazon.com/tools) with links to all the key coding tools you'll need to more readily apply a language's rich features to the AWS world. These tools include the following:

- *Software development kits (SDKs)*—Programming frameworks designed to ease application creation using all major programming languages (Java, .NET, Python, and so on) and platforms (Android, iOS, and so on) from any major OS.
- *Integrated development environment (IDE) toolkits*—Developers who already do their coding on either the Eclipse or Visual Studio IDE can add an AWS Toolkit as a plug-in to allow direct integration with an AWS account and all its resources.

The Tools page also links to four developer-oriented services: Code-Commit, CodeBuild, CodeDeploy, and CodePipeline.

20.2.1 CodeCommit

Programming code can be complicated, and the complication is compounded when you have multiple team members contributing updates and fixes. Keeping track of revisions and ensuring that only the right people have access can easily make the difference between a project's success and failure.

Although it may feel as though it's been part of developers' resource kits forever, the Git version control system was only created by Linus Torvalds in 2005. Since then, GitHub, the flagship Git host, has become by far the most popular place to push code and other digital data to common repositories.

With CodeCommit, AWS provides a Git-based service for individuals and teams developing for the Amazon cloud. Of course, you need to have Git installed on your local workstation. The value proposition? Complete integration with AWS services—especially IAM for access control. Figure 20.2 shows the instructions for connecting to a Code-Commit repository.

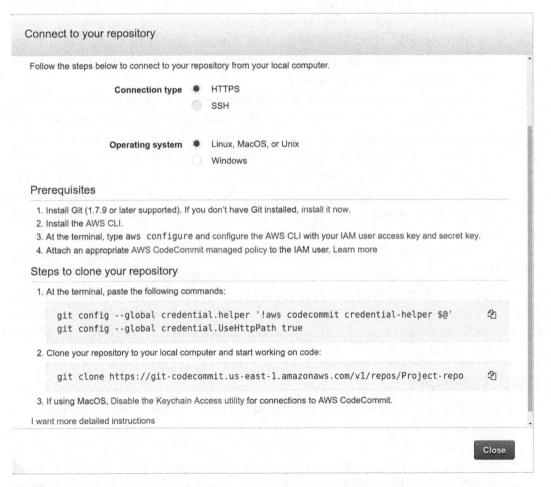

Figure 20.2 Instructions for connecting to a CodeCommit repository and cloning the repository's contents

Unlimited repositories and 50 GB of storage per month are available free for the first five active users. Each extra user costs $1/month.

20.2.2 CodeBuild

Continuous integration and continuous deployment (CI/CD) pipelines: now there's a term you can add to your LinkedIn profile without fear of scaring away employers. It's become a buzz phrase that can take on more than one meaning, but I think it's fair to say that CI/CD attempts to automate the process of moving a project from source code to a deployment-ready build (aka *compiled*) state.

Why would you want to automate builds? Well, if it was just you slaving deep into the night over a hot keyboard, then perhaps you wouldn't. It would probably make sense to compile and package your code manually. But if you're part of a team trying to complete a complex, multimodule project, then allowing each developer to run their own builds can end in chaos.

One solution is to create a *build farm* server to which all team members have appropriate levels of access. That approach can work well but can also be expensive and time consuming (and often under-utilized).

AWS's CodeBuild is a virtual build farm that, in the venerable AWS tradition, generates costs only when it's used. And true to its cloud roots, CodeBuild will automatically scale up to meet the seasonal heavy demands of major releases or product fixes, and then scale back down when calm descends on your team.

CodeBuild can handle workloads based on Java, Python, Node.js, Ruby, Go, Android, and Docker runtimes, and it works with code coming from CodeCommit, GitHub, and S3. A CodeBuild environment can be configured with a number of AWS-centric environment settings, including the target location for the artifacts that the build will generate (see figure 20.3).

20.2.3 CodeDeploy

Once you have a working application (either built using CodeBuild or put together manually), you can use CodeDeploy to push it to live servers. Here's the executive summary version of how CodeDeploy works. So that the service will know what's what, you include an application specification file called AppSpec among the project files you upload to a repository or an S3 bucket. From the CodeDeploy end (either

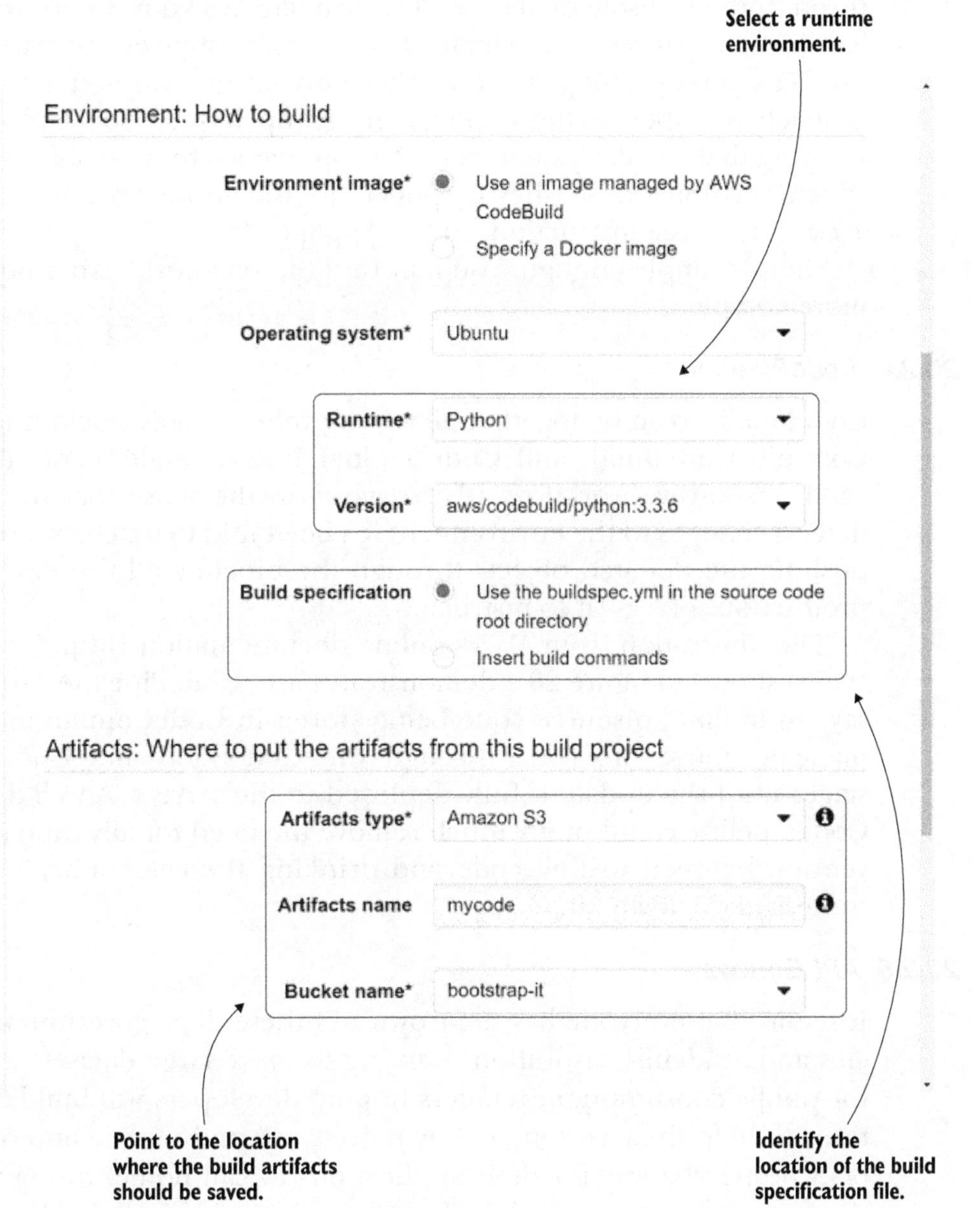

Select a runtime environment.

Environment: How to build

Environment image* ● Use an image managed by AWS CodeBuild
○ Specify a Docker image

Operating system* Ubuntu ▼

Runtime* Python ▼

Version* aws/codebuild/python:3.3.6 ▼

Build specification ● Use the buildspec.yml in the source code root directory
○ Insert build commands

Artifacts: Where to put the artifacts from this build project

Artifacts type* Amazon S3 ▼ ⓘ

Artifacts name mycode ⓘ

Bucket name* bootstrap-it ▼

Point to the location where the build artifacts should be saved.

Identify the location of the build specification file.

Figure 20.3 Configuring a CodeBuild project. Note how, as it's currently set, CodeBuild will expect to find a buildspec.yml file in the source code root directory.

through the Console or via the CLI), you let AWS know where your project files are stored and which of your EC2 instances are part of the project's deployment group and, therefore, targets for updates.

Each member of the deployment group has a CodeDeploy agent running that regularly queries (polls) the service for available revisions. When revisions exist, they're pulled to the instances and deployed according to the instructions in the AppSpec file.

Sounds simple enough. You may find the real-world experience a bit more complex.

20.2.4 *CodePipeline*

CodePipeline can tie together all your developer tools (including Code-Commit, CodeBuild, and CodeDeploy) into a single, centrally managed, responsive workflow. It's *responsive* in the sense that the service detects changes to the environment it's been told to watch and reacts by pushing the updated objects through the pipeline all the way to your production servers (if so instructed).

The illustration from AWS's online documentation (http://mng.bz/Wt65) shown in figure 20.4 demonstrates how CodePipeline can detect, say, an update to source code being stored in CodeCommit and automatically move the code through the CodeBuild and CodeDeploy stages until the update is fully deployed to the servers. A well-designed CodePipeline could pretty much remove the need for any human intervention between writing code and drinking the celebratory beers on successful deployment.

20.2.5 *API Gateway*

It seems that everyone has their own API these days: government agencies and academic institutions wanting to make large datasets available for public consumption, retailers hoping developers will build applications to help their customers buy more stuff, and mobile app developers who need a way for their applications to call home. In many ways, the application program interface figures prominently in developers' dreams—and nightmares.

Amazon's API Gateway can manage the opening and closing of any API doors you want associated with your applications. Whether those apps are hosted on EC2 instances or running on Lambda, API Gateway can be configured to accept, authorize, direct, process, and monitor your API call traffic. Like many AWS tools, API Gateway is a pay-per-user service.

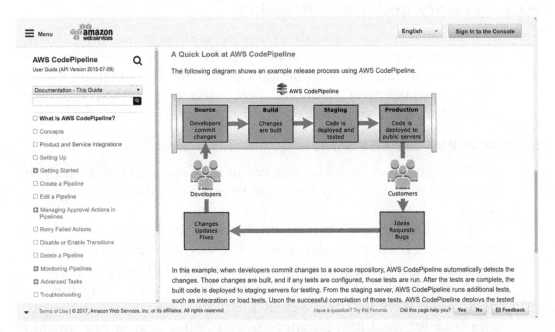

Figure 20.4   Part of AWS's CodePipeline documentation showing a CodePipeline-fueled update cycle

20.2.6 *CloudFormation*

Although technically it's more of an infrastructure-management service, AWS CloudFormation lends itself nicely to developer workflows, so I'll include it here in my list of developer tools. CloudFormation templates—either sample templates provided by AWS or custom templates you write yourself—define a stack of resources that you can quickly deploy and administer. Because the templates exist within the CloudFormation environment, you can be sure that, once launched, each individual element will be appropriately integrated with the rest and that all the dependencies and parameters you define will be met.

By way of comparison, Elastic Beanstalk, discussed in chapter 19, automatically and invisibly handles your application's infrastructure for you. By contrast, CloudFormation expects you to fully understand all the infrastructure elements your application will require, but it simplifies the *process* by automating their practical *coordination*.

20.3 Security and authentication

Not enough can be written about internet and network security. Even if you follow all the recommended best practices, you can still find yourself on the wrong end of some kind of breach. The following services can help secure your resources' perimeters and the way your users authenticate their way inside.

20.3.1 AWS WAF and AWS Shield

AWS WAF and AWS Shield are like two peas in a pod. As two separate services sharing a single web page (see figure 20.5), they seem to belong together.

If I told you that the WAF acronym stands for *web application firewall*, would it make you wonder whether it was developed by Amazon's Department of Redundancy Department? Think about it: a firewall is a way to closely control access to a resource based on a packet's origin or destination. Well, isn't that exactly what the security groups associated with your EC2 and RDS instances and VPCs do? And in case anything

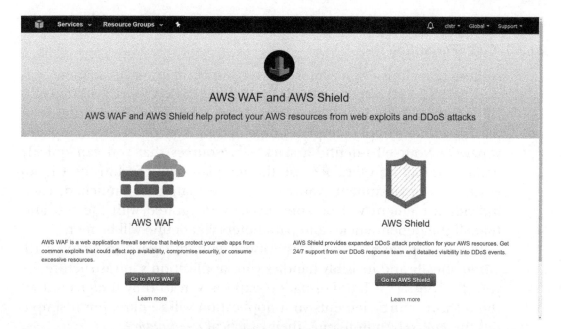

Figure 20.5   The AWS WAF and AWS Shield start page, letting you choose between two distinct select actions

manages to sneak past a security group, the odds are that it will be caught by any network access control lists (ACLs) you've configured.

So what could yet *another* firewall-type tool do for you? Ooh! Ooh! Ask me!

Ok, I'll answer. Think of a WAF (also known as a *web ACL*) as a tool that can define the traffic you want to allow, using just about any characteristic. A WAF goes far further than testing for a particular network protocol or origin IP address; it can read request headers and content strings and check them against any conditions you set. This kind of filtering—which is far more detailed than anything possible using security groups and network ACLs—is designed to fight back against a modern problem: malicious website attacks.

When you configure your WAF, you specify conditions that can be added to rules. One rule might state that if Condition A and Condition B are both present in an incoming web request, then access will be denied; otherwise, access will be granted.

The key to the power of a WAF is in the kinds of conditions you can test for. You can, for instance, identify SQL injection strings in the URI or query string (something you definitely *don't* want to allow through). Malicious bots and suspicious origin IP ranges can also be defined for conditions. With conditions and rules defined, a WAF is associated with an AWS resource (a load-balancer endpoint, for instance), and it's ready to get to work protecting your applications.

What about Shield—and something else called Shield Advanced? If there's a Shield Advanced, doesn't that mean there's a Shield Basic somewhere to go with it? Yup. *AWS Shield* is a distributed denial of service (DDoS) protection tool that's automatically and freely active for resources on all AWS accounts; see figure 20.6.

Shield Advanced is an optional (and for-purchase) service that offers more-robust service whose features include DDoS response-team support and cost protection for any attack-related service charges to Route 53, CloudFront, and ELB. When tens of thousands of zombie servers start up against you during a DDoS attack, it's not uncommon to face thousands of dollars of usage charges. That said, Shield Advanced protection isn't cheap, starting at $3,000/month.

278 CHAPTER 20 *Everything else (nearly)*

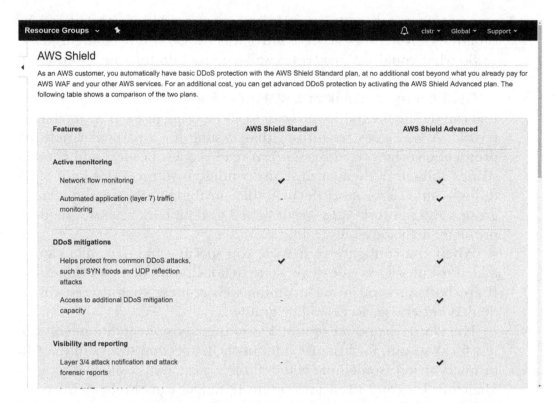

Figure 20.6 Part of a page from AWS's product documentation site showing the differences between AWS Shield Standard and AWS Shield Advanced coverage

20.3.2 Cognito

WAFs—and to some degree security groups and network ACLs—defend your resources from misuse. In other words, they prevent anyone from using your applications in ways those apps weren't meant to be used. Amazon Cognito, on one level at least, solves an entirely different problem: how to distinguish among your users so you can serve each of them appropriately.

What's the big deal about that? Well, people using an online gaming site will expect to be able to log back in after taking a break and pick up where they left off. And individuals who purchase a premium account on a video-streaming site will want access to the perks they paid for, regardless of whether they're logging in to the web application from a mobile smart phone or home PC. So you need a way to figure out who's who.

How does Cognito work? You can create a user directory (or *user pool,* as Amazon calls it) and define what kind of information and verification you'll require from users when they sign up. As with everything Amazon, Cognito's user pools can easily scale into the millions of accounts. You can also enable *federated identities* to allow users to sign up using their existing accounts with third-party identity providers like Google and Facebook. Finally, although activating it can be complicated, you can also use Amazon Cognito Sync to ensure that every user gets a full account experience regardless of the device used to log in.

20.4 Messaging

When you're building and maintaining complicated projects involving large teams and thousands or millions of users, strong communication is king. Reliable messaging is sometimes the only thing that can hold all the gears together and keep them turning productively. These days, messaging isn't the exclusive concern of human beings; machines and machine processes want seats at the table, too.

20.4.1 SNS

You encountered AWS's Simple Notification Service back in chapter 5, when you told SNS to alert you if a Route 53 health check on a web server failed. That was a pretty good illustration of the ways SNS can be neatly integrated into your cloud workflow. In general terms, a publisher (the Route 53 health check, in the example) sends a message to an existing topic that's already been associated with individual or multiple recipients through a subscription (in the example case, my email address).

In addition to alerting human administrators through emails or SMS text messages, SNS messages can also be directed at and consumed by AWS services like Lambda and SQS, prompting them to spawn new processes in response. And in addition to targeting AWS services in subscriptions, you can push messages to mobile devices using one of a number of available third-party push-notification services, including Google Cloud Messaging for Android, Apple Push Notification Service, and Windows Push Notification Service. Figure 20.7 shows the main SNS dashboard from which you can create and manage topics, subscriptions, and platform applications, or send a one-time message.

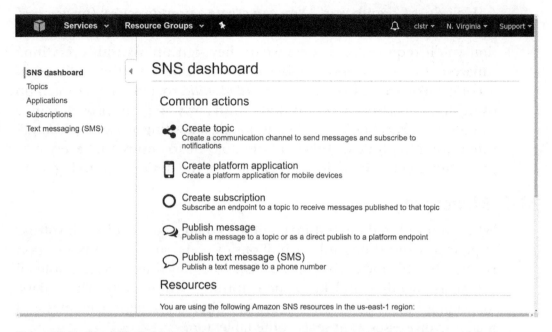

Figure 20.7   The SNS dashboard. Links to the Topics, Applications, Subscriptions, and Text Messaging (SMS) pages are found in the left panel.

20.4.2 SQS

Amazon Simple Queue Service (SQS) is all about coordination and ensuring that complex processes don't break down due to broken communication among multiple parts. Imagine an online business whose users upload their favorite digital pictures so the photos can be printed and shipped back to them. A number of separate steps must all succeed if the process is going to work, including these:

- Storing the image in an S3 bucket
- Processing (resizing, filtering) the image
- Associating the customer's shipping address with the shipping order
- Sending the image to the printer
- Processing customer payment
- Green-lighting the shipping order
- Closing the transaction and processing the payment
- Sending a confirmation email to the customer

Some of those steps (like shipping and sending the confirmation email) may begin only after preceding steps are complete. But others (like processing the shipping address and storing the image in S3) are independent. So that no dependent process will start before its prerequisites have been satisfied, and so that *no* process will ever be unnecessarily delayed, you need a reliable way to transmit success notifications. By *reliable*, I mean the message will be received even if the recipient process happens to be busy at the time of transmission.

SQS addresses this problem by decoupling message producers and consumers. In the example, the image-processing module (wearing its "message producer" hat) can send a message to the printer (acting as the consumer), telling it that the image is ready to print. If the printer is currently busy on a different job, the message won't fail but will wait patiently in the queue until the printer (or a different printer, if there's more than one) is free. Until that happens, the job status will be reported as "incomplete." Either way, the producer is immediately free to take on new tasks without having to worry about the ultimate destiny of the one it just completed.

20.4.3 SES

While your servers are happily chatting with each other via SNS and SQS, perhaps you can have a quick word with your customers. Being able to reach out to current and potential customers (without spamming them, of course) is a huge business requirement. You want to efficiently manage large email lists to ensure that emails are delivered at the right time, and to analyze rich data on how each campaign was received.

Looking for a single email marketing service to handle the heavy lifting (think: MailChimp)? Amazon Simple Email Service (SES) offers a full-featured, mature platform that—of course—is both scalable and integrated with the rest of your AWS infrastructure.

20.5 Shortcuts

Why reinvent the wheel if there's an entire internet of helpful templates out there? If you need to do something on AWS that involves a bewildering combination of services and configuration settings, you may not always be in the mood to start from scratch. It's worth a web search to see if someone has already created a helpful guide or a script that can get you on your feet fast.

20.5.1 *AWS Quick Starts*

The first place you should look is on the AWS Quick Starts page (https://aws.amazon.com/quickstart). Quick Starts are fully documented guides to common solutions, provided by AWS partners. But they're more than guides: each Quick Start includes a link to launch the template in your account using the AWS CloudFormation service.

The templates are organized by category (DevOps, Databases & Storage, and so on, as shown in figure 20.8). The DevOps category, for instance, includes templates for firing up a Chef or Puppet server, a Docker Datacenter, or an Atlassian JIRA deployment. Databases include Microsoft SQL server and SAP HANA. Naturally, the template assumes that you already have any licenses needed to run the software.

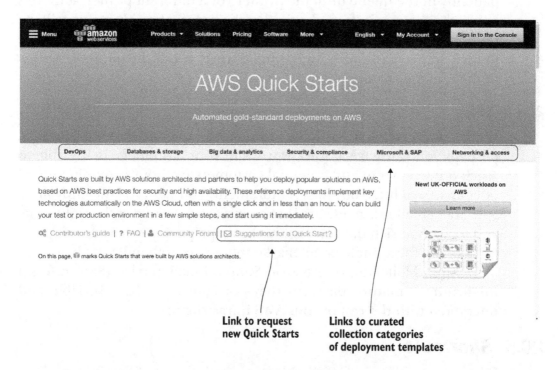

Figure 20.8   The AWS Quick Starts page, including category link shortcuts. Note the Suggestions link, allowing you to request a new Quick Start.

20.5.2 *Migration shortcuts*

You want to get your data and servers up and running on AWS as quickly and painlessly as possible. As it turns out, that's pretty high on AWS's wish list, too. After all, the sooner you're online, the sooner AWS is earning revenue from your deployment. This pleasant confluence of shared goals is probably what has driven Amazon to create migration tools to help you over some of the more common transition hurdles.

The AWS Database Migration Service (DMS) claims to have successfully migrated more than 16,000 databases. Considering that DMS is a relatively new service and that moving large, active databases halfway across the planet can be a massively complex task, I'll assume that's a pretty impressive number. (It's also just refreshing to see an AWS-related metric under a billion.)

You start DMS by identifying your local (source) database, a target database on AWS, and a replication database that will exist only to support the migration operation. DMS can migrate a live database running just about any popular engine. Using the AWS Schema Conversion Tool, you can even convert to a different engine as part of the process.

Of course, AWS suggests that you consider converting to its MySQL-compatible Aurora database engine. And based on everything I've heard about it so far, Aurora does rank as a serious contender.

Finally, you should be aware of the AWS Server Migration service, which can simplify migrating local VMware virtual machines into EC2. You're never entirely on your own!

Never the end

Are we there yet?

Of course not. Even if you were to commit yourself to mastering the 100+ services AWS currently has online, by the time you were half done, there would probably be at least a handful of new ones. And that's not including the dozens of new service *features* added each month.

Having said that, if you've worked through the entire book—following along with the demos and labs in each chapter on your own AWS account—then you're not doing too badly. You may still lack the confidence that comes with lots of experience, but lack of experience is a condition with a simple cure. Think problems through carefully, plan ahead, and dive in. Rinse and repeat.

Here are a few ideas about where you might want to go from here.

21.1 Keeping up

Even if you won't be working on AWS deployments every day, it can be useful to stay plugged in. One good way to do that without having to invest an insane amount of time is to subscribe to the AWS Announcements email list. I don't remember ever getting more than two or three emails a week. It takes only a few seconds to visually scan the list of headlines to see if there's anything close enough to your interests to justify clicking through to the web page.

Figure 21.1 shows the What's New at AWS page (https://aws.amazon .com/new), where recent AWS announcements and news are neatly displayed. You never know what will spark the next Great Project Idea or solve a crippling problem.

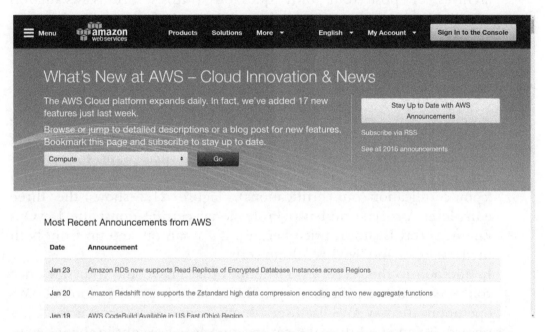

Figure 21.1   The What's New at AWS page. Note the Stay Up to Date link, which you can use to subscribe to the announcements email list.

21.2 *Where to turn for help*

Amazon spends an enormous amount of money on its documentation (https://aws.amazon.com/documentation). I don't know how many people are working on it full time, but they're really productive. Intelligent links to context-relevant material appear on all service pages, the content appears in globally uniform formats, and it's just about always up to date.

If I have a complaint with the in-house documentation, it's that there may be too much of it. It's true that you'll never please everyone; but more often than not, I find myself impatiently scanning documentation pages for specific information rather than reading them from end to end.

As a rule, I'm more likely to quickly grab what I'm looking for by using an internet search engine. From there, I usually find what I need courtesy of existing questions on Server Fault (http://serverfault.com).

AWS hosts its own discussion forums, and it can't hurt to search the archives or post your own question (https://forums.aws.amazon .com/index.jspa). In my experience, the AWS forum isn't the most active of user communities, and there's no guarantee you'll find satisfaction there, but this might change over time.

21.3 Certifications

A well-designed certification exam is its own reward. Grades and diplomas have value, but the real payoff is in what you learn while working through the process. For that reason, you may want to consider attempting one or more of AWS's certifications (https://aws.amazon .com/certification/our-certifications). Figure 21.2 shows the three entry-level Associate and two Professional certifications; the DevOps Engineer cert is shown twice because it's a natural step up from both the Developer and SysOps Admin certs.

In addition to the career opportunities that may come your way once you've earned a certification, you'll also have learned to look at AWS operations the way AWS itself sees them. Again: the process is the main reward. Having said that, the certifications carry weight in the job market, if only because AWS requires its APN Partner companies to have a minimum number of certified employees on staff.

And just think: tens of thousands of businesses of all sizes are either already using AWS services or are about to migrate. Anyone who can demonstrate a solid understanding of the way AWS works and the tools it makes available will have a significant advantage.

21.4 Lab: the steroid overdose edition

Here we go, one last lab—and it's a monster. You've been hired by Big Corp to move most of its IT resources online. Your job, should you decide to accept it, isn't to create the infrastructure, but to explain exactly *how* you'd do it (which tools you'd use) and how much per month it would

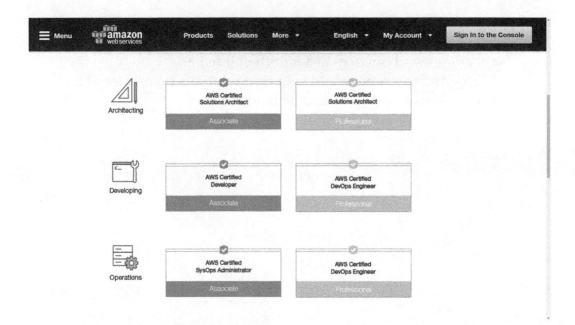

Figure 21.2   The main AWS Certifications page

likely cost. Assume that, each month, the application will transfer about 500 GB of data out to the internet and 50 GB of data in.

Here's what Big Corp needs:

- Highly available virtual servers running a web application 24 hours a day for a global audience. The application service includes streaming a large and growing number of videos.
- A MySQL database to support the web application.
- A second (separate) MySQL database for the HR department that must remain onsite for regulatory compliance. But both remote employees and processes on the application server will need to securely access the database. The database will also need to be regularly and securely backed up to the cloud.
- Frequent and complete backups of all data.
- Security infrastructure meeting or exceeding current best practices.
- DNS management of the company domain.

I've posted my suggested solution to the problem on the *Learn AWS in a Month of Lunches* book forum: https://forums.manning.com/forums/learn-amazon-web-services-in-a-month-of-lunches.

Please feel welcome to add your own solutions to the thread and join the discussion. Good luck, and be in touch!

appendix
Connecting to
your EC2 instance

The only way "in" to manage a Linux EC2 instance is through the Secure Shell (SSH) protocol—and from time to time, at least, you'll definitely need access. SSH isn't hard to use, but if you haven't done it before, it can be a bit intimidating. In case you're not familiar with how the process works from your operating system, this appendix tells you what you need to know.

Accessing the instance from a Linux or macOS machine

Open a terminal window through which you can connect to your new AWS instance. Depending on the Linux distribution running on your machine, you may use the Ctrl-Alt-T key combination or a desktop menu. Type `ls` to list the contents of your current directory, to confirm that the key-pair .pem file is there:

```
ls
```

If the key isn't there, you'll have to find it. On a Linux machine, predictably enough, you can do that using the `find` tool. Assuming that keyname is the name you gave your .pem file, type `find` followed by a tilde (~) to indicate that you're looking only within your user's home directory hierarchy. -name tells find that you're looking for a file named keyname.pem:

```
find ~ -name keyname.pem
```

Once you find your key, you need to tighten up the file's permissions (that is, set them so that only its owner—you—has access of any kind). Otherwise, your AWS Ubuntu server won't let you log in. On either Linux or macOS, you can change the file permissions using a Unix command-line program called Change Mode that's part of the basic Bash environment on all Unix-based systems. Substitute the name you gave your key for keyname:

```
chmod 400 keyname.pem
```

Make a note of the path to the file (probably something like /home/yourname/Downloads), because you'll need it later.

You can now log in to your instance using your key pair (using the full path you found through locate, if it's not in the current directory), the username *ubuntu,* and the IP address you just saw on the EC2 dashboard:

```
ssh -i keyname.pem ubuntu@54.152.9.184
```

You're asked to authenticate the host by typing the word yes—all three letters of the word *yes* (see figure A.1). I remember a very smart DevOps professional turning to me for help after being unable to log in to a remote server after 10 or 15 frustrating minutes; it turned out he was responding with just a *y*.

Figure A.1   SSH login screen to an AWS EC2 instance

> **TIP** The two most common mistakes preventing successful SSH logins involve permissions and the system path. In the former case, you (or, more often, I) forgot to change the permissions of the key file to

400; and in the latter case, the key file is in a different directory than your current work directory and isn't on the system path.

If you receive an error telling you something like "openssh not installed," then, obviously, you'll have to install it. On an Ubuntu, Mint, or Debian system, do that as follows:

```
sudo apt install openssh-server
sudo systemctl start ssh
```

On some older Ubuntu systems, the previous command should be `sudo service ssh start`.

On CentOS Linux, use `yum` instead:

```
sudo yum -y install openssh-server openssh-clients
chkconfig sshd on
service sshd start
```

What is this sudo thingy?

For many practical reasons, using an OS account that enjoys full administrative powers is unnecessarily risky: anyone who finds themselves logged in (including work colleagues who wander by a momentarily unattended computer) will have automatic complete control. On the other hand, restricting yourself to a non-administrative account will make it pretty much impossible to get anything done.

Many flavors of Linux solve this problem by providing selected accounts with admin authority that under most circumstances is purely theoretical, but that can be invoked when necessary by prefacing a command with the word `sudo` (like the earlier `sudo yum` example). Once you confirm your identity by providing your password, your command will be treated as though it was issued by the root user.

Want to see how it works? Try running the earlier command without `sudo`.

Accessing the instance from a Windows machine

Although Windows 10 now allows you to install a Linux Bash interface (run as a subsystem for Linux using Ubuntu user-mode binaries) through which you can use SSH as you saw in the previous section, you may prefer to work with the Windows SSH client, PuTTY. You first need to download the free PuTTY remote-access program from its website: www.chiark.greenend.org.uk/~sgtatham/putty.

Next, you'll convert the .pem key that you generated in AWS to PuTTY's .ppk format. From the Start menu, choose All Programs > PuTTY > PuTTYgen.

For Type of Key to Generate, I'd choose the most commonly used encryption algorithm, SSH-2 RSA. Most of the others are there for backward compatibility. Then click Load, make sure All Files (.) will be displayed, and select your .pem file. Click Save Private Key to start the conversion (make sure you use the same name for your key that you used for the .pem version). You don't need to add a passphrase if you don't want to, but getting your local machine to prompt you for a passphrase each time for initiating a remote SSH login does add an extra layer of security.

You can now open the PuTTY program by choosing All Programs > PuTTY > PuTTY. Because the instance you're running on AWS is an Ubuntu server, Host Name is ubuntu. Choose SSH for Connection Type, and make sure your port is set to 22 (the default port used by SSH connections). Select your .ppk file through the Category pane on the left. Click to expand Connection, and then SSH, and then click Auth. From there, browse to the folder where you saved your .ppk file, and select it. Finally, click Yes, and your session should open.

index

Symbols

* (asterisk) character 234
/ (forward slash) 206
^ (caret) character 26
~ (tilde) character 107, 289

A

access keys 117, 126
accounts
  administering resources with AWS
    CLI 167–169
  AWS IAM with 118–126
    configuring groups 124–126
    creating admin users 118–122
    creating groups 124–126
    locking down root user
      accounts 123–124
    signing in as IAM user 122
  AWS, setting up 5–7
  of root users
    locking down 123–124
    protecting 114
  threats to 98–100
    admins 99–100
    hackers 98–99
ACL (access control list) 183
AD-compatible system 249
addressing
  with NAT 191–194
  with TCP/IP 190–191

add-user-to-group command 167
admin users, creating 118–122
AdministratorAccess policy 121
admins, threats to AWS accounts 99–100
Akamai 226
alarms 155
alerts, in CloudWatch monitoring service
  billing 154–157
  usage 157–158
alias record set 74
Amazon CloudFront
  costs of using 232–234
  creating distributions 228–236
    final steps 235–236
    SSL/TLS certificates 234–235
    SSL/TLS encryption 230
    TTL settings 230–232
  overview 226–227
Amazon Web Service. See AWS
AMI (Amazon Machine Image) 10, 18,
    100, 167
Apache 31
API Gateway. See AWS API Gateway
APN (AWS Partner Network)
    Technology 246
applications, assessing 35–38
AppSpec file 272
archives
  compressed, generating 106–107
  overview 111
ARN (Amazon Resource Name) 113
Attach Policy page 125

authenticated users 88
authentication 276–279
  AWS Cognito service 278–279
  AWS Shield protection service 276–277
  AWS WAF 276–277
authentication code 116
auto scaling
  creating auto scaling groups 218–223
    configuring scaling policies 220–223
    integrating load balancers 219
  creating launch configurations 214–218
  shutting down 224
auto scaling groups, creating 218–223
  configuring scaling policies 220–223
  integrating load balancers 219
availability monitoring 70
availability zones 189–194, 201
  deploying websites across two 195–197
  NAT addressing 191–194
  network design 189–190
    data reliability 189–190
    data security 189
  TCP/IP addressing 190–191
availability. See high availability capability
AWS (Amazon Web Service)
  accounts, setting up 5–7
  finding help 8
  infrastructure of 10–11
  instances
    accessing 23–24
    launching 17–22
  overview 8–11
AWS API Gateway 274
AWS CLI (command-line interface)
  administering account resources with
    167–169
  benefits of 160–161
  configuring 164–166
    choosing output formats 165
    choosing regions 164–165
    working with multiple AWS profiles
      166
  installing 107–110, 161–163
    on Linux 162
    using bundled installers 162–163
    with Python pip package management
      system 163

  with Windows MSI files 161
  overview 159–160
  using help system 166–167
AWS CloudFormation service 275
AWS CodeBuild build service 272
AWS CodeCommit control service
  270–272
AWS CodeDeploy deployment service
  272–274
AWS CodePipeline delivery service 274
AWS Cognito service 278–279
aws command 109
aws configure command 164
AWS Console 17
AWS Direct Connect, for hybrid
  infrastructures 246
AWS Directory Service, for hybrid
  infrastructures 248–249
AWS DMS (Database Migration
  Service) 283
AWS DynamoDB database service 268
AWS EC2 (Elastic Compute Cloud)
  Docker on, cloud automation with
    258–261
  with hybrid infrastructures 250–251
AWS Elastic Beanstalk, cloud automation
  with 254–258
AWS ElastiCache web service 269–270
AWS IAM (Identity and Access
  Management) 113–117
  best practices 116–117
    access keys 117
    MFA 116
  groups 115
  policies 113
  roles 115–116
  signing in as user 122
  users 113–114
  with AWS accounts 118–126
    configuring groups 124–126
    creating admin users 118–122
    creating groups 124–126
    locking down root user accounts
      123–124
    signing in as IAM user 122
AWS Lambda, cloud automation
  with 261–265
AWS Quick Starts page 282

AWS RDS (Relational Database Service)
   building instances 58–63
   migrating databases to 57–58
AWS Redshift hosting service 268–269
AWS region 49
AWS SES (Simple Email Service) 281
AWS Shield protection service 276–277
AWS Snowball service, for hybrid
      infrastructures 245
AWS SNS (Simple Notification Service)
      279
AWS SQS (Simple Queue Service)
      280–281
AWS Storage Gateway, for hybrid
      infrastructures 244
AWS WAF (web application firewall)
      276–277

B

backups
   importance of 98–100
   to S3
      manually 105–110
      with snapshots 100–105
balancers
   of loads
      associating with security groups
         208–209
      associating with target groups 210
      creating 208–209
      integrating 219
   of multizone loads 201–210
bandwidth 35
Beanstalk. See AWS Elastic Beanstalk
billing alerts, in CloudWatch monitoring
      service 154–157
buckets, S3
   creating 85–86
   uploading files to 86–91
budgets 147–153
   creating 148–149
   using tags with 150–153
build farm server 272
burst capable 57
burstable performance 39

C

ca-certificates 162, 170
cache 237, 269
canonical name 74
capacity
   calculating for websites 33–34
   overview 212
Capex (capital expenses) 127, 135
cd command 44
CDN (content-delivery network) 226
   creating Amazon CloudFront
         distributions 228–236
      CloudFront costs 232–234
      final steps 235–236
      SSL/TLS certificates 234–235
      SSL/TLS encryption 230
      TTL settings 230–232
   using Amazon CloudFront 226–227
certificate signing request. See CSR
certificates, SSL/TLS 234–235
Change Mode program 290
Choose an Instance Type page 19
CI/CD (continuous integration and con-
      tinuous deployment) 272
CIDR (Classless Inter-Domain Routing)
      194, 198
class types, RDS 67
CLI (command-line interface).
         See AWS CLI
cloud automation
   with AWS Elastic Beanstalk 254–258
   with AWS Lambda 261–265
   with Docker on AWS EC2 Container
         Service 258–261
cloud computing 1, 177
cloud projects, estimating costs of
      128–131
CloudFlare 226
CloudFormation service. See AWS Cloud-
      Formation service
CloudFront. See Amazon CloudFront
CloudWatch monitoring service 153–158
   billing alerts 154–157
   budgets 147–153
      creating 148–149
      using tags with 150–153
   usage alerts 157–158

clusters 211, 265
CMS (content management system) 41
CNAME record 75
CodeBuild build service.
        See AWS CodeBuild build service
CodeCommit control service. See AWS
        CodeCommit control service
CodeDeploy deployment service. See AWS
        CodeDeploy deployment service
CodePipeline delivery service. See AWS
        CodePipeline delivery service
Cognito service. See AWS Cognito service
command-line interface. See AWS CLI
compiled state 272
compliance restrictions 242
compressed archives, generating 106–107
compression 111
Configure Instance Details page 19
Configure Security Group page 20
configuring
    AWS CLI 164–166
        choosing output formats 165
        choosing regions 164–165
        working with multiple AWS profiles
            166
    groups 124–126
    hosted zones 71–76
        configuring record sets 72–75
        using Elastic IP addresses 75–76
    record sets 72–75
    scaling policies 220–223
    security group settings 63–64
    WordPress 43–45
connectivity, hybrid 246–249
    AWS Direct Connect 246
    AWS Directory Service 248–249
    virtual private gateways 246–247
Console page 5
Consulting Partners 246
container 258
content management system. See CMS
content-delivery network. See CDN
continuous integration and continuous
        deployment. See CI/CD
costs
    of cloud projects 128–131
    of databases 56–57
    of using Amazon CloudFront 232–234
    tracking with resource tags 146

cp command 44
CPU credits 39
Create Auto Scaling Group page 218
CSR (certificate signing request) 234
curl 108, 162, 170
customer gateway device 247

D

data
    reliability of 189–190
    security of 189
data accessibility 54
data transfers, cost of 242
data warehouses 268
database dump 67
Database Migration Service. See AWS DMS
databases 268–270
    AWS DynamoDB database service 268
    AWS ElastiCache web service 269–270
    AWS Redshift hosting service 268–269
    building AWS RDS instances 58–63
    configuring security group settings
        63–64
    estimating costs of 56–57
    infrastructure of 54–55
    migrating to AWS RDS 57–58
    models of 52–53
        choosing 53
        NoSQL 53
        relational 52
    overview 51
    populating new 64–66
DDoS (distributed denial of service) 277
demand of users
    automating high availability capability
        175–177
    cloud computing 177
    elasticity vs. scalability 177–179
deploying websites, across zones 195–197
Dev/Test environment 60
developer tools 270–275
    AWS API Gateway 274
    AWS CloudFormation service 275
    AWS CodeBuild build service 272
    AWS CodeCommit control service
        270–272

developer tools *(continued)*
  AWS CodeDeploy deployment service
      272–274
  AWS CodePipeline delivery service 274
DevOps Engineer cert 286
DHCP (Dynamic Host Configuration
      Protocol) 192
Direct Connect usage 246
Direct Connect. *See* AWS Direct Connect
Directory Service. *See* AWS Directory
      Service
disaster recovery, for hybrid infrastructures
      249–250
distributions, creating with Amazon
      CloudFront 228–236
  final steps 235–236
  SSL/TLS certificates 234–235
  SSL/TLS encryption 230
  TTL settings 230–232
DMS (Database Migration Service).
      See AWS DMS
dnf 162
DNS (domain name system) 68
  adding names to public indexes 70–71
  configuring hosted zones 71–76
    configuring record sets 72–75
    using Elastic IP addresses 75–76
  routing policies 76–82
    creating 79–82
    creating health checks 77–78
Docker container 265
Docker on AWS EC2, cloud automation
      with 258–261
Dockerrun.aws.json file 256
documentation 285–286
domain 82
domain name system. *See* DNS
domain registration 70, 82
downloading WordPress 43–45
droplet 11
dumps, creating for MySQL database
      management 58
Dynamic Host Configuration Protocol.
      See DHCP
dynamic IP addresses 21
DynamoDB database service. *See* AWS
      DynamoDB database service

E

EBS (Elastic Block Store) 34–35
EBS volumes 10, 34
EC2 (Elastic Compute Cloud) service
  core compute services 34–35
    bandwidth 35
    EBS 34–35
    memory 35
    vCPUs 34
  instances, launching with AWS CLI
      167–169
    families 39
  overview 16–17
  web server
    accessing AWS instances 23–24
    building Ubuntu Linux web servers
        24–30
    launching AWS instances 17–22
    troubleshooting 30–31
  websites
    adding WordPress 41–49
    assessing applications 35–38
    calculating capacity needs 33–34
    choosing instances for 38–41
  websites, integrating S3 resources into
      91–92
EC2 Container Registry 265
EC2 instance, connecting to 291–292
  from Linux or macOS machine 289–291
  from Windows machine 291–292
ECS-optimized Amazon Linux AMI 260
edge caching 226
edge locations 237
Elastic Beanstalk. *See* AWS Elastic Beanstalk
Elastic Compute Cloud service. *See* EC2
Elastic IP addresses
  overview 82
  using for hosted zones 75–76
ElastiCache web service. *See* AWS Elasti-
      Cache web service
elasticity
  overview 3, 11
  scalability vs. 177–179
encryption
  overview 237
  SSL/TLS 230
encryption key 89
endpoint 55, 67

F

Failover 61, 80, 199, 211
failover rule 77
federated identities 279
files, uploading to S3 buckets 86–91
filesystems, WordPress 46
Filter parameter 158
find tool 289
forward slash 206
Free Tier 4, 31
Free Usage Tier 129

G

gateways. *See* AWS API Gateway; virtual private gateways
Geolocation Routing policy 80
geolocation rule 77
Glacier cloud storage service, for hybrid infrastructures 243–244
groups
  configuring 124–126
  creating 124–126
  of AWS IAM 115
growth, managing
  estimating costs of cloud projects 128–131
  using TCO Calculator 131–135

H

hackers, threats to AWS accounts 98–99
hardware 54
hardware virtual machine. *See* HVM
health checks, creating 77–78
help
  using system for AWS CLI 166–167
  with AWS 8
help command 167
high availability capability
  auto scaling
    creating auto scaling groups 218–223
    creating launch configurations 214–218
    shutting down 224
  automating 175–177

content-delivery networks
  creating Amazon CloudFront distributions 228–236
  using Amazon CloudFront 226–227
load balancing
  building multizone load balancer 201–210
  definition of 199–201
  testing clusters 210–211
with networking tools
  availability zones 189–194
  deploying websites across two availability zones 195–197
  network subnets 189–194
  organizing resources in VPCs 181–189
horizontal scaling 179
hosted zones, configuring 71–76
  configuring record sets 72–75
  using Elastic IP addresses 75–76
HVM (hardware virtual machine) 104
hybrid infrastructures
  AWS EC2 Systems Manager 250–251
  connectivity 246–249
    AWS Direct Connect 246
    AWS Directory Service 248–249
    virtual private gateways 246–247
  disaster recovery 249–250
  storage solutions 243–245
    AWS Snowball service 245
    AWS Storage Gateway 244
    Glacier cloud storage service 243–244
    S3 243–244
  VMware integration 252
  when to use 242

I

i (information) icon 134
IAM (identify and Access Management) 148
icons 228
IDE (integrated development environment) toolkits 270
- -ignore-installed six argument 163
igw object 186
images
  creating 103–105
  re-creating instances using 105

index document 96
indexes, public 70–71
infrastructure 242
  of AWS 10–11
  of databases 54–55
infrastructures, hybrid
  AWS EC2 Systems Manager 250–251
  connectivity 246–249
  disaster recovery 249–250
  storage solutions 243–245
  VMware integration 252
  when to use 242
install script 163
installing
  AWS CLI 107–110, 161–163
    on Linux 162
    using bundled installers 162–163
    with Python pip package management
      system 163
    with Windows MSI files 161
  Ubuntu Linux web servers software
    25–28
instance class types, RDS 67
Instance details page, EC2 23
instance types 39, 49
instances
  AWS RDS, building 58–63
  AWS, accessing 23–24
  choosing for websites 38–41
  EC2, launching with AWS CLI 167–169
  launching four 202–204
  re-creating with images 105
  registering in target groups 206–207
integrating, S3 resources into EC2-based
  websites 91–92
internet gateway 198
IOPS (input/output operations per
  second) 61
IP address 31
IPv4 190, 198
IPv6 198
iSCSI device 244

J

JDBC (Java Database Connectivity) 269
JSON (JavaScript Object Notation) 170

K

Kerberos 249
- -key-name plural 169
key 146
key pairs 22, 24, 31
keys and salts 49
keys, access 117

L

Lambda. See AWS Lambda
LAMP (Linux, Apache, MySQL, PHP) 26
Latency Routing Policy 80
latency rule 77
launch configurations, creating for auto
  scaling 214–218
Launch Instance button, EC2 dashboard
  18
launching
  AWS instances 17–22
  four instances 202–204
  new EC2 instances using AWS CLI
    167–169
Linux
  connecting to EC2 instance from
    289–291
  installing AWS CLI on 162
loads
  balancers
    associating with security groups
      208–209
    associating with target groups 210
    creating 208–209
  balancing, definition of 199–201
  building multizone balancers 201–210
    associating target groups with load
      balancer 210
    creating target groups 204–206
    launching four instances 202–204
    registering instances in target groups
      206–207
locking down, root user accounts 123–124
logs 31, 85
ls command 28, 44, 107

M

M4 instance type 40
macOS
  connecting to EC2 instance from
      289–291
  installing AWS CLI on 162–163
managed services 67
manual backups 105–110
  choosing what to back up 106
  generating compressed archives
      106–107
  installing AWS CLI 107–110
manual method, to create VPCs 185–186
measured service 177
memory 35
memory optimized class type 57
messaging 279–281
  AWS SES 281
  AWS SNS 279
  AWS SQS 280–281
metric 154, 158
MFA (multi-factor authentication) 116
migrating databases to AWS RDS 57–58
migration 252
Multi-AZ 67
multizone load balancers, building
    201–210
  associating target groups with load
      balancer 210
  creating load balancers 208–209
  creating target groups 204–206
  launching four instances 202–204
  registering instances in target groups
      206–207
mv (move) command 28
My AMIs tab, WordPress 214
MySQL database management system
  creating dumps 58
  preparing for WordPress 42–43
mysql-common package 48
mysql-server package 48

N

NACL (network access control list) 30
names
  adding to public indexes 70–71
  designing naming schemes 140–141

nano 31–32
NAT (network address translation)
    191–194
netmask 194
networking tools
  availability zones 189–194
    NAT addressing 191–194
    network design 189–190
    TCP/IP addressing 190–191
  deploying websites, across two availabil-
      ity zones 195–197
  network subnets 189–194
    NAT addressing 191–194
    network design 189–190
    TCP/IP addressing 190–191
  organizing resources in VPCs 181–189
networks
  design of 189–190
    data reliability 189–190
    data security 189
  for content delivery
    creating Amazon CloudFront
        distributions 228–236
    using Amazon CloudFront 226–227
  subnets of 189–194
    NAT addressing 191–194
    TCP/IP addressing 190–191
NIST (National Institute of Standards)
    177
node 11
NoSQL (Not Only SQL) 53, 66
NS (name servers) 72

O

object storage 84, 96
octets 194
ODBC (Open Database Connectivity) 269
on-demand pricing 224
on-demand self service 177
operating systems, Ubuntu Linux 24–30
Opex (operating expenses) 135
OpsWorks 265
origin server 227, 237
output formats, choosing 165

P

performance monitoring 158
permission management 86
permissions 96
PHP (Hypertext Preprocessor) 31–32
pilot-light model 250
pip install package 163
pip method 163, 170
policies, for scaling 220–223
populating new databases 64–66
primary-server value 142
production environment 60
production tag 151
- -profile argument 166
profiles, multiple 166
programmatic, defined 116
projects, cloud 128–131
public indexes, adding names to 70–71
PuTTY 49, 292
PV (paravirtual) 104
Python 111
Python pip package management system 163

Q

Quick Starts page. See AWS Quick Starts page

R

-r flag 46
RADIUS-based authentication 249
rapid elasticity 177
RDS (Relational Database Service) 7, 55, 137
record sets, configuring 72–75
record type 82
recovery-point objectives 249
recovery-time objectives 249
Redshift hosting service. See AWS Redshift hosting service
Reduced Redundancy storage 88, 96
regions, choosing 164–165
registering instances, in target groups 206–207
relational database elements 66

Relational Database Service. See AWS RDS
relational databases 52
reliability of data 189–190
reserve pricing 224
resource groups, resource tags and 143–146
resource pooling 177
resource tags 137–142
    applying 137–140
    creating 137–140
    defined 136–137
    designing naming schemes 140–141
    resource groups and 143–146
    searching 141–142
    tracking costs with 146
resources
    of accounts, administering with AWS CLI 167–169
    organizing 181–189
    S3, integrating into EC2-based websites 91–92
    searching tagged 141–142
roles, of AWS IAM 115–116
root account 49
root device 100, 111
root users
    locking down accounts of 123–124
    protecting accounts of 114
Route 53 82
route table 182, 198
routing policies 76–82
    creating 79–82
    creating health checks 77–78
routing policy 77, 82
RPO (recovery-point objective) 252
RTO (recovery-time objective) 252

S

S3 (Simple Storage Service)
    backing up to
        importance of 98–100
        manually 105–110
        with snapshots 100–105
    creating buckets 85–86
    creating static websites with 93–95
    for hybrid infrastructures 243–244

S3 (Simple Storage Service) *(continued)*
  integrating resources into EC2-based
      websites 91–92
  overview 84–91
  uploading files to buckets 86–91
s3 command 109
scalability 3
  elasticity vs. 177–179
  overview 11
scaling out 179
scaling policy 224
scaling up 179
scaling, configuring policies 220–223
SDKs (software development kits) 270
searching resources tags 141–142
secret access key 126
secret-key page, WordPress 45
secure sockets layer. *See* SSL/TLS
security 54, 189, 276–279
  AWS Cognito service 278–279
  AWS IAM 113–117
    best practices 116–117
    groups 115
    policies 113
    roles 115–116
    users 113–114
    with AWS accounts 118–126
  AWS Shield protection service 276–277
  AWS WAF 276–277
Security Credentials page 164
security groups
  associating load balancers with 208–209
  configuring settings 63–64
Server Fault 286
serverless architectures 262
servers, preparing for WordPress 42
server-side encryption 96
SES (Simple Email Service). *See* AWS SES
Shared Responsibility Model 98
Shell 170
Shield Advanced 277
Shield protection service. *See* AWS Shield
      protection service
shortcuts 281–283
  AWS DMS 283
  AWS Quick Starts page 282
shutting down, auto scaling 224
signing in, as user of AWS IAM 122

Simple Email Service. *See* AWS SES
Simple Monthly Calculator 56, 128–129
Simple Notification Service. *See* AWS SNS
Simple Queue Service 265
Simple Routing Policy 80
Simple Storage Service. *See* S3
snapshots 100–105
  creating 101–103
  creating images 103–105
  using images to re-create instances 105
Snowball. *See* AWS Snowball service
SNS (Simple Notification Service) 78, 158
SOA (start of authority) 72
software 55, 100
software development kits. *See* SDKs
sort key 268
spot pricing 224
spreadsheets 134
SQL (Structured Query Language) 52
SQS (Simple Queue Service) 280
SSD (solid state drive) 20
SSH (Secure Shell) protocol 289
SSL (Secure Sockets Layer) 230
SSL/TLS (secure socket layer/transport
      layer security)
  certificates 234–235
  encryption 230
staged migrations 242
standard class type 57
Standard storage option 88
Standard-IA storage 88, 96
static websites, creating with S3 93–95
Storage Gateway. *See* AWS Storage Gateway
storage space, EBS 34
storage, hybrid 243–245
  AWS Snowball service 245
  AWS Storage Gateway 244
  Glacier cloud storage service 243–244
  S3 243–244
subnets, of networks 189–194
  NAT addressing 191–194
  network design 189–190
  TCP/IP addressing 190–191
sudo apt update 25
sudo command 31
sudo service ssh start command 291

T

Tag Editor 146
Tag Instance page 20
tags 31
  overview 85
  using with budgets 150–153
tar 49
tar program 106
target groups
  associating with load balancers 210
  creating 204–206
  registering instances in 206–207
TCO (total cost of ownership) 15, 128, 131–135
TCO Calculator 131–135
TCP/IP (transmission control protocol/internet protocol) 190–191
Technology Preview stage 252
testing WordPress applications 47–48
time-to-live settings. *See* TTL settings
TLS (Transport Layer Security) 230
tools for developers 270–275
  AWS API Gateway 274
  AWS CloudFormation service 275
  AWS CodeBuild build service 272
  AWS CodeCommit control service 270–272
  AWS CodeDeploy deployment service 272–274
  AWS CodePipeline delivery service 274
top command 36
Total Estimated Charge metric 155
traffic management 70
transactions-primary value 143
TTL (time-to-live) 73, 230–232, 237

U

Ubuntu Linux operating system, web servers
  building 24–30
  creating websites 28–30
  installing software 25–28
unused Elastic IP 76
unzip 163, 170
updates 284–285
uploading files to S3 buckets 86–91

URL (uniform resource locator) 31
usage alerts, in CloudWatch monitoring service 157–158
user data 224
user demand
  automating high availability 175–177
  cloud computing 177
  elasticity vs. scalability 177–179
user management 86
users 126
  admins, creating 118–122
  of AWS IAM 113–114
    protecting root user account 114
    signing in as 122
  root
    locking down accounts of 123–124
    protecting accounts of 114
UTF-8 characters 138

V

value 146
vCPUs (virtual central processing units) 34, 49
versioning 85
vertical scaling 179
virtual private gateways, for hybrid infrastructures 246–247
virtualization 8, 11
VM (virtual machine) 9, 11
VMware integration, with hybrid infrastructures 252
volume 110
VolumeIdleTime value 158
VPCs (virtual private clouds) 6, 11, 62, 175, 198, 246
  creating new 185–189
    using manual method 185–186
    using wizard 187–189
VPN (virtual private network) 246, 252

W

w3techs.com 41
WAF (web application firewall) 276
warm-standby model 250
web ACL 277

web root directory 27
web servers
  EC2 service
    accessing AWS instances 23–24
    launching AWS instances 17–22
    troubleshooting 30–31
  Ubuntu Linux operating system
    building 24–30
    creating websites 28–30
    installing software 25–28
website encryption 237
websites
  deploying across two availability zones
      195–197
  EC2-based 91–92
  static 93–95
  with EC2 service
    adding WordPress 41–49
    assessing applications 35–38
    calculating capacity needs 33–34
    choosing instances for 38–41
  with Ubuntu Linux operating system
      28–30
Weighted Routing Policy 80
weighted rule 77
wget program 43

Windows MSI (Microsoft Installer), install-
    ing AWS CLI with 161
Windows, connecting to EC2 instance
    from 291–292
WordPress 41–49
  configuring 43–45
  downloading 43–45
  preparing MySQL 42–43
  preparing servers 42
  setting up filesystems 46
  shutting down 48–49
  testing applications 47–48

X

Xen 261

Y

yum 162

Z

ZIP format 108
ztf flags 107